JAMES CITY PARISH
JAMESTOWN, VIRGINIA
1607
FIRST PROTESTANT CHURCH IN AMERICA

# The
# Colonial Clergy of Virginia, North Carolina and South Carolina

By

THE REVEREND FREDERICK LEWIS WEIS, TH.D.

*Historian of the Society of the*
*Descendants of the Colonial Clergy*

Southern Historical Press, Inc.
Greenville, South Carolina

Please direct all correspondence and orders to:

**www.southernhistoricalpress.com**
or
**SOUTHERN HISTORICAL PRESS, Inc.**
**PO BOX 1267**
**Greenville, SC    29601**
**southernhistoricalpress@gmail.com**

Originally published: Boston, MA.   1955
Copyright 1955 by: Frederick L. Weis
ISBN #978-1-63914-031-2
All rights Reserved.
*Printed in the United States of America*

# THE COLONIAL CLERGY OF AMERICA

THE history of the towns of the British Colonies in North America during the colonial period was in large measure that of their churches, and the history of these churches was largely that of their clergy. The ministers of that period were the leaders in theology, law, medicine, education, and to a considerable degree, in politics and Indian warfare. Often they were the only educated persons in a community.

Harvard College was founded in 1636 to provide a literate ministry for the churches of New England, and it is to be noted that of the thousand colonial ministers in Massachusetts nine-tenths of them were college graduates and many others were privately tutored by college-trained clergymen.

The Society of the Descendants of the Colonial Clergy was incorporated by the Commonwealth of Massachusetts, on February 9, 1933. Its major purposes are "to cherish and maintain the memory of the lives and works of the colonial clergy of America; to perpetuate their spirit and the religious freedom which they sought in the New World; to keep in remembrance the churches which they served; to promote the fitting celebration of anniversaries both of colonial ecclesiastical bodies and churches, and of events in the lives of their clergy; to collect and preserve documents, histories, biographical sketches and memorials pertaining to the colonial clergy of America and the parishes which they served; and to promote social intercourse and friendship among the descendants of the colonial clergy now and hereafter."

The first endeavor of the founders of these colonies, which later formed the United States of America, was the continuance of the Christian institutions under which they had been born. As Francis Baylies said: "The clergy were the principal instruments in keeping alive the spirit and enterprise of the English race in the wilds of America. Nor did they confine themselves to ecclesiastical functions. Their influence was felt in the civil affairs of Government, and even in the transactions of ordinary life."

There were nearly five thousand settled ministers in colonial America, each of whom, according to his ability, education and station, was an unquestioned leader in his time and place. With the passage of many decades some of the ancient parishes which they served have ceased to exist; many are still strong and flourishing. It is to ensure the perpetuation of the memory of these leaders of colonial times, the founders and shapers of our national character and institutions, that this Society of the Descendants of the Colonial Clergy was formed.

### ELIGIBILITY

"Any person shall be eligible for membership who is at least twenty-one years of age, and a lineal descendant of an ancestor who was a clergyman regularly ordained, installed or settled over any Christian church within the limits of the thirteen colonies prior to July 4, 1776."—*From the By-laws.*

The Society includes the descendants of Colonial Clergymen of all denominations.

# OFFICERS

## 1954

*Governor*:

John Chandler, Esquire.

*Deputy-Governor*:

George William Wheelwright III.

*Secretary*:

Dudley Huntington Dorr, Esquire,

60 State Street, Boston 9, Massachusetts.

*Historian*:

The Reverend Frederick Lewis Weis, Th.D.,

R. F. D. 2, Peterborough, New Hampshire

*Treasurer*:

Francis Wilson Fleischner,

The Clinton Trust Company, Clinton, Massachusetts.

*Chaplain*:

The Reverend John Henry Wilson.

*Chancellor*:

Haven Parker, Esquire.

*Marshal*:

Colonel George Alanson Parker.

*Surgeon*:

Franklin Greene Balch, M.D.

*Signet*:

Richard Gibson Dorr, Esquire.

JOHN AGNEW, son of Jacob Agnew of Kirmanock, Galloway; matric. Univ. of Glasgow; lic. for Va., 17 June 1753; K.B. for Va., 27 June 1753; sett. Suffolk Par. (Nansemond) Va., 1754-1775; ejected as a royalist; British chaplain; captured during the Rev. war and sent to France; Ep.*

WILLIAM AGUR, lic. for Va., 21 June 1768; sett. Nottoway Par. (Southampton) Va., 1773-1774; Ep.

JOHN ALDERSON, b. Yorkshire, England, 1719, son of Rev. John Alderson (an Anglican clergyman); sett. Germantown, Pa., as a Bapt., ca. 1755; sett. Smith and Lynville's Creek (Rockingham) Va., 6 Aug. 1756-1772; Botetourt co., Va., 1772-1781; Bapt.; d. Botetourt co., Va., 1781.

JOHN ALDERSON, JR., b. New Jersey, 5 Mar. 1738, son of Rev. John Alderson; ord. Smith's and Lynville's Creek (Rockingham) Va., Oct. 1775-1777; sett. Alderson (Greenbriar) Va., 1777-1821; founder of Greenbriar Ch., 24 Nov. 1781; Bapt.; d. Alderson, Va., 5 Mar. 1821.

JOHN ALEXANDER (poss. son of John Alexander of Scotland, gent., b. 1665, Balliol Coll., Oxford, matric. 16 Dec. 1687, a. 22); signed a petition to Gov. Andros, 1696; sett. Sittingbourne Par. (King George) Va., before 1732; Ep.

GEORGE ALFORD, A.B., b. ca. 1611, son of John Alford of Heavitree, Devon, matric. Exeter Coll., Oxford, 3 Feb. 1631/2, a. 20; A.B., 21 June 1632; sett. Lynnhaven Par. (Princess Anne) Va., 1658; Ep.

THOMAS ALLARDS, ord. for Va., 27 Sept. 1699; Ep.; d. Williamsburg, Va., 1701.

ALMONER, see Armeraud.

CHARLES ANDERSON, b. ca. 1670; inducted by order of Council, 1693; sett. Westover Par. (Charles City) Va., 1692-1718; signed a petition to Gov. Andros, 1696; Ep.; d. Westover Parish, Va., 1718.

JAMES ANDERSON (See C.C.Del.), b. Scotland, 17 Nov. 1678; sett. Rappahannock, Va., 22 Apr. 1709-1710; Presb.; d. Donegal, Pa., 16 July 1740.

JOHN ANDREWS, b. Scotland; ord. 1749, lic. for Va., 12 Apr. 1749; K.B. for Va., 17 Apr. 1749; sett. Cameron Par. (Loudoun) Va., 1749-1767; in 1765 he was paid for two sermons in Truro Parish; Ep.

* K.B., King's Bounty, i.e., passage money paid to America. The location of churches and parishes in the South is given by counties rather than by towns. The county (indicated by parentheses) follows the name of the parish.

ROBERT ANDREWS, A.M., b. Pa.; Univ. of Pa., 1766, A.B., A.M.; ord. England, 1772, lic. for Ware Parish, Va., 26 Dec. 1772, K.B. for Va., 19 Jan. 1773; chaplain, Va. regt., Rev. war; commissioner to extend the Mason & Dixon line, 1779-1784; Prof. of Moral Philosophy, Wm. & Mary Coll., 1779, Prof. of Mathematics, 1784; deputy, 1787-1799; sett. York-Hampton Par. (York) Va., 1785; Ep., d. 1804.

WILLIAM ANDREWS, A.B. (perhaps b. 1671, son of John Andrews of Bishops Canning's, Wilts; matric. Lincoln Coll., Oxford, 15 July 1690, a. 24 y; A.B., 1695); ord. for Va., 4 Oct. 1700; sett. St. Mary's Par. (Caroline) Va., 1702-1703; sett. Albany, N.Y. (missionary to the Indians), 1712-1719; translator of a primer and prayers into the Mohawk language; Ep.

WILLIAM ANDREWS, b. Ireland (perhaps admitted sizer, Trinity Coll., Dublin, 27 May 1766); ord. (Bsp. London), 1770; missionary at Schenectady, N.Y., 1770-1773; sett. Nottoway Par. (Southampton) Va., 1775-1776; Tory; Ep.

JOSEPH ANTHONY, itinerant preacher in Va.; sett. Chesterfield (Chesterfield), Va., 1770-1771; later at Otter Creek and Burton's Creek, Va.; Bapt.

JOHN ARMERAUD (Armourier or Almoner), sett. Hungar's Par. (Northampton) Va., before 1651; sett. Wicomico Par. (Northumberland) Va., before 1653; sett. at Christ Church Par. (Lancaster) Va., on 3 Dec. 1653; Ep. (He may have been: John Armanar, of Wilts, b. 1590; matric. Hart Hall, 19 June 1910, a. 20).

JONATHAN ARNOLD, A.M. (See C.C.N.E.) b. Haddam, Conn., 11 Jan. 1700/1, son of Jonathan and Elizabeth Arnold, Y.C., 1723, A.B., A.M.; A.M., Oxf., 1735/6; ord. West Haven, Conn. (Cong. Ch.), 1725-1734; ord. England (Ep.), 1735; K.B. for N.E., 19 Mar. 1735/6; sett. West Haven and Derby, Conn. (Ep. Ch.), 1736-1740; sett. St. Andrew's Ch., Staten Island, N.Y., 1740-1745; sett. Fredericksville Par. (Albemarle) Va., 1747-1754; Cong.-Ep.; d. Fredericksville, Va., 1754.

ARCHIBALD AVENS (or Avon), ord. 1767; lic. for Va., 2 Feb. 1767, K.B. for Va., 10 Feb. 1767; sett. Cameron Par. (Loudoun) Va., 1767-1776; Ep.

JUSTINIAN AYLMER, sett. Elizabeth City Par. (Elizabeth City) Va., 1645-1667; sett. James City Par. (James City) Va., 1671; Ep.

JOHN BAGGE (prob. b. Kilkee (Waterford) Ireland, 1682, son of Wm., pensioner, Univ. of Dublin, 26 July 1698, A.B., 1703), came to Va. as a deacon, 1709; ord. (Ep.) England, 1717, K.B., Va., 13 Nov. 1717; sett. St. Anne's Par. (Essex) Va., 1709-1712; sett. Hanover Par. (King George), 1713-1716; Sittingbourne Par. (Richmond), 1716-1716; St. Anne's Par. (Essex), 1717-1725; Ep.; d. Williamsburg, Va., 1725.

ELIJAH BAKER, b. Lunenburg co., Va., 1742; baptized, 1769; ord. (Bapt.) Mecklenburg County, Va., 1773; sett. Geneto Ch.,

Maloane's (Mecklenburg) and Boar Swamp Ch. (Henrico), and as an itinerant preacher in Charles City, James City and York counties, Va., 1773-1773, and in Henrico, New Kent and Warwick counties, 1773-1775; sett. Lower Northampton Ch. (Northampton) Va., 1778-1798; Bapt.; d. Northampton co., Va., 6 Nov. 1798.

THOMAS BAKER (A.B., Oxford, 1758 or 1761), lic. for Va., 24 Aug. 1769; K.B., Va., 8 Sept. 1769; applied for Kingston Par. (Mathews) Va., 1770; poss. sett. there, 1770-1774; Ep.

WILLIAM BALFOUR, K.B. for Va., 23 Jan. 1738/9; sett. Upper Parish (Nansemond) Va., 1744-1745; Ep.

JOHN BALL (A.B., Oxford 1670 or 1677), sett. Henrico City Par. (Henrico) Va., 1679-1684; St. Peter's Par. (New Kent), 1685-1689; signed the address to Gov. Nicholson, 1700; Ep.

ALEXANDER BALMAINE, b. near Edinburgh, Scotland, 1740; matric. St. Andrews, Edinburgh, 23 Feb. 1757/8; ord. 1772, lic. for Cople Par. (Westmoreland) Va., 11 Oct. 1772, K.B., 20 Oct. 1772; sett. Augusta Par. (Augusta) Va., Nov. 1773-1775; member, Committee of Safety, Augusta co.; chaplain, 13th Va. regt. throughout the Rev. war; sett. Frederick co., Va., 1785-1820; Ep.; d. Frederick, Va., ca. 1820.

JOHN BANISTER, A.M., b. ca. 1650, son of John Banister of Twigworth, co. Gloucester, Eng.; matric. Magdalen Coll., Oxford, 21 June 1667, a. 17; A.B., 1671, A.M., 1674, clerk, 1674-1676, chaplain, 1676-1678; original Trustee of Wm. & Mary Coll, Va., 1691; sett. Charles City Par. (Charles City), Va., 1678-1692; a distinguished botanist; Ep.; d. Roanoke Falls, Va., 1692.

JOHN BARCLAY, A.M. (See C.C.Md.), b. Windsor, Eng., 28 Mar. 1732, son of Rev. James Barclay, Canon of Windsor; A.B., King's Coll., Camb., 1755, A.M., 1758; sett. Cumberland Par. (Lunenburg) Va., 1756-1757; sett. Oxford and St. Peter's Parish (Talbot) Md., 1758-1770; Ep.

THOMAS BARGRAVE, D.D., matric. Clare Coll., Camb., ca. 1596; A.B., 1599/1600, A.M., 1603, B.D., 1610, D.D., 1621; Rector of Jevington (Sussex) Eng., 1614-1621; came to Va. with his brother, Capt. George Bargrave, 1619; sett. Henrico City Par. (Henrico) Va., 1619-1621; he was nephew to the Dean of Canterbury; gave his library to the proposed College at Henrico, Va.; Ep.; d. Henrico City, Va., 1621.

HENRY BARLOW, K.B. for Va., 4 June 1725; sett. Warwisqueake Par. (Isle of Wight) Va., 1726-1729; Lynnhaven Par. (Princess Anne) Va., 14 Nov. 1729-14 Oct. 1747; Hungar's Par. (Northampton) Va., 1747-1761; Ep.; d. Hungar's Parish, Va., 1761.

SAMUEL BARNARD (possibly b. 1683, son of William Bernard of Winchfield, Hants, matric. Univ. Coll., Oxford, 12 Mar. 1699/1700, a. 17); came to Va., 1716; sett. by Gov. Spotswood in a parish near Williamsburg; was sick in 1719; Ep.

JOSEPH BARNET, lic. 19 Mar. 1775; ord. June 1775; sett. Patterson's Creek (Mineral) W.Va., 1775 et post; Bapt.

JOHN BARNETT (See *C.C.N.C.*), lic. for N.C., 2 May 1765, K.B. for N.C., 10 May 1765; S.P.G. missionary in N.C., Oct. 1765-1770; sett. St. Thomas's Par. (Orange) Va., 1771-1774; Ep.

ROBERT BARRETT, b. in Va., son of Charles Barrett of Louisa co., Va.; K.B. for Va., 5 Dec. 1737; master of the Indian School, Wm. & Mary Coll., 1737; sett. St. Martin's Par. (Hanover) Va., 1738-1787; Ep.; d. Albemarle co., Va., 1805.

DAVID BARROW, b. in Va., ca. 1753; preached in Brunswick co., Va., 1771; ord. Mill Swamp (Isle of Wight) Va., 2 July 1774-1797; also preached at Black Creek, Va.; went to Ky., 1797; Bapt.; d. Kentucky, ca. 1814.

JAMES BATES, b. Middletown, Va., 1650, son of George Bates of York County, Va.; sett. Skimino Creek, Va., Friend's Meeting, 1712-1723; Quaker; d. Skimino Creek, Va., 1723.

THOMAS BAYLEY (See *C.C.Md.*), K.B. for Narragansett (R.I.), 27 Mar. 1712; itinerant minister in N.C.; sett. St. Paul's Parish, Baltimore, Md., 1713-1723; sett. Newport Par. (Isle of Wight) Va., 1724-1728; Lynnhaven Par. (Princess Anne) Va., 1728; Ep.; sent back to Eng., 1729.

JOHN BEATTY (prob. matric. Univ. of Glasgow, 14 Nov. 1729); K.B. for Va., 27 Feb. 1732/3; sett. St. Andrew's Par. (Brunswick) Va., 1733-1750; Ep.

THOMAS BECKETT, K.B. for Va., 10 May 1727; sett. St. James's Par. (Goochland) Va., 1727-1733; St. Mark's Par. (Culpeper) Va., May 1733-1739; officiated in Fredericksville Par. (Albemarle) Va., 1754; Ep.

JAMES BELL, b. Sussex co., Va., 1735; sett. Sappony (Sussex) Va., 1773-1778; Bapt.; d. Sappony, Va., Sept. 1778, a. 43.

JOHN BELL (possibly b. 1671, son of William Bell of Sowton, Salop; matric. Pembroke Coll., Oxford, 18 Nov. 1691, a. 20); came to Va., 1711; K.B. for Va. 21 Jan. 1711/2; sett. St. Mary's White Chapel Par. (Lancaster) Va., 1713-1743; Christ Ch. Par. (Lancaster), 1713-1743; St. Stephen's Par. (Northumberland) Va., 1723; Ep.; d. Christ Church Parish, Va., 1743.

THOMAS BENNETT, A.B., matric. sizar, Trinity Coll., Camb., 1621, A.B., 1624/5; ord. priest by the Bishop of Peterborough, 9 Apr. 1628; sett. West Parish (Nansemond) Va., 1648; became head of an Independent (Puritan) congregation, 1648; banished by Gov. Berkeley, 1648; Ep.-Independent.

WILLIAM BENNETT, A.M., matric. sizar, St. John's Coll., Camb., 1569, A.B., 1570/1, A.M., 1574; Rector, Suffield (Norfolk) Eng., 1581-1621; Puritan clergyman who came to Va., 1621; was minister at Edward Bennett's plantation at Warwisqueake, 1621-1624; Independent; d. Warwisqueake Parish, Va., 1624.

JOHN BERKELEY, A.B. (probably b. Limerick, Ireland, 1708, son of Rev. Henry Berkeley; matric. pensioner, Trinity Coll., Dublin, 15 June 1730, A.B., 1734); sett. Cornwall Par. (Charlotte)

Va., 1755-1762; Cumberland Par. (Lunenburg) Va., 1756; perhaps at Jamestown, 1758; Ep.

JOHN BERTRAND, fled from France as a Huguenot under Louis XIV; ord. in Eng.; sett. in King George and Lancaster counties, Va.; sett. Sittingbourne Par. (King George) Va., 1701; Ep.; d. Sittingbourne Parish, 1701.

JOSEPH BEWSHER, A.B., b. 1720, son of Launcelot Bewsher of Barton (Westmoreland) Eng.; matric. Queen's Coll., Oxford, 27 Mar. 1740, a. 20; A.B., 1743; S.P.G. missionary at Barbadoes; lic. for Va., 2 Mar. 1752; declined a call to Henrico Parish, Va., 1752; Ep.

SAMUEL BLACK, came from Ireland, ord. Brandywine Manor, Pa., 10 Nov. 1736; sett. Brandywine Manor, Pa., 18 Nov. 1735-May 1741; installed, Mount Joy, formerly Franklin, now Geinburg, Conewago (Adams) Pa., May 1742; sett. Mount Joy, Pa., 1741-4 Apr. 1745; sett. Londonderry (Lebanon) Pa., 1741-1745; sett. Rockfish and Mountain Plains (Nelson) Va., 1752-1770; Old Side Presb.; d. Rockfish (Nelson) Va., 9 Aug. 1770.

WILLIAM BLACK (See C.C.Del.), b. Dumfries, Scotland, ca. 1679; S.P.G. missionary at Lewes and Cedar Creek Hundred, Del., 1708-1709; sett. Accomac Par. (Accomac) Va., 1709/10-1724; Ep.

ARTHUR BLACKAMORE, b. ca. 1679, son of Arthur Blackamore of London; matric. Christ Church Coll., Oxford, 7 May 1695, a. 16; K.B. to Va., 26 Sept. 1707; master of the grammar school, Wm. & Mary Coll., Va., 1710-1716; Ep.

JOHN BLACKNALL, A.B., b. 1692, son of John Blacknall of Wiccham, Bucks, gent., matric. Christ Church Coll., Oxford, 31 Mar. 1710, a. 18; A.B., 1714; K.B. for N.C., 7 June 1725; missionary, S.P.G., in N.C., 1725-1726; sett. St. Stephen's Par. (Northumberland) Va., 1726-1726; sett. Kingston Par. (Mathews) Va., 1740-1747 (and possibly 1726-1747); Ep.; d. Kingston Parish, Va., 1747.

BENJAMIN BLAGROVE, b. 1746, son of John Blagrove of Oxford; matric. St. Mary's Hall, 15 Oct. 1764, a. 18; lic. for Va., 5 Mar. 1772, K.B. for Va., 10 Mar. 1772; sett. Southwark Par. (Surry) Va., 1774-1776; member of the county Committee of Safety for Surry co., Va.; chaplain, Gen. Assembly, 1783; sett. Martin's Brandon Par. (Prince George) Va., 1785-1787; sett. Westover Par. (Charles City) Va., 1787; sett. St. Peter's Par. (New Kent) Va., 1789-1793; Ep.

COMMISSARY JAMES BLAIR, D.D., b. Scotland, 1653; A.B., Univ. of Edinburgh, A.M., D.D.; Rector, Cranston, Scotland, before 1682; in England, 1682-1685; came to Va., 1685, as missionary, S.P.G.; founder and first President, William & Mary Coll., 1693-1743; Commissary to the Bishop of London for Va., 1689-1743; sett. Henrico Par. (Henrico) Va., 1685-1694; James City Parish (James City) at Jamestown, Va., 1694-1710; Bruton Par. (James City) at

Williamsburg, 1710-1743; President of the Council of the Colony; acting Governor of Va., 1740-1741; Ep.; d. Williamsburg, Va., 18 Aug. 1743, a. 87; buried at Jamestown.

WILLIAM BLAND, b. Va.; ed. William & Mary Coll., 1758-1763; ord. London, 1767, lic. for Va., 24 June 1767, K.B. for Va., 15 July 1767; sett. James City Par. (James City) Va., 1767-1777; Warwick Par. (Warwick) Va., 1785; Elizabeth City Par. (Elizabeth City) Va., 1786; Norfolk Par. (Norfolk) Va., 1791-1803; Ep.; d. Norfolk, Va., 1803.

AARON BLEDSOE, sett. North Fork of Pamunkey (Orange) Va., 1774-1806; excluded, 1806; Bapt.; d. before 1809.

JOSEPH BLEDSOE, sett. Upper Essex (Essex) Va., 1772-1773; Bapt.

THOMAS BLUETT (or Blewer) (See C.C.Del.), sett. North Farnham Par. (Richmond) Va., 1739-1742; S.P.G. missionary in Kent co. and at Dover and Milford, Del., 1745-1749; Ep.; d. Dover, Del., 25 Jan. 1749.

JOSEPH BLUMFIELD (or Bloomfield), b. Eyrecourt (Galway), 1710, son of Benjamin Blumfield; pens. Trinity Coll., Dublin, 14 Oct. 1726, a. 16; A.B., 1731; K.B. for Va., 3 July 1735; sett. St. Paul's Par. (Hanover) Va., 1736; Truro Par. (Fairfax) Va., 1737; Ep.

JAMES BOISSEAU, taught at the Huguenot Academy in Montauban, France; came to Va., 1689; K.B., 11 Nov. 1689; sett. St. John's Par. (King William) Va., 18 Mar. 1689/90-1692/3; Charleston, S.C., Huguenot Ch., 1712-1712; Hug.-Ep.; living at Charleston, S.C., 1712.

FRANCIS BOLTON, A.B., King's Coll., Camb., 1613/4, perhaps Vicar at Goodeston, Norfolk, England, 1613; came to Va., 1621; sett. Elizabeth City Par. (Elizabeth City) Va., 1621-1623; Kecoughtan Par. (Elizabeth City), 1621-1623; sett. Hungar's Par. (Northampton) Va., 1623-1630; James City Par. (James City) Va., at Jamestown, 1630 et post; Ep.

JOHN BOLTON, sett. Cople Par. (Westmoreland) Va., 1693-1698; Ep.

JONATHAN BOUCHER, A.M. (See C.C.Md.), b. Blencogo, Cumberland, England, 12 Mar. 1737/8; A.M., Columbia (Hon.), 1771; ord. 1762; arriv. Urbana, Va., 12 July 1759; taught school at Port Royal, Va.; resided at Mt. Church (Essex) Va.; K.B. Va., 30 Mar. 1762; sett. St. Mary's Par. (Caroline) Va., 1759-1762, 1763-1770; sett. Hanover Par. (King George) Va., 1762-1770; Annapolis, Md., 1770-1775; loyalist, ret. to England, Sept. 1775; Ep.; d. Carlisle, Cumberland, Eng., 27 Apr. 1804.

JAMES BOWKER, b. Blakeley, Lancashire, England, 1665, son of the Rev James Bowker (and brother of Rev. Ralph Bowker, q.v.); adm. sizar, St. John's Coll., Camb., 5 June 1684, a. 19; sett. Kingston Par. (Mathews) Va., 1690-1691; sett. St. Peter's Par. (New Kent) Va., 1698-1703; Ep.; d. St. Peter's Par., Va., 1703.

RALPH BOWKER, b. Caton, Lancashire, 1671, son of Rev. James Bowker; adm. sizar St. John's Coll., Camb., 27 June 1678, a. 17; sett. St. Stephen's Par. (King & Queen) Va., 1702-1714; member of the convention of the clergy, 1719; Ep.

ROBERT BRACEWELL, A.B., b. ca. 1612, son of Richard Bracewell of London; matric. Hart Hall, Oxford, 22 Feb. 1627/8, a. 15; A.B., 3 Nov. 1631; came to Va. before 1651; chosen Burgess from Isle of Wight co., Va., 1653; in Isle of Wight co., 1653-1668; Ep.; d. ca. 1668.

JOHN BRACKEN, D.D., lic. for Amelia co., Va., 6 July 1772; K.B. Va., 28 July 1772; sett. Bruton Par. (James City) Va., at Williamsburg, 1773-1818; master of the grammar school, William & Mary Coll., 1775-1779; President and Prof. of Moral Phil., William & Mary Coll., 1812-1814; chosen Bishop of Virginia, 1812, but never consecrated; Ep.; d. Williamsburg, Va., 15 July 1818.

JOHN BRAIDFOOT, b. Scotland, lic. for Va., 25 Apr. 1772; K.B. Va., 28 Apr. 1772; sett. Portsmouth Par. (Norfolk) Va., 1774-1784; chaplain throughout the Rev. war; Ep.; d. Portsmouth, Va., ca. 1785.

JOHN BRANDER, lic. for Va., 11 Mar. 1759; K.B. Va., 14 Mar. 1759; sett. Russell Par. (Bedford) Va., 1773-1776; Ep.

JAMES BREECHIN (See *C.C.Md.*), K.B. to Md., 10 Dec. 1695; sett. All Hallow's and Coventry Parishes, Md., 1696-1698; ret. to England; K.B. again, to Va., 16 Nov. 1702; sett. St. Paul's Par. (Hanover) Va., 1704-1705; Cople Par. (Westmoreland), 1709-1722; Ep.; living in Va., 1722.

CHARLES BRIDGES, sett. St. Martin's Par. (Hanover) Va., 1734-1738; Ep.

WILLIAM BRODEY (or Brodie), ord. for Va., 17 June 1709; K.B. Va., 25 June 1709; sett. St. Peter's Par. (New Kent) Va., 1710-1720; Ep.; d. St. Peter's Parish, Va., 1720.

CLEMENT BROOKE (See *C.C.Md.*), b. Prince George co., Md., ca. 1730; sett. in Md., 1759-1762; came to Va. from Md., 1762; sett. Overwharton Par. (Stafford) Va., 1764-1776; member, Committee of Safety, Stafford co., Va.; sett. Cople Par. (Westmoreland) Va., 1765; Ep.; d. Prince George co., Md., 1800, aged over 70 years.

ZACHARIAH BROOKE, A.M., b. Yeldham, Essex, Eng., 1676, son of Rev. John Brooke; matric. Sidney Coll., Camb., 30 June 1690, a. 14; A.B., 1693/4, A.M., 1697; ord. (Bsp. of Ely), 20 Sept. 1702; vicar of Hauxton and Newton, Cambridgeshire; came to Va. ca. 1710; K.B. for Va., 24 July 1719; sett. St. Peter's Par. (New Kent) Va., May to Oct. 1721; sett. St. Paul's Par. (Hanover) Va., 1721-1736; sett. Dale Par. (Chesterfield) Va., 1737-1738; sett. King William Par. (Powhatan) Va., 1737-1738; Ep.; d. Manakintown, Va., 1738.

JOHN BROWN, A.B., b. 1728; A.B., Princeton, 1749; ord. Fagg's Manor, Pa., 11 Oct. 1753; sett. Timber Ridge (Rockbridge) Va., 1753-1767; New Providence (Rockbridge) Va., 1753-1796;

moved to Ky.; New Side Presb.; d. Frankfort, Ky., 1803. a. 75.

JOHN BRUNSKILL, Sr. (I), K.B. for Va., 6 May 1715, came to Va., 1715; attended the convention in 1719; sett. Wilmington Par. (James City) Va., 1715-1723; sett. St. Margaret's Par. (Caroline) Va., 1738-1758; Ep.

JOHN BRUNSKILL, A.B. (II), b. 1718, son of Richard Brunskill of Upmanhall, Westmoreland, Eng.; adm. sizar Pembroke Coll., Camb., 13 Oct. 1737, a. 19; A.B., 1741/2; sett. Cumberland Par. (Lunenburg) Va., 1748; sett. Raleigh Par. (Amelia) Va., 1754-1804 (vacant 1776-1785); Ep.; d. Raleigh Parish, Va., 1804.

JOHN BRUNSKILL, Jr. (III), b. 1731, son of Rev. John Brunskill of Va.; adm. sizar Pembroke Coll., Camb., 16 Mar. 1750/1, a. 20; lic. for Va., 29 Sept. 1752; K.B. Va., 11 Oct. 1752; sett. Hamilton Par. (Fauquier) Va., 1754-1758; Ep.

ROBERT BUCHAN, lic. for Va., 16 Mar. 1772; K.B., Va., 20 Mar. 1772; sett. Amherst Par. (Amherst) Va., 1780; Overwharton Par. (Stafford) Va., 1785-1804; Ep.

JOHN BUCHANAN, D.D., b. near Dumfries, Scotland, 1743; A.B., Edinburgh, A.M., D.D., before 1812; ord. London, 1775; lic. for Va. (Henrico Par.), 13 Aug. 1775; K.B. Va., 5 Sept. 1775; sett. Lexington Par. (Amherst) Va., 1780-1785; sett. Henrico Par. (Henrico) Va., 10 May 1785-1822; Ep.; d. Richmond, Va., 19 Dec. 1822, a. 74.

RICHARD BUCKE, b. Wymondham, Norfolk, Eng., ca. 1582, son of Edmund Bucke; adm. sizar Caius Coll., Camb., 26 Apr. 1600, a. 18; came to Va. with Sir Thomas Gates, landing at Jamestown, 23 May 1610; sett. James City Par. (James City) at Jamestown, 1610-1623/4; Ep.; d. Jamestown, Va. before Feb. 1623/4.

HENRY JOHN BURGES, b. Va., 28 Nov. 1744, son of Rev. Thomas Burges of Va.; lic. (Bsp. of London), 1 Nov. 1768; K.B. for N.C., 11 Nov. 1768; S.P.G. missionary, St. Mary's Par. (Edgecomb) N.C., 1769-1770; sett. Newport Par. (Isle of Wight) Va., 1770-1776; sett. Nottoway Par. (Southampton) Va., 1776-1785, 1789-1797; Suffolk Par. (Southampton) Va., 1778; Southwark Par. (Surry) Va., 1785-1789; Ep.; d. Nottoway Parish, Va., 1797.

THOMAS BURGES, Sr., b. Staffordshire, Eng., 6 Sept. 1712; K.B. for N.C., 2 Oct. 1741; came to Va.; sett. Nottoway Par. (Southampton) Va., 1754-1758; sett. St. Mary's Par. at Tarboro (Edgecomb) N.C., 1759-1779; kept school both in Va. and N.C.; Ep.; d. Edgecomb, N.C., 1779.

BENJAMIN BURGHER, b. ca. 1744; ord. Va., ca. 1774; sett. Mt. Ed (formerly Whitesides) (Albemarle) Va. (1774 et post?); Bapt.; d. Mt. Ed, Va., 12 Nov. 1822, a. 78.

THOMAS BURNET (possibly A.B., Queen's Coll., Camb., 1690, A.M., 1694), ord. for Va., 30 Aug. 1700; K.B. for Va., 18 Sept. 1700; sett. Lawn's Creek Par. (Surry) Va., 1702 (et post?); North Farnham Par. (Richmond) Va., 1741-1742; Ep.

JOHN BURRUS, sett. Middlesex co., Va., 1770; Bapt.

JAMES BUSHNELL, sett. Weyanoke Par. (Charles City) Va., 1702 ff.; Ep.

AMORY BUTLER, b. Montacute, Somersetshire, England, 1648, son of Rev. Almeric Butler, vicar of that parish; adm. sizar Sidney Coll., Camb., 7 May 1667, a. 18; sett. Sittingbourne Par. (King George) Va., 1671-1678; Ep.; d. King George co., Va., 1678.

THOMAS BUTLER, A.M. (prob. A.M., Oxford, 1631, or Camb., 1623); sett. Denbigh Par. (Warwick) Va., 1635 *et post;* Ep.

WILLIAM BUTLER, A.B., b. Moorlinch, Somerset, Eng., 1647, son of Rev. Almerica Butler; adm. sizar Sidney Coll., Camb., 25 Apr. 1664, a. 17; A.B., 1667/8; sett. Washington Par. (Westmoreland) Va., 1677-1681; Ep.; brother of Rev. Amory Butler.

JEAN CAIRON, b. Figeac, Guyenne, France; escaped to Zurich, Switzerland, 1688, at the time of the revocation of the Edict of Nantes; sett. Pays de Vaud; K.B. to Va., 10 Oct. 1710; sett. Manakintown, King William Par. (Powhatan) Va., 1710-1715; Hug.-Ep.; d. Manakintown, Va., 1715.

SAMPSON CALVERT, A.B., b. ca. 1603, son of Rev. George Calvert, of Meere, Somersetshire, Eng.; matric. St. Edmund's Hall, Oxford, 23 Jan. 1623/4, a. 20, A.B., 14 Feb. 1624/5; sett. Elizabeth River Par. (Norfolk) Va., 1649; Ep.

JOHN CAMERON, D.D., educ. at King's Coll., Aberdeen; D.D., William & Mary Coll.; ord. (Bsp. of Chester), 1770; came to Va., 1770; sett. St. James's Par. (Mecklenburg) Va., 1770-1784; Bristol Par. (Dinwiddie) Va., 1784-1793; Nottoway Par. (Nottoway) Va., 1793-1795; Cumberland Par. (Lunenburg) Va., 1795-1815; Ep.; d. Cumberland Parish, Va., 1815.

JOHN CAMM, D.D., b. ca. 1718, son of Thomas Camm of Hornsea, co. York, Eng.; adm. sizar Trinity Coll., Camb., 16 June 1738, a. 20, A.B., 1741/2, A.M.; ord. (Bsp. of Lincoln), 28 Mar. 1742; sett. Newport Par. (Isle of Wight) Va., 1745-1749; York-Hampton Par. (York) Va., 1749-1771; 1774-1778; sett. Bruton Par. (James City) Va., at Williamsburg, 1771-1773; Prof. of Divinity, William & Mary Coll., 18 Sept. 1749-1757; 1763-1772; Bishop's Commissary in Va., 1771-1776; Pres., William & Mary Coll., 1771-1777; member, Colonial Council of Va., 1774; Ep.; d. Williamsburg, Va., 1778.

ICHABOD CAMP, A.M. (See *C.C.N.E.*), b. Durham, Conn., 15 Feb. 1725/6, son of John Camp; Y.C., A.B., 1743, A.M.; ord. (Bsp. of London), 25 Mar. 1751/2; lic. 26 Mar. 1752; K.B., N.E., 7 Apr. 1752; S.P.G. missionary at Middletown and Wallingford, Conn., Aug. 1754-June 1760; sett. St. Anne's Par. (Albemarle) Va., 1752-1753; Amherst Par. (Amherst) Va., 1761-1776; Lexington Par. (Amherst) Va., 1761-1776; had been settled as a Congregationalist at Sharon, Conn., 27 May 1746-May 1748; physician; Ep.; d. Kaskaskia, Ill., 20 Apr. 1786.

ARCHIBALD CAMPBELL, b. Kirnan, Scotland; came to Va., 1730; K.B. for Va., 4 Feb. 1745/6; sett. Washington Par. (Westmoreland) Va., 1754-1775; Ep.

JAMES CAMPBELL, lic. by Hanover Presbytery, Va., 10 Oct. 1771; sett. Cub Creek (Charlotte), Forks of the James (Rockingham), Hat Creek (Campbell), Sinking Spring (Washington), and Timber Ridge (Rockingham), all in Va., 1771-1772; Presb.; d. Va., 15 Oct. 1772.

ANDREW CANT, K.B., Leeward Islands, 29 June 1692; in Va., 1696; signed a petition to Gov. Andros for more salary; Ep.

JOHN CARGILL, K.B., Leeward Islands, 21 Apr. 1708; ord. for Va., 28 Apr. 1708; sett. Southwark Par. (Surry) Va., 1708-1732; Ep.; d. (will probated in Surry co.), Va., 1732.

JOHN CARNEGIE, A.M., b. Scotland, ca. 1673, son of David Carnegie, gent.; Glasgow Univ.; matric. Balliol Coll., Oxford, 28 Sept. 1695, a. 22, as A.M., of Aberdeen; K.B. for Va., 11 Oct. 1700; ord. for Va., 26 Oct. 1700; sett. St. Mary's White Chapel Par. (Lancaster) Va., 1702-1706; Ep.

JOHN CARR, A.B., b. Geggleswick, Eng., 1643, son of John Carr; adm. sizar Christ's Coll., Camb., 4 Mar. 1660; A.B., 1664/5; ord. Deacon (Archbsp. of York) Sept. 1664; sett. St. Peter's Par. (New Kent) Va., 1684-1685; Ep.; d. St. Peter's Parish, Va., 1685.

ROBERT CARR, sett. Stratton-Major Par. (King & Queen) Va., 1680-1686; Ep.

JESSE CARTER, lic. for Southampton Par., Va., 21 Oct. 1772; K.B. Va., 3 Nov. 1772; applied for St. James Southam Par. (Powhatan) Va., 1773, but not chosen; sett. Drysdale Par. (Caroline) Va., 1778-1804; Ep.

ROBERT CHAPLIN, resigned a parish (unknown) in Va., 1740; Ep.

RÉNÉ CHASTAIN, b. Powhatan co., Va., 28 June 1741, of French parents; ord. Buckingham (Buckingham) Va., Apr. 1772-1825; Bapt.; d. Buckingham, Va., 1825.

WILLIAM CHICHELEY, A.M., b. 1691, son of Sir John Chicheley, Knt., of Wimpole, Cambridgeshire; adm. pens. Trinity Coll. Camb., 28 June 1709, a. 18; A.B., 1712/3, A.M., 1716, college librarian, 1716; Rector, Widley, Hants, 1726, and of Farlington, 1726; K.B. Va., 24 Sept. 1729; Ep.; d. 1737.

JAMES CHILES (or Childs), sett. Louisa co., Va., 1770; sett. Rocky River (Anson) N.C., 1770-1776; Bapt.

HENRY CHRISTALL, went to Eng. for Holy Orders, 1741; sett. St. Stephen's Par. (Northumberland) Va., 1742-1743; Ep.

JAMES CLACK, b. England; K.B. for Md., 10 Dec. 1695; sett. Ware Par. (Gloucester) Va., 1679-1723; Ep.; d. Ware Parish, Va., 1723.

CHARLES CLAY, b. Hanover co., Va., 1744 (first cousin of Henry Clay); lic. for Va., 7 June 1769; ord. London, 1769; K.B. Va., 8 June 1769; sett. St. Anne's Par. (Albemarle) Va., 22 Oct. 1769-1785; Manchester Par. (Chesterfield) Va., 1785-1786; farmer after 1785 in Bedford co.; delegate to the Constitutional Convention of Va., 1788; Ep.; d. Bedford co., Va., ca. 1824.

ELEAZER CLAY, b. 2 May 1744; ord. Chesterfield (Chesterfield) Va., 1775-1836; Bapt.; living in Chesterfield, Va., 2 May 1836, a. 92 yrs.

JOHN CLAY, sett. Chickahominy, Va., 1776-1780; Bapt.; d. Chickahominy, Va., 1780.

JOHN CLAYTON, Fellow of the Royal Soc.; sett. James City Parish (James City) Va., at Jamestown, 1684-1686; ret. to Eng.; naturalist and writer; Ep.

JAMES CLOUGH (or Gough) (perhaps Magdalen Coll., Oxford, 1664; A.M.; Fellow at Oriel Coll., 1665-1672); sett. James City Par. (James City) Va., at Jamestown, 1676-1684; sett. Southwark Par. (Surry) Va., 1684; condemned to death by Beacon, but released; Ep.; d. Jamestown, Va., 15 Jan. 1683/4.

MR. CLUVERIUS (a Philip Cluver was at Exeter Coll., Oxford, 1609); sett. Hampton Par. (York) Va., ca. 1644; Ep.

ROSCOW COLE, lic. for Va., 19 Jan. 1748/9, K.B. for Va., 21 Feb. 1748/9; usher at the William & Mary Coll. grammar school, 1744-1747; sett. Warwick Par. (Warwick) Va., 1754; Ep.

SAMUEL COLE, sett. Pianketank Par. (Middlesex); Christ Church Par. (Lancaster); and Lancaster Parish (Middlesex), all in Va., 1657-1659; Ep.; d. Lancaster co., Va., 1659.

PETER COLLIER, A.B., adm. sizar, Christ's Coll., Camb., 10 May 1686, A.B., 1689/90; in Va. 1700 (K.B. for Md., 28 July 1698); sett. Hungar's Par. (Northampton) Va., 1702-1703; Ep.

HENRY COLLINGS, K.B. for Va., 8 May 1722; sett. St. Peter's Par. (New Kent) Va., 1722-1725; Ep.; d. St. Peter's Parish, Va., 1725.

ALEXANDER COOKE, sett. Christ Church Par. (Lancaster) Va., 26 Sept. 1652-*ante* 1 Apr. 1657; Ep.

WILLIAM COTTON (possibly, Fellow at Exeter Coll., Oxford, 1629-1639; A.B., 7 July 1632; A.M., 30 Apr. 1635); sett. Hungar's Par. (Northampton) Va., 1632-1645; Ep.; prob. Rector, Nether Broughton, co. Leicester, Eng., 1646.

JOHN COURTNEY, b. King and Queen co., Va., ca. 1744; sett. Upper College (King William) Va., 1774-1778; sett. Richmond, Va., 1788-1810; Bapt.; d. Richmond, Va., 18 Dec. 1824.

WILLIAM COUTTS, lic. for Va., 7 June 1768; sett. Martin's Brandon Par. (Prince George) Va., 1773-1776; resigned, 1776; Ep.

JAMES COX, D.D. (See *C.C.Md.*), b. St. Giles in the Fields, London, England, 27 Mar. 1693, son of Rev. Henry Cox; matric. Merton Coll., Oxford, 20 May 1708, a. 15, A.B., 1713, A.M., 1716, B.D. & D.D., 1731; Curate, Pinner, Herts, 1716; Master, Harrow Free Grammar School, 1722; K.B., Md., 21 June 1723; sett. Charles City county, Va., 1723-1729; sett. St. Paul's Par. (Queen Annes) Md., 1729-1753; St. John's Par. (Caroline) Md., 1748-1753; (Upper Master, Harrow School, 1730-1746); Ep.; d. St. Paul's Parish, Md., 1753.

ELIJAH CRAIG (brother of Lewis Craig), ord. Blue Run

(Orange) Va., May 1771; sett. Blue Run, 1769-1786; member of the N.C. Separatist Bapt. Assn., 1772; sett. Crooked Run (Culpeper) Va., 1772-1774; removed to Ky., 1786; Bapt.; d. Kentucky, 1808.

JAMES CRAIG, A.B., b. ca. 1724, son of Philip Craig of London, gent., matric. Christ Church Coll., Oxford, 17 June 1742, a. 18; A.B., 1746; lic. for Va., 31 Mar. 1755; K.B. Va., 4 Apr. 1755; sett. St. Stephen's Par. (Northumberland) Va., 1758-1758; sett. Cumberland Par. (Lunenburg) Va., 1759-1795; physician and preacher; Ep.; d. Cumberland Parish, Va., 1795.

JAMES CRAIG (possibly the same), sett. Hamilton Par. (Fauquier) Va., 1774 et ante- ca. 1799; Ep.

JOHN CRAIG, A.M., b. Dunagor, co. Antrim, Ireland, 17 Aug. 1709; A.M., U. of Edinburgh, 1732; came to New Castle, Del., 17 Aug. 1734; lic. Donegal, 30 Aug. 1738; ord. Augusta, Va., 3 Sept. 1740; sett. Tinkling Spring (Augusta) Va., near Waynesboro, 1740-1774; sett. Augusta (Augusta) Va., Old Stone Church at Fort Defiance, 1740-1774; first settled Presbyterian minister in Va.; d. Augusta Church (Augusta) Va., 21 Apr. 1774, a. 63.

LEWIS CRAIG (brother of Elijah Craig), b. Va., 1740; began preaching 1767; ord. Upper Spotsylvania, Va., Nov. 1770; sett. Craig's Chh., Upper Spotsylvania, 1770-1781; sett. Tuckahoe (Caroline), Upper King & Queen (King & Queen), and Upper Essex (Essex) Va., ca. 1781; Gilbert Creek (Lincoln) Va., 1781-1783; South Elkhorn, Ky., 1783-1795; Bapt.; d. Bracken co., Ky., 1826, a. 86.

WILLIAM CRAIGH, sett. Cornwall Par. (Charlotte) Va., ca. 1755; Ep.

ALEXANDER CRAIGHEAD, son of Rev. Thomas Craighead (See C.C.N.E.), lic. 8 Oct. 1734; ord. Bart, Middle Octorora, Pa., 18 Nov. 1735-1741; was a Cameronian, 1745-1753; sett. Windy Creek (Augusta) Va., on Cow Pasture River, 1749-1755; sett. Sugar Creek and Rocky River Center (Muhlenburg) N.C., inst. 27 Sept. 1758-1766; only minister in 1766 between the Yadkin and Catawba rivers; third minister to sett. in N.C.; Presb.; d. Rocky Creek, N.C., Mar. 1766.

JOHN CREEL, came from Fauquier co., Va., 1765; sett. Brick Church, Mill Creek (Pittsylvania) Va., 1770-1795; Bapt.; d. Mill Creek, Va., ca. 1795, a. 52.

ALEXANDER CRUDEN, b. Aberdeen, Scotland, lic. for Va., 14 Mar. 1749; K.B. Va., 22 Mar. 1749/50; sett. South Farnham Par. (Essex) Va., 1752-1774; Ep.; ret. to Great Britain at the beginning of the Rev. war.

CHARLES CUMMINGS, b. Ireland, 1732; came to America in early manhood; lic. Tinkling Spring (Augusta) Va., 18 Apr. 1767; ord. North Mountain (Augusta) Va., 14 May 1767-Apr. 1772; sett. Holston (Washington) Va., 30 miles east of Abingdon, as first minister, with churches at Sinking Spring, Ebbing Spring and Royal Oak, 1772-1812; member, Committee of Safety, Fincastle and Washington counties, Va., 1776; Chaplain, 1776; Presb.; d. Holston, Va., Mar. 1812, a. 80 y.

DAVID CURRIE, b. Edinburgh, Scotland; came to Va., 1730; ord. for Va., 1740 or 1742; sett. Christ Church Par. (Lancaster) Va., 1743-1780; sett. St. Mary's White Chapel Par. (merged with Christ Church Par., 1752) (Lancaster) Va., 1743-1752; supply, Wicomico Par. (Northumberland) Va., 1745; Ep.; d. Christ Church Parish, Va., 1792.

CHARLES DACRES, sett. Wicomico Par. (Northumberland) Va., 1683; Ep.; see Charles Davies, prob. the same.

TOWNSHEND DADE, lic. for Va., 13 Aug. 1765, K.B. Va., 15 Aug. 1765; ord. London, Eng., for Fairfax Parish, Va., 1765; sett. Fairfax Par. (Fairfax) Va., 1765-1777; sett. St. Peter's Par. (Montgomery) Md., 1791-1794; Ep.

JOSEPH DAVENPORT, b. Williamsburg, Va.; educated at William & Mary Coll.; lic. for Va., 12 Oct. 1755; K.B. Va., 23 Oct. 1755; sett. Charles Par. (York) Va., 1757-1785; Ep.

CHARLES DAVIES (or Davis, see also Dacres), sett. Old Farnham Par. (Richmond) Va., ca. 1680 and ff.; sett. Wicomico Par. (Northumberland) Va., ca. 1680-1683; Ep.

PRICE DAVIES, A.B., b. 1732, son of Rev. Edward Davies of Moughtrey, co. Montgomery; matric. Jesus Coll., Oxford, 13 June 1750, a. 18; A.B., Christ Church Coll., 1754; sett. Blissland Par. (New Kent) Va., 1763-1792; Ep.

SAMUEL DAVIES, A.M., b. near Summit Ridge, New Castle co., Del., 3 Nov. 1723, son of David Davies, of Welsh extraction; A.M., Princeton, 1753 (Hon.); attended Mr. Blair's school at Fagg's Manor; lic. 30 July 1746; ord. Hanover (Hanover) Va., 19 Feb. 1746/7, as an evangelist; missionary to Hanover co., Va., 1747; sett. Hanover (Hanover) Va., seven miles from Richmond, 1747-1759; visited Scot. and Eng. to solicit funds for Princeton Univ., 1753-1755; arriv. N.Y., 13 Feb. 1755; Pres., Princeton Univ., 26 Sept. 1759-1761; minister, 1st Chh., Princeton, N.J., 1759-1761; Presb.; d. Princeton, N.J., 4 Feb. 1761, a. 36 (GS).

WILLIAM DAVIES (or Davis), sett. Hanover Par. (King George) Va., 1752-1758; Master, grammar school, William & Mary Coll., 1758; sett. Westover Par. (Charles City) Va., 1758-1773; sett. Hanover Par. (King George) Va., 1773-1777; Ep.

JONATHAN DAVIS, preached at New Poquoson Par. (York) Va., 1680; Ep.

PETER DAVIS, lic. for Va., 11 June 1751, K.B. Va., 25 June 1751; sett. Southwark Par. (Surry) Va., 1754-1758; Ep.

SUPERIOR DAVIS, supply, Christ Church Par. (Middlesex) Va., 1682-1683; Ep.

THOMAS DAVIS, lic. for Va., 22 Sept. 1754; K.B. Va., 25 Sept. 1754; sett. Warwick Par. (Warwick) Va., 1758; Ep.

THOMAS DAVIS, from Charles City co., Va.; usher, William

& Mary Coll., 1768; ord. London, Sept. 1773; lic. for Norfolk Parish, Va., 21 Sept. 1773; K.B. Va., 13 Oct. 1773; sett. Elizabeth River Par. (Norfolk) Va., 1773-1776; St. Stephen's Par. (Northumberland) Va., 1779-1792; Fairfax Par. (Fairfax) Va., 1792-1806; Elizabeth River Par. (Norfolk) Va., 1806-1808; Hungar's Par. (Northampton) Va., 1808; chaplain, 1st Continental Dragoons, Am. Rev.; officiated at Washington's funeral; Ep.; d. Hungar's Parish, Va., after 1808.

MARTIN DAWSON, b. 1744; sett. Ballenger's Creek, Totier (Albemarle) Va., 1774-1809; Bapt.

MUSGRAVE DAWSON, A.B., b. 1723, son of William Dawson of Aspatria, Cumberland, Eng.; matric. Queen's Coll., Oxford, 2 Mar. 1743/4, a. 20; A.B., 1747; lic. for Va., 1 Feb. 1747; K.B. Va., 4 Feb. 1747; sett. St. Mary's Par. (Caroline) Va., 1751-1758; Ep.

THOMAS DAWSON, A.M., b. 1713, son of Edward Dawson of Soulby, Cumberland; matric. Queen's Coll., Oxford, 6 Mar. 1731/2, a. 19; ord. 1740; master, Indian School, William & Mary Coll., 1738-1755; sett. Bruton Par. (James City) Va., at Williamsburg, 1743-1759; Bishop's Commissary, 1752-1761; Pres., William & Mary Coll., 1755-1761; member, Governor's Council, 1755-1761; called brother of William, but prob. son of Edward; Ep.; d. 1761.

WILLIAM DAWSON, D.D., b. 1705, son of William Dawson of Aspatria, Cumberland; matric. Queen's Coll., Oxford, 11 Mar. 1719/20, a. 15; A.B., 22 Feb. 1724/5, A.M., 1728; D.D., Oxford, 10 Feb. 1746/7; Prof. of Moral Philosophy, William & Mary Coll., 1729-1749; Bishop's Commissary for Va., 1743-1752; Pres., William & Mary Coll., 1743-1752; member, Governor's Council, 1743-1752; Ep.; d. Williamsburg, Va., 1752.

WILLIAM DEAN, sett. Forks of the James (Rockbridge) Va., 1747-1748; sett. Timber Ridge (Rockbridge) Va., 1747-1748; Presb.

LAURENCE DE BUTTS (See C.C.Md.), b. 1693, matric. Trinity Coll., Dublin, 1721; K.B. for Va., 1721; sett. Washington Par. (Westmoreland) Va., 1721-1730; St. Stephen's Par. (Northumberland) Va., 1723-1726; St. Mark's Par. (Culpeper) Va., 1731-1733; Pohick Church, Truro Par. (Fairfax) Va., 1733-1734; sett. in Md., (q.v.), 1735-1763; Ep.; d. 1763.

BENJAMIN De JOUX, minister at Fenestrelle (Waldensian Valleys), 1659-1662; later sett. at Die, Lyon and London; refugee minister in London, 30 Mar. 1691; came in the "Peter and Anthony," to Jamestown, Va., 20 Sept. 1700; Ord. (Bsp. of London) for King William Parish, Va., as its first minister; sett. King William Par. (Powhatan) Va., 1700-1704; first Waldensian minister in America; Ep.; d. Manakintown, King William Parish, Va., 1703/4 (adm. bond signed, 24 Aug. 1704).

THOMAS DELL, b. ca. 1696, matric. Merton Coll., Oxford, 21 May 1713, a. 17; K.B. for Va., 2 June 1721; sett. Hungar's Par. (Northampton) Va., 1721-1729; Ep.

CLAUDE PHILIPPE de RICHEBOURGE (See *C.C.N.C.* and *C.C.S.C.*), came to Va., 1700; sett. King William Par. (Powhatan) Va., at Manakintown, 1700-1707; sett. N.C., 1708-1711; sett. S.C., 1712-1719; Hug.-Ep.; d. St. James's Santee, S.C., 1719 (will made 15 Jan. 1718/9).

ARCHIBALD DICK, lic. for Va., 26 Mar. 1762; ord. 1762; K.B. for Va., 26 Mar. 1762; sett. St. Margaret's Par. (Caroline) Va., 1773-1801; Ep.

ADAM DICKIE, K.B. for Va., 12 Apr. 1731; sett. Va., 1731, as minister, parish unknown; Ep.

ROBERT DICKSON, b. Northumberland, Eng., ca. 1716; adm. sizar Peterhouse, Camb., 16 Apr. 1734, a. 18; lic. for Va., 22 Oct. 1746; sett. Lynnhaven Par. (Princess Anne) Va., 13 July 1748-23 Feb. 1776; Ep.; d. Lynnhaven Parish, Va., 1776 (will probated, Va., 14 Feb. 1777).

JOHN DIXON, educated, William & Mary Coll.; usher, Wm. & Mary Coll., 1747; lic. for Va., 4 Aug. 1748; K.B. Va., 7 Sept. 1748; sett. Kingston Par. (Mathews) Va., 1754-1770, resigned; sett. Stratton-Major Par. (King & Queen) Va., 1773; Prof. of Divinity, Wm. & Mary Coll., 1770-1777; Tory; Ep.; d. Kingston Parish, Va., 1777.

THOMAS DOBSON, b. Essex co., Va.; sett. Hunting Creek (Halifax) Va., 1775-1809; Bapt.; living Hunting Creek, Va., 1809.

BENJAMIN DOGGETT, A.M., b. Ipswich, Eng., ca. 1637, son of William Doggett; adm. sizar St. John's Coll., Camb., 27 Jan. 1654/5, a. 18, A.B., 1658/9, A.M., 1662; curate, Stoke, Suffolk, Eng., 1662; came to Va., 1669 or earlier; sett. Christ Church Par. (Lancaster) Va., 1669-1682; St. Mary's White Chapel Par. (Lancaster) Va., 1669-1682; Ep.; d. 1682.

WILLIAM DOTSON, sett. Ebenezer (Campbell) Va., 1773-1775; sett. Millstone, Va., ca. 1787; Bapt.

FRANCIS DOUGHTY (See *C.C.N.E.*), son of Francis Doughty, merchant and alderman of Bristol England; had been vicar of Sodbury in co. Gloucester; came to N.E., as a non-conformist, 1638; preached in Taunton, Mass., 1638-1639; sett. Newport, R.I., 1640-1642; sett. Newtown and Flushing, L.I., N.Y., 1642-1647; preached in English in New York, N.Y., 1643-1646; lived in Maryland, 6 Aug. 1648-12 Oct. 1659; sett. Patuxent River and Charles City co., Md., 1659-1662; sett. as an Ep. minister at Hungar's Par. (Northampton) Va., 1655-1659; sett. Northampton co., Va., 1662-1665; sett. Sittingbourne Par. (King George) Va., 1665-March 1669; was in N.Y.C., 19 Apr. 1669; but d. soon after this; Ep.-Cong.-Ep.

WILLIAM DOUGLASS, b. Scotland; lic. for Va., 24 Sept. 1749; K.B. Va., 5 Oct. 1749; sett. St. James-Northam (Goochland) Va., 1750-1777; resigned, 1777; removed to a farm in Louisa co.; Ep.; d. Louisa co., Va., ca. 1780.

COPE D'OYLEY, A.B., b. Southrop, Gloucester co., Eng.,

1658, son of Charles D'Oyley; matric. Wadham Coll., Oxford, 10 Mar. 1675/6, a. 17; A.B., Merton Coll., Oxford, 1680; sett. Elizabeth City Par. (Elizabeth City) Va., 1687; sett. Denbigh Par. (Warwick) Va., 1688-1696; sett. Bruton Par. (James City) Va., at Williamsburg, 1697-1702; chaplain, General Assembly, 1702; Ep.; d. Williamsburg, Va., 1702.

SAMUEL DUDLEY, b. ca. 1654, son of Thomas Dudley of Coventry, Eng.; matric. St. Edmund's Hall, Oxford, 24 Mar. 1670/1, a. 17; sett. Sittingbourne Par. (King George) Va., 1680-1684; sett. South Farnham Par. (Essex) Va., 1684; Ep.

HANDCOCK DUNBAR, A.B., b. Twiford, near Athlone, Ireland, 1702, son of Rev. David Dunbar; sizar, Trinity Coll., Dublin, 6 June 1721, a. 19; A.B., 1725; K.B. for Va., 20 Dec. 1725; sett. St. Stephen's Par. (King and Queen) Va., 1754-1776; Ep.

WILLIAM DUNLOP, from Philadelphia, Pa., lic. Barbadoes, 25 Feb. 1766; sett. Stratton-Major Par. (King and Queen) Va., 4 Apr. 1768-1779; sett. St. Paul's Par. (Hanover) Va., 1779; Ep.; d. St. Paul's Parish, Va., 25 Sept. 1779.

WILLIAM DUNN, b. ca. 1677, came from Clogher, Ireland; ord. (Bsp., of Down and Connor); K.B. for Carolina, 10 Dec. 1705; came to S.C., 1705; sett. St. Paul's Par. (Colleton) S.C., 1706-1707, resigned and left S.C., 1707; sett. Hungar's Par. (Northampton) Va., 1710 (and possibly 1707-1710); Ep.

ROBERT DUNSTER, sett. Isle of Wight co., Va., 1651-1656; Ep.; will made Isle of Wight co., Va., 1656.

WILLIAM DURAND, b. Cornwall, Eng., ca. 1624, son of Thomas Durand of Bodmin; matric. Exeter Coll., Oxford, 12 Sept. 1640, a. 16; sett. Elizabeth River Par. (Norfolk) Va., 1648; became a non-conformist; went to Boston.

NATHANIEL EATON, Ph.D., M.D. (see *C.C.N.E.*), b. 1609; came to Va., 1639; sett. Hungar's Par. (Northampton) Va., 1645-1646; ret. to Eng., 1646; Rector of Biddeford, Devon, 1668; Cong.-Ep.; d. a prisoner for debt, 1674.

SAMUEL EBURNE, b. London, ca. 1645, son of Richard Eburne of St. Antholin's, London, adm. pensioner, St. John's Coll., Camb., 3 Oct. 1663, a. 18; ord. 1 June 1667; Rector of Stocking-Pelham, Eng., 1667; sett. Setauket, L.I., N.Y., 1685-1688; sett. Bruton Par. (James City) Va., at Williamsburg, 1688-1697; returned to L.I., N.Y., where he lived 1697-1705; S.P.G. missionary at Isles of Shoals, N.H., 1703; Ep.

OBADIAH ECHOLS, sett. Wynn's Creek (Halifax) Va., 1773-1775 *et post*; Bapt.; d. before 1809.

DR. SAMUEL ECKERLING, b. Strasbourg, Alsace, son of City Councillor Michael Eckerling; arrived in Pa., 1725; ejected from Ephrata, Pa., 1745; sett. Strasburg, Va., 1750-July 1764; German Bapt. or Dunkard; d. 15 Jan. 1781.

SAMUEL EDMUNDSON, lic. Rockfish (Nelson) Va., 14 Oct. 1773; sett. at Cook's Creek, Linville's Mountain, Peeked Mountain, and Mossy Creek, all in Rockingham co., Va., 1773-1775; removed to S.C., 1775; Presb.

THOMAS EDWARDS, ord. 1702; K.B. for Va., 30 Nov. 1702; sett. St. Anne's Par. (Essex) Va., 1712-1716; Ep.; d. St. Anne's Parish, Va., 1716.

ESDRAS THEODORE EDZARD (or Edgard) (See *C.C.Md.*), sett. Hanover Par. (King George) Va., 1727-1731; gave up the ministry and kept a tavern at Falmouth, Va. 1757-1763; Ep.; d. Falmouth, Va., 1763.

HENRY ELEBECK, K.B. for Va., 11 Jan. 1731/2; sett. Southwark Par. (Surry) Va., 1747-1751; Ep.; d. Southwark Parish, Va., 2 Nov. 1751.

ROBERT ELKIN, b. Brunswick co., Va., 1745, son of Nathaniel Elkin; sett. as a Bapt. preacher in Orange co., Va., 1771-1779; took oath of allegiance in Orange co., Va., 25 Mar. 1779; sett. Winchester, Ky.; Bapt.; d. Winchester, Ky., 1822.

ARTHUR EMMERSON, SR., A.B., b. ca. 1711, son of John Emmerson of Newcastle-upon-Tyne, Eng.; matric. Univ. Coll., Oxford, 3 July 1729, a. 18; A.B., 1733; K.B. for Antigua, 19 Mar. 1735/6; sett. Accomac Par. (Accomac) Va., 1754-1755 *et post;* Ep.

ARTHUR EMMERSON, Jr., prob. son of Rev. Arthur Emmerson, Sr., student, William & Mary Coll., 1758, lic. for Va., 29 Sept. 1768; K.B. Va., 11 Nov. 1768; sett. Meherrin Par. (Greenville) Va., 1773-1776; sett. Suffolk Par. (Nansemond) Va., 1785; sett. Portsmouth Par. (Norfolk) Va., 1785-1801; Ep.

GEORGE EVE, b. Culpeper, Va., 1748; ord. 1778; sett. Rapidan (Culpeper) Va., 1775-1790; sett. Blue Run (Orange) Va., 1786-1790; sent to Ky., 1790; sett. Georgetown, Ky., 1790-1800; Bapt.; d. Kentucky after 1800.

JAMES FALCONER, K.B. for Va., 8 Oct. 1718; sett. Hungar's Par. (Northampton) Va., 1719-1720; sett. Elizabeth River Par. (Norfolk) Va., 1720-1724; sett. Elizabeth City Par. (Elizabeth City) Va., 1720-1724; sett. Charles Par. (York) Va., 1725-1727; Ep.; d. Charles Par. (York) Va., 1727.

PATRICK FALCONER, K.B. for Va., 29 Apr. 1710; arriv. in Va., Aug. 1710; sett. Hungar's Par. (Northampton) Va., 1710-1718; Ep.; d. Hungar's Parish, Va., 1718.

THOMAS FALKNER (or Faulkner), sett. Warwisqueake Par. (Isle of Wight) Va., 1642; Ep.

JOHN FARNIFOLD, A.B., son of Sir Thomas Farnifould of Steyning, Sussex, M.P., 1624-1626, 1640-1645; matric. New Coll., Oxford, 2 Oct. 1652, A.B., 19 Apr. 1656; sett. Old Fairfield Par. (later known as St. Stephen's Par.) (Northumberland) Va., 1670-1702; sett. Boutracey Par. (Northumberland) Va., 1690-1702; member, first Board of Trustees, William & Mary Coll., 1691-1693; Ep.; d. Fairfield Parish, Va., 1702 (will dated and proved 1702).

FENDALL, see Trendall.

MR. FENTON, Ep. clergyman, d. Elizabeth City co., Va., 1624

(possibly Matthew Fenton of London, gent., matric. Trinity Coll., Oxford, 13 Dec. 1616, a. 17, A.B., 24 Feb. 1619/20; or Johnson Fenton, of Wilts, matric. Queen's Coll., Oxford, 6 Feb. 1600/1, a. 18).

ROBERT FERGUSON, sett. Bristol Par. (Dinwiddie) Va., 1740-1748; Ep.; d. Bristol Parish, Va., 1748.

NICHOLAS FERRERS, ord. by Bsp. Laud, 1626; sett. James City (James City) Va., 1626-1637; Ep.; d. Jamestown, Va., 1637.

THOMAS FIELD, lic. 2 Aug. 1770; K.B. for America, 16 Aug. 1770; sett. Kingston Par. (Mathews) Va., 1774-1778; Ep.

ALEXANDER FINNEY, K.B. for Va., 17 Dec. 1724; sett. Rector of Martin's Brandon Par. (Prince George) Va., 1724-1770; Ep.; d. Martin's Brandon Parish, Va., 17 Nov. 1770.

THOMAS FINNEY, A.B., son of Rev. Thomas Finney, matric. New Inn Hall, Oxford, 9 Dec. 1650, A.B., 11 Oct. 1653; vicar of Perran Zabuloe, 1661; sett. Charles Par. (York) Va. 1686-1687; Ep.; d. Charles Parish, Va., 1687.

WILLIAM FINNEY, A.M. (Glasgow); came to Va., 1710; sett. Henrico Par. (Henrico) Va., 1711-1727; sett. King William Par. (Powhatan) Va., 1718-1727; sett. St. James-Northam Par. (Goochland) Va., 1720-1724; Ep.; d. Henrico Parish, Va., 1727.

PHILIP VICKERS FITHIAN, A.B., Princeton, A.B., 1772; preached at Opequon, Va., 11 June 1775; chaplain, Heard's Brigade, N.J. Militia, 1776; Presb.; d. 1776.

EDWARD FOLLIOTT, B.C.L., b. 1610, son of Sir John and Elizabeth (Aylmer) Folliott of Naunton, Worcestershire, Knt.; matric. Hart Hall, Oxford, 13 Apr. 1632, a. 22; B.C.L., 24 Nov. 1632; Rector, Foots Cray, Kent., 1634; Rector, Alderton, Northants, 1634-1640; came to Va., 1652; sett. York Par. (York) Va., 1652-1690; sett. Cople Par. (Westmoreland) Va., ca. 1673; Ep.; d. York Parish, Va., 1690 (will proved 1690). (Also spelled Foliot).

FRANCIS FONTAINE, b. 1697, son of James Fontaine; K.B. for Va., 30 Dec. 1720; sett. Manakintown, King William Par. (Powhatan) Va., 1720-1721; sett. St. Margaret's Par. (Caroline) Va., 1721-1722; sett. St. Peter's Par. (New Kent) Va., 1722; sett. Yorkhampton Par. (York) Va. 1722-1749; Prof. of Oriental languages, William & Mary Coll., 1729; Hug.-Ep.; d. Yorkhampton Par., 1749.

JAMES MAURY FONTAINE, son of Francis Fontaine; student at William & Mary Coll.; ord. in England, 1762, for Petsworth Parish; lic. for Va., 10 Oct. 1763; K.B. Va., 8 Dec. 1763; sett. Petsworth Par. (Gloucester) Va., 1762-1764, 1790-1795; sett. Ware Par. (Gloucester) Va., 1764-1795; sett. Abingdon Par. (Gloucester) Va., ca. 1792; Ep.; d. Ware Parish, Va., 1795.

PETER FONTAINE, b. 1691, son of James Fontaine; K.B. for Va., 30 Mar. 1716; sett. James City Par. (James City) Va., 1716-1720; Martin's Brandon Par. (Charles City) Va., 1716-1720; Wallingford Par. (Charles City) Va., 1716-1720; Weyanoake Par. (Charles City) Va., 1716-1720; King William Par. (Henrico) Va.,

1719-1720; sett. Westover Par. (Charles City) Va., 1720-1757; Chaplain, Col. Byrd's Commission to survey the Va.-N.C. line, 1728-1729; Hug.-Ep.; d. Westover Parish, Va., July 1757.

ALEXANDER FORBES, ord. for Va., 6 Mar. 1709/10; K.B. for Va., 25 Mar. 1709/10; arriv. in Va., Aug. 1710; sett. Warwisqueake Par. (Isle of Wight) Va., 1710-1727; Ep.

EDWARD FORD, B.D., b. ca. 1715, son of Rev. Thomas Ford, Bishop's Palace, Bristol, Gloucestershire, Eng.; matric. Corpus Christi Coll., Oxford, 16 Dec. 1729, a. 14; A.B., 1733, A.M., 17 Feb. 1736/7, B.D., 1744; master, grammar school of William & Mary Coll., 1737-1739; sett. Petsworth Par. (Gloucester) Va., (1739-1741); went to Eng., for priest's orders, 1739, to qualify for holding a Fellowship at Oxford; Ep.

REUBEN FORD, b. 1742, son of William Ford; ord. Goochland (Goochland) Va., 1771-1823; sett. Licking Hole (Goochland) Va., 1776-1780; sett. Hopeful (Goochland) Va., 1807-1823; Bapt.; d. Goochland, Va., 1823.

STEPHEN FOUACE, came to Va., 1685, member, first Board of Trustees, William & Mary Coll., 1691; sett. Yorkhampton Par. (York) Va., 1690-1702; sett. Martin's Hundred Par. (James City) Va., 1702; Walloon-Ep.; ret. to Eng., 1702.

JAMES FOULIS, lic. for Va., 28 Dec. 1750; K.B. for Va., 24 Jan. 1750/1; sett. Antrim Par. (Halifax) Va., 1753-1759; went to S.C., 1770; sett. St. David's Parish at Cheraw Hill, S.C., 1770-1770; left S.C., 1779; Ep.

GEORGE FOX, founder of the Society of Friends; preached at the Old Somerton meetinghouse (Nansemond) Va., 1672; Quaker.

JOHN FOX, b. in Va., possibly the son of Henry Fox of King William co.; student at William & Mary Coll.; went to Eng. for Holy Orders, May 1731; lic. for Va., 11 Sept. 1731; master, Indian School, William & Mary Coll., 1729-1736; sett. Ware Par. (Gloucester) Va., before 1737-1764; Ep.

JOHN FRASER (See C.C.Md.), ord. 29 Aug. 1700; K.B. Va., 18 Sept. 1700; arriv. in Va., 1 Nov. 1701; sett. Overwharton Par. (Stafford) Va., 1702-1705; sett. St. Paul's Par. (King George) Va., 1702-1705; sett. in Md., 1705-1742; Ep.; d. Piscataway Parish, Md., Nov. 1742.

GEORGE FRAZIER (See C.C.Del.), res. Overwharton Par. for a time before going to Eng. for ordination; K.B. for Va., 20 Aug. 1738; sett. Dale Par. (Chesterfield) Va., 1742-1754, and poss. 1738-1758; Ep.

DANIEL FRISTOE (See C.C.Md.), b. Chappawomsick, Stafford co., Va., 7 Dec. 1739, brother of William Fristoe; ord. 15 June 1771; sett. Brenttown (Fauquier) Va., 1774-1774; Bapt.; d. Marcus Hook, Pa., 1774, a. 35.

WILLIAM FRISTOE, b. Stafford co., Va., 1742, brother of Daniel Fristoe; lic. 1761; sett. Chappawomsick (Fauquier) Va., 1761-1810; sett. Potomac Church, Hartwood (Stafford) Va., 1771-

1776; sett. Buck Marsh (Frederick) Va., 1771-1776; also Zion and Salem (Shenandoah) Va., time not given; Bapt.; d. Broad Run (Shenandoah) Va., 14 Aug. 1828, a. 85.

WILLIAM FYFE, schoolmaster, Elizabeth City, Va., 1724; K.B. for Va., 24 Sept. 1729; sett. Elizabeth City Par. (Elizabeth City) Va., 1731-1755; Ep.; d. Elizabeth City, Va., 1755.

JOHN GAMMILL, K.B. for Va., 24 Sept. 1729; sett. Warwisqueake Par. (Isle of Wight) Va., 1729-1744; Ep.; d. Newport, Va., 1744.

JAMES GARDEN, lic. for Va., 22 Sept. 1754; K.B. Va. 25 Sept. 1754; sett. St. Patrick's Par. (Prince Edward) Va., 1755-1773; Ep.; d. St. Patrick's Parish, Va., 19 Feb. 1773.

ROBERT GARNER (K.B. for Va., 23 Sept. 1735 as Robert Gardner ?), sett. Wicomico Par. (Northumberland) Va., 1739-1740; Ep.

JAMES GARNET, b. Culpeper co., Va., Nov. 1743, son of Capt. Anthony Garnet; sett. Crooked Run (Culpeper) Va., 1774-1830; Bapt.; d. Crooked Run, Va., 1830.

JOHN GARRARD, b. Pa.; sett. Mill Creek, Opequon (Berkeley) Va., 1755-1756; sett. Ketockton Creek (Loudoun) Va., 1756-1766; sett. Buck Marsh (Frederick) Va., prob. 1766-1770; Presb.; d. ca. 1784.

JOHN GARZIA, K.B. for Va., 8 Apr. 1724; sett. Elizabeth River Par. (Norfolk) Va., 1724-1739; missionary of S.P.G. from Va. to N.C., 1739-1744; sett. Bath, N.C., St. Thomas's Church, 1739-1744; Ep.; d. Bath (Beaufort) N.C., 29 Nov. 1744, by a fall from a horse.

ANTHONY GAVIN, K.B. for Va., 17 June 1735; sett. Henrico Par. (Henrico) Va., 1735-1736 (9 months); sett. St. James-Northam Par. (Goochland) Va., 1736-1750; preached four times in French and six times in English each year in the Huguenot Church at Manakintown, King William Par. (Powhatan) Va., 1736-1750; Hug.-Ep.; d. St. James-Northam Parish, Va., 1750 (will probated in Goochland co., 18 Sept. 1750).

JAMES GELSTON, sett. Opequon (Frederick) Va., 1737-1738; Presb.

ISAAC WILLIAM GIBERNE, b. Westminister, London, Eng., nephew of the Bsp. of Durham; lic. for Va., 30 Sept. 1758; came to Va., 1759; K.B. for Va., 12 Feb. 1765; Rector, Hanover Par. (King George) Va., 1759-1762; sett. St. Thomas's Par. (Orange) Va., 1759-1761; sett. Lunenburg Par. (Richmond) Va., Jan. 1762-1795; member, Committee of Safety, Richmond co., Va.; Ep.

THOMAS GILBERT, sett. Buffaloe (Halifax) Va., 1776-1777; Bapt.

NICHOLAS GLOVER, A.M., matric. sizar Jesus Coll., Camb., Easter, 1584, A.B., 1587/8, A.M., 1591; preached in counties Bedford and Huntingdon, Eng.; came to Va., with Sir Thomas Gates, Aug. 1611; sett. Jamestown, Va., 1611; Ep.; d. soon after 1611.

MORGAN GODWIN, A.B., bapt. at English Bicknor, Gloucestershire, 2 Dec. 1640, son of Archdeacon Morgan Godwyn, LL.D., grandson of Bishop Francis, D.D., Bishop of Hereford, and great-grandson of Bishop Thomas, D.D., of Bath and Wells; matric. Brasenose Coll., Oxford, 27 June 1662, a. 21; A.B., Christ Church Coll., 16 Mar. 1664/5; came to Va., 1665; sett. James City Par. (James City) Va., 1665-1666; sett. Marston-York Par. (York) Va., 1665-1666; ret. to Eng.; vicar of Wendover (Bucks) Eng., 1666. Rector of Woldham (Kent) Eng., 1680; vicar of Bulkington (Warwick) Eng., 1681; Ep.

BENJAMIN GOODWIN, ord. for Va., 5 Mar. 1708/9; sett. St. Peter's Par. (New Kent) Va., 1709-1710; chaplain, General Assembly, 1714; sett. Yorkhampton Par. (York) 1714-1722; Ep.; d. Yorkhampton Parish, Va., 1722.

JOHN GOODWIN (possibly b. Horley, Oxfordshire, 1690, son of John Goodwin; matric. Christ Church Coll., Oxford, 22 Feb. 1707/8, a. 18; A.B., New Inn Hall, Oxford, 1711; Rector of Salford, Oxfordshire, 1710-1725); sett. St. Stephen's Par. (King and Queen) Va., 1725; Ep.

ALEXANDER GORDON, b. Scotland, sett. Antrim Par. (Halifax) Va., 1763-1775; sett. Petersburg, Va.; Tory; Ep.

JOHN GORDON (perhaps b. 1663, son of John Gordon of Oxford; matric. Brasenose Coll., Oxford, 29 Jan. 1679/80, a. 16; A.B., 1683); K.B. for Md., 27 Dec. 1695; supply at St. Peter's Par. (New Kent) Va., 1695; sett. Wilmington Par. (James City) Va., 1695-1702; Ep.

JOHN GORDON, sett. Frederick Par. (Frederick) Va., *before* 1765; Ep.

THOMAS GORDON (perhaps A.M., Trinity Coll., Camb.; vicar of Wolston (Warwick) Eng., 1665); sett. Farnham Par. (King George) Va., 1671; Ep.

JOHN GORSUCH (perhaps son of the Rev. John Gorsuch, D.D., d. Eng., 1649, and his wife Anne (Lovelace) Gorsuch, d. Va., 1657); sett. Lancaster Par. (Middlesex) Va., 1654-1657; Ep.

MATTHEW GOTTLIEB GOTTSCHALK (See *C.C.Md.*), b. 1716; sett. South Branch of the Potomac, West Va., 1745-1747; Moravian; d. Bethlehem, Pa., Aug. 1748.

GOUGH, see Clough.

ISAAC GRACE, ord. for Va., July 1703; K.B. Va., Aug. 1703; invited to preach at Bruton Par. (James City) Va., 1704; ret. to Eng.; Ep.

WILLIAM GRAHAM, A.B., b. Paxton (near Harrisburg) Pa., 19 Dec. 1745, son of Michael and Susanna (Miller) Graham; A.B., Princeton, 1773; lic. for Va., 26 Oct. 1775; sett. Timber Ridge (Rockbridge) Va. and Forks of the James (Rockbridge) Va., 1775-1789; founder and Rector, Washington Coll., now Washington & Lee Coll., Lexington, Va., teacher of Theology, 1775-1789, president,

1776-1796; Captain in Rev. war, 1778; Presb.; d. Richmond, Va., 9 June 1799 (GS).

SAMUEL GRAY, K.B. for Va., 1 Dec. 1689; on first Board of Trustees, William and Mary Coll., 1693; sett. Christ Church Par. (Middlesex) Va., 1690-1698; sett. Cople Par. (Westmoreland) Va., 1699-1708; sett. St. Peter's Par. (New Kent) Va., 1708-1709; Ep.

MR. GRAYBILL, sett. Woodstock (Shenandoah) Va., 1754-1754; Mennonite.

SPENCE GRAYSON, b. 1734, son of Benjamin Grayson of Dumfries, Prince William co., Va., and brother of Senator William Grayson; ord. 1771; K.B. for Va., 27 June 1771; sett. Cameron Par. (Loudoun) Va., 1773-1776; sett. Dettingen Par. (Prince William) Va., 1784-1798; chaplain, Grayson's Continental Regiment, Rev. war; Ep.; d. Dettingen Parish, Va., 1798.

DR. CHARLES GREEN, A.M., b. ca. 1710, son of Moor Green of Monmouth, Wales; matric. Balliol Coll., Oxford, 15 Mar. 1727/8, a. 18, A.B., 1731, A.M., 15 Jan. 1735/6; ord. for Truro Par., 1737; sett. Cople Par. (Westmoreland) Va., 1734-1738; sett. Truro Par. (Fairfax) Va., 1737-1764; physician; Ep.; d. Truro Parish, Va., 1764.

ROGER GREEN, A.M., came from Norfolk, Eng., matric. sizar St. Catharine's Hall, Camb., Easter, 1631, A.B., 1634/5, A.M., 1638; ord. (Bsp. of Norwich) 9 Mar. 1638/9; sett. West Par. (Nansemond) Va., 1653-1671; sett. Jamestown, Va., 1671; Ep.; author of *Virginia's Cure . . .,* 1661.

JAMES GREENWOOD, b. lower Va., 1749; began preaching 1769; sett. Piscataway (Essex) Va., 1769-1809 (40 yrs.); (lay preacher in 1772; prob. ord. 13 Mar. 1774, when the church was organized); Bapt.; living at Piscataway, Va., 1809, a. 60.

STEPHEN GREGG, sett. Abingdon Par. (Gloucester) Va., 1695; expelled; Ep.

JOHN GREGORY, sett. Upper Par. (Nansemond) Va., 1680; Ep.

DAVID GRIFFITH, D.D., M.D., b. N.Y. City, 1742; K.B. N.J., 3 Sept. 1770; M.D., D.D., Univ. of Pa., 1786; physician, 1763-1770; ord. London, 19 Aug. 1770; S.P.G. Missionary at Gloucester and Waterford, N.J., 1770-1771; sett. Shelburne Par. (Loudoun) Va., 1771-May 1776; chaplain, 3rd Va. regt., 1776-1779; surgeon, Rev. army; sett. Fairfax Par. (Fairfax) Va., 1780-1789; Bsp. elect of Va., May 1786; Ep.; d. Philadelphia, Pa., 3 Aug. 1789, a. 48.

CHARLES GRIMES (or Grymes), b. Ightham, Kent, England, 1612; adm. sizar Pembroke Coll., Camb., 1631, a. 19; sett. York Par. (York) Va., 1644-1648; inducted, New Poquoson Par. (later Charles Par., 1692) (York) Va., 20 Feb. 1644/5; sett. 1644-1648; Ep.; d. Gloucester co., Va.

LEWIS GUILLIAM, b. ca. 1743, son of Morgan Guilliam of Llanavon Vawe, Brecon, Wales; matric. Jesus Coll., Oxford, 18 Mar. 1763, a. 20; sett. Camden Par. (Pittsylvania) Va., 1771-1777; member, Committee of Safety, Pittsylvania co., Va., 1774; Ep.

GEORGE GURLEY, K.B. for Va., 4 Oct. 1764; sett. St. Luke's Par. (Southampton) Va., 1773-1792; Ep.

JOHN GWINN (or Gwynn), matric. New Hall Inn, Oxford, 25 Mar. 1659; sett. Ware Par. (Gloucester) Va., 1672-1674; sett. Abingdon Par. (Gloucester) Va., ante 26 Sept. 1674-1688; Ep.

JOHN HENRY HAEGER, b. Anzhausen, Nassau, Germany, 25 Sept. 1644, son of Henry Haeger; professor of the Latin School at Siegen, 25 Sept. 1678-1703; installed minister, Oberfischbach, 12 June 1703-13 Apr. 1711 (resigned 16 Feb. 1711); in London, 2 Oct. 1713; came to Va., Apr. 1714; sett. Germania Ford (Orange) Va., St. George's Parish, 1714-1718; sett. Weaversville i.e. Germantown, 8 miles south of Warrentown (Fauquier) Va., 1718-1733; Germ.-Ref.; Ep.; d. Germantown, Va., Feb. 1733 (will probated 28 Mar. 1733), a. 88.

NATHANIEL HALL, sett. Upper Banister (Pittsylvania) Va., 1774-1774; Bapt.

THOMAS HALL, lic. for St. Martin's Par. in Va., 6 Apr. 1774; K.B. Va., 20 May 1774; sett. Trinity Par. (Louisa) Va., 1775-1776; sett. St. James-Northam Par. (Goochland) Va., 1781; chairman, Louisa Committee of Safety, 1775; Ep.

ARTHUR HAMILTON, lic. for Va., 11 June 1768; sett. Petsworth Par. (Gloucester) Va., 1768-1777; sett. Stratton-Major Par. (King & Queen) Va., 1778; chaplain to the Governor, 1769; Ep.

THOMAS HAMPTON, A.B., b. ca. 1609, son of Rev. William Hampton of Reigate, Surrey, Eng.; matric. New Coll., Oxford, 11 Mar. 1624/5, a. 16; A.B., Corpus Christi Coll., 3 Jan. 1626/7; came to Va. before 1637; sett. James City Par. (James City) Va., at Jamestown, 1640-Feb. 1644/5; sett. Hampton Par. (York) Va., Mar. 1645/6-1 Apr. 1658; sett. Wallingford Par. (Charles City) Va., ca. 1680; Wilmington Par. (James City) Va., ca. 1680; Ep.

JOHN GEORGE HANTSCH, Sr., came from Oltendorf, Saxony; ord. Deacon, 1750; itinerant minister in Md. and W. Va.; Moravian; d. Bethlehem, Pa., Jan. 1754.

Col. SAMUEL HARISS, b. Hanover co., Va., 12 Jan. 1724; baptized, 1758; ord. Sandy Creek, N.C., 1769; missionary to Va. and N.C., 1759-1795; sett. County Line (Pittsylvania) Va., 1771-1771; Church warden; Sheriff; Justice-of-the-Peace; Burgess; Col. in the militia; Captain of Fort Mayo and Commissary; Bapt.; d. Va., 1795.

THOMAS HARRISON, D.D. (See C.C.N.E.), b. Hull, Yorkshire, Eng., ca. 1616, son of Robert Harrison; adm. pens. Sidney Coll., Camb., 12 Apr. 1634, a. 16, A.B., 1637/8, D.D., Univ. of Dublin, 1658; came to Va., 1640; sett. Seawell's Point, Elizabeth River Par. (Norfolk) Va., 25 May 1640-summer 1648; chaplain to Gov. Berkeley; perhaps in Indian wars, 1644; turned non-conformist and banished, 1648; sett. Boston, Massachusetts, 1648-1650; ret. to Eng.; sett. St. Dunstan-in-the-East, London, 1651-1653; chaplain to Henry Cromwell, in Dublin, Ireland, 1654-1658; minister, St. Oswald's Church, Chester, Eng., 1658-1662; sett. Cook St. Church,

Dublin, Ireland, 1662-1682; lic. to preach in Cheshire, 1672; Ep.-Cong.; d. Dublin, Ireland, between 16 June 1682 (will made) and 22 Sept. 1682 (admin. granted).

WILLIAM HARRISON, b. 1730; sett. Bristol Par. (Dinwiddie) Va., 1762-1780; Ep.; d. Petersburg, Va., 1814, a. 84.

RICHARD HARTWELL, A.B. (See *C.C.Md.*), A.B., Trinity Coll., Dublin, 1729; sett. Bristol Par. (Dinwiddie) Va., 1739-1739; sett. Md., 1749-1751; Ep.

JOHN CHRISTOPHER HARTWIG (See *C.C.Md.*), preached at Winchester, Va., 1762, 1769, 1781; Lutheran; d. Claremont, N.Y., 17 July 1796, a. 82.

SAMUEL HEATON, b. Wrentham, Mass., 18 Nov. 1711, son of Samuel and Sarah Heaton; sett. N.J., ca. 1734; ord. N.J., 1751; sett. Opequon Creek (or Mill Creek) (Berkeley) W.Va., 1751-1754; sett. Pa. and N.J., 1754-1777; Bapt.; d. Dividing Creek, N.J., 26 Sept. 1777, a. 65.

JOHN WILLIAM HENDEL, D.D., b. Duerkheim, Palatinate, Germany, 20 Nov. 1740, son of John Jacob and Anna Sybilla (Otten) Hendel; educated at Univ. of Heidelberg, 10 May 1759-10 Feb. 1762; D.D., Princeton, 1787; came to Am., 1764; preached to 16 congregations in Pa.; sett. Stephentown (Frederick) Va., 1766-1770; V.P., Franklin Coll., 1787-1794; Pres. Council, G.R. Church, 1768, 1779, 1789, 1791; German-Ref.; d. Philadelphia, Pa., 29 Sept. 1798.

GERHARD ANTHONY JACOB HENKEL (or Henckel), bapt. Mehrenberg, Germany, 27 Oct. 1668, son of George and Anna Eulalia (Dentzer) Henckel; graduated in theol. at the Univ. of Giessen, 16 Mar. 1692; ord. Eschelbronn, Germany, 28 Feb. 1692; sett. near Frankfort-on-the-Main; sett. Massanutton Church at Germanna (Orange) Va., 1714-1716; ret. to Germany, 1716-1717; sett. St. Michael's Chh., Luth., Germantown, Pa., 1717-1728; also at Falkner's Swamp Chh., New Hanover, Pa., 1717-1728; and for 1723-1728: Mill Creek (Lebanon) Pa., Reed's or Old Tulpehocken Chh., and the Luth. chhs. at Manatawny, Oley Hills or Colebrookdale, Moselem and Rockland, all in Pa.; Luth.; d. Germantown, Pa., 12 Aug. 1728 (will dated same day).

SAMUEL HENLEY, lic. for Va., 24 Dec. 1769; K.B. Va., 8 Jan. 1770; Prof. of Moral Phil., William & Mary Coll., 1770-1777; sett. Bruton Par. (James City) Va., prob. as a curate; ret. to Eng., 1777; Ep.

FREDERICK LEWIS HENOP (See *C.C.Md.*), b. Kaiserslautern, 7 Oct. 1740; matric. Heidelberg, 1758; arriv. Am., 1765; sett. in Pa. and N.J., 1765-1769; sett. Md. and Va., 1770-1784; Va. settlements, 1770-1784: Lovettsville (Loudoun), Stephenstown (Frederick), Strasburg, at Staufferstown (Shenandoah), Winchester (Frederick), Woodstock, at Millerstown (Shenandoah), and Roeder's Chh. at Timberville; Germ.-Ref.; d. Frederick, Md., Sept. 1784.

PATRICK HENRY, K.B. for Va., 31 July 1732; sett. St.

George's Par. (Spotsylvania) Va., 1732-Apr. 1734; sett. St. Paul's
Par. (Hanover) Va., 1737-1777; Ep.; d. St. Paul's Parish, Va., 11
Apr. 1777.

ROBERT HENRY, A.M., b. Scotland; A.B., Princeton, 1751,
A.M.; ord. (Presby. of N.Y.), 1753; inst. Round Oak Chh., Cub
Creek (Charlotte) Va., 4 June 1755-1766; sett. Briery (Prince
Edward) Va., 1755-1766; sett. New Providence (Mecklenburg)
N.C., 1766-1767; Steel Creek (Mecklenburg) N.C., 1766-1767;
Presb.; d. Cub Creek (Charlotte) Va., 8 May 1767.

JAMES HERDMAN, lic. for Va., 23 Sept. 1770; K.B. Va.,
27 Sept. 1770; sett. Bromfield Par. (Culpeper) Va., 1774-1791; Ep.

RICHARD HEWITT, William & Mary Coll., 1753-1755; lic.
for Va., 30 Sept. 1760; sett. Hungar's Par. (Northampton)
Va., 1761-1774; Ep.; d. Hungar's Parish, Va., 1774.

WILLIS HEYLEY, sett. Mulberry Island (Warwick) Va.,
1634-1635 et post; Ep.

THOMAS HIGBY, sett. Hungar's Par. (Northampton) Va.,
1651-1656; Ep.

JAMES HILL, sett. Catawba (Halifax) Va., 1773-1777; Bapt.

MATTHEW HILL, ord. York, Eng., 3 June 1652; Rector of
Thirsk, Yorkshire, Eng.; ejected 1662; sett. Charles City co., Va.,
1669-1679; Ep.-Presb.-Independent.

JOHN HINDMAN, ord. in Pa. as a Presb. missionary to Va.,
11 Nov. 1742; sett. Opequon (Frederick) Va., 1743-1745; called to
Rockfish (Nelson) Va. and Mountain Plains (Nelson) Va., 26 Mar.
1745; became an Ep.; lic. for Va. by Bsp. of London, 22 Sept. 1746;
sett. Augusta Par. (Augusta) Va., 1747-1748, as the first minister of
that parish; Presb.-Ep.; d. Augusta Parish, Va., 1748.

JOHN HOGE, A.B., b. Scotland, son of William Hoge of
Pertha Amboy, N.J.; A.B., Princeton, 1749; lic. 10 Oct. 1753; ord.
1755; sett. Pennsylvania near the Susquehanna River, 1755; sett.
Opequon (Frederick) near Winchester, Va., 1755-1780; sett. Cedar
Creek (Frederick) Va., 1755-1780; sett. Tuscarora, Va., 1760-1776;
sett. Back Creek (Berkeley) W.Va., 1760-1780; ret. to Pa.; Presb.;
d. Pa. after 1795.

JOHN HOLBROKE (See C.C.Md.), came to Va., 1729; sett.
Hungar's Par. (Northampton) Va., 1729-1747; Ep.

N. HOLLOWAY, sett. Guinea's Bridge (Spotsylvania) Va.,
1774-1774; Bapt.

JOSEPH HOLT, A.B. (See C.C.Md.), b. Lancashire, Eng.,
1668; A.B., Jesus Coll., Camb., 1688/9; sett. Stratton-Major Par.
(King & Queen) Va., 1696-1700; supply, Petsworth Par. (Gloucester) Va., 1697-1700; sett. All Faith's Parish, Md., 1701-1703; William
and Mary Par., Md., 1701-1705; St. Mary's City, Md., 1701-1705;
ret. to Eng.; K.B. for Barbadoes, 11 Mar. 1712/3, as the first S.P.G.
missionary to the West Indies; chaplain and physician at Barbadoes,
1713-1714; supply, Wicomico Par. (Northumberland) Va., 1712-
1720; name often spelled Hoult; Ep.

GEORGE HOPKINS (prob. Camb. U., 1598/1600); came to Va., 1618/23; sett. Hampton Par. (then Chiskiack Par.) (York) Va., 1643-1645; Ep., d. York co., Va., 1645.

THOMAS HOPKINSON, A.M., b. Philadelphia, Pa., 7 Sept. 1747, son of the Hon. Thomas and Mary Hopkinson, A.B., Univ. of Pa., 1766, A.M., 1770; K.B. for Pa., 3 Oct. 1773; sett. St. Thomas's Par. (Baltimore) Md., 1775-1776; sett. Shrewsbury Par. (Kent) Md., 1777 et post; sett. Kingston Par. (Mathews) Va., 1784; Ep.; Charles co., Md., 26 May 1784.

JAMES HORROCKS, A.M., b. Wakefield, Yorks, Eng., ca. 1734, son of James Horrocks; adm. sizar Trinity Coll., Camb., 3 June 1751, a. 17; A.B., 1755, A.M., 1758, Fellow, 1756; ord. (Bsp. of Peterborough) 1757; usher at Wakefield School, 1757; lic. for Va., 5 Nov. 1761; K.B. Va., 5 Nov. 1761; master, grammar school, William & Mary Coll., 1763; sett. Bruton Par. (James City) Va., at Williamsburg, 1764-1771; Pres., William & Mary Coll., 1764-1771; Bishop's Commissary for Va., 1768-1771; member, Governor's Council; started for Eng., 1772; Ep.; d. Portugal, 27 Mar. 1772.

RICHARD HOTCHKISS, K.B. for Md., 30 Dec. 1720; sett. Southwark Par. (Surry) Va., 1753-1754; Ep.

WILLIAM HOUSDEN, sett. Newport Par. (Isle of Wight) Va., ca. 1680; sett. West Par. (Nansemond) Va., ca. 1680; Ep.

WILLIAM HUBARD (or Hubbard), son of James Hubard; William & Mary Coll., 1759-1762; ord. 1766; lic. for Va., 28 Apr. 1766; K.B. Va., 1 May 1766; sett. Warwick Par. (Warwick) Va., 1773-1776; sett. Newport Par. (Isle of Wight) 1780-1802; Ep.; d. Newport Par. (Isle of Wight) Va., 1802.

GEORGE HUDSON, adm. sizar Trinity Coll., Camb., 22 June 1686; K.B. for Va., 25 July 1694; minister in Va., 1694-1696, parish not given; Ep.; d. Williamsburg, Va., 1696.

THOMAS HUGHS, K.B. for Va., 31 Jan. 1715/6; sett. Upper Par. (Nansemond) Va., 1716-1719; sett. Abingdon Par. (Gloucester) Va., 1719-1744; Ep.

ROBERT HUNT, LL.B., b. Hants, ca. 1568; prob. matric. Magdalen Hall, Oxford, 14 Feb. 1588/9, a. 20, A.B., 23 Nov. 1592, A.M., 4 July 1595; LL.B., Trinity Hall, Camb., 1606; vicar of Reculver, 18 Jan. 1594/5-1602; sett. Heathfield, co. Sussex, 1602-1606; member, London Company, 10 Apr. 1606; embarked for Va., 19 Dec. 1606, as chaplain; sett. Jamestown (James City) Va., 1607-1608; first Anglican minister to settle in America; Ep.; d. Jamestown, Va., before 12 June 1608 (will probated 14 July 1608).

JOHN HURT, lic. for Va., 21 Dec. 1774; K.B. Va., 18 Jan. 1775; sett. Jefferson co., Va., 1775; chaplain, 6th Va. regt. in Rev. war; sett. St. Stephen's Par., S.C., 1783-1786; Ep.

ROBERT INNES, lic. for Va., 6 July 1747; sett. Drysdale Par. (Caroline) Va., 1754-1758; Ep.

WILLIAM IRWIN, student of the Rev. John Todd, Louisa co., Va., 1769; ord. Rockfish (Nelson) Va., 9 Apr. 1772-1775; sett.

Mountain Plains (Nelson) Va., 1772-1775; sett. Rich Cove (Albemarle) Va., 1775 *et post;* Presb.; d. Rich Cove, Va.

ANDREW JACKSON (said to have been not ordained episcopally), sett. Christ Church Par. (Lancaster) Va., 1683-1710; sett. St. Mary's White Chapel Par. (Lancaster) Va., 1683-1710; Ep.; d. Lancaster co., Va., 1710.

THOMAS JACKSON, came to Va. from N.Y.; ord. Cook's Creek (Rockingham) Va., 3 May 1770-1773; sett. Peaked Mountain (Rockingham) Va., 1770-1773; sett. Linville's Mountain (Rockingham) Va., 1770-1773; sett. Mossy Creek (Rockingham) Va., 1770-1773; Presb.; d. Rockingham co., Va., 10 May 1773.

HENRY JACOB, A.M., b. Kent co., Eng., 1563; matric. St. Mary's Hall, Oxford, 27 Nov. 1581, a. 18, A.B., 1583, A.M., 1586; sett. Leyden, Holland (Independent Chh.), 1607-1616; sett. London, Eng., 1616-1624 (called the *first* Congregational Chh. in the world); came to Va., 1624; sett. Warwisqueake Par. (Isle of Wight) Va., (Cong. Chh.), 1624 *et post;* Cong.; d. Isle of Wight co., Va., after 1624.

DEVEREUX JARRATT, b. New Kent co., Va., 6 Jan. 1732/3, son of Robert and Sarah (Bradley) Jarratt; lic. for Va., 28 Dec. 1762; ord. London, Eng., 1 Jan. 1763; K.B. for Va., 26 Jan. 1763; sett. Bath Par. (Dinwiddie) Va., 29 Aug. 1763-1800; Ep.; d. Bath Par., Va., 29 Jan. 1801, a. 69.

EDWARD JOHNSON (matric. New Coll., Oxford, 2 July 1658 ?); minister in York co., Va., before 1665, parish not known; Ep.; d. York co., Va., ca. 1665.

JOSIAH JOHNSON, lic. for Va., 10 July 1766, K.B., Va., 20 July 1766; master of the grammar school, William & Mary Coll., 1767-1772; Ep.; d. Williamsburg, Va., 1772-1773.

THOMAS JOHNSON, b. 1748, son of Thomas Johnson of Instones, Staffordshire, Eng.; matric. Magdalen Coll., Oxford, 17 Dec. 1770, a. 22 (A.B., Trinity Coll., Dublin, 1772); sett. Cornwall Par. (Charlotte) Va., 1773-1787; Ep.

WILLIAM JOHNSON, sett. Rocks (Prince Edward) Va., 1772-1776; Bapt.

EDWARD JONES, son of Richard Jones of Gloucester; student at William & Mary Coll., 1767; lic. for N.C., 29 May 1769; K.B. N.C., 6 June 1769; missionary for S.P.G. at St. Stephen's Par. (Johnston) N.C., 1769-1770; sett. St. Mark's Par. (Culpeper) Va., 1772-Feb. 1780; sett. North Farnham Par. (Richmond) Va., 1786-1787; Ep.

EMMANUEL JONES, Sr., A.B., b. Anglesea, Eng., 1668, son of John Jones; A.B., Oriel Coll., Oxford, 1691/2; ord. for Va., 28 May 1700; sett. Petsworth Par. (Gloucester) Va., 1700-1738; Ep.; d. Petsworth Parish, Va., 1739.

EMMANUEL JONES, Jr., son of Rev. Emmanuel Jones; master of the Indian School, William & Mary Coll., 1755-1777; Ep.; d. before 1782.

EMMANUEL JONES III, grandson of Rev. Emmanuel Jones, Sr., lic. for Va. (St. Bride's Parish), 21 Sept. 1774; K.B. Va., 16 Nov. 1774; student, William & Mary Coll., 1772-1774; sett. St. Bridge's Par. (Norfolk) Va., 1776-*ante* 1787; Ep.; d. before 1787.

HUGH JONES, A.M. (See *C.C.Md.*), b. Wales, 1671, son of Thomas Jones; sett. in Md., 1696-1702; prof., William & Mary Coll., 1702-1722; sett. James City Par. (James City) Va., 1720-1722; in England, 1722-1724; K.B. Va., 14 Sept. 1724; sett. St. Stephen's Par. (King & Queen) Va., 1724-2 Feb. 1726; sett. in Md., 1726-1760; Ep.; author, *Present State of Virginia,* 1724; d. North Sassafras Parish, Md., 8 Sept. 1760, a. 91.

JOHN JONES (possibly b. Holyhead, co. Anglesey, 1711, son of John Jones, gent., pens., Trinity Coll., Dublin, 6 June 1729, a. 18; A.B., 1734; A.M., 1736); lic. for Va., 19 June 1750; sett. Augusta Par. (Augusta) Va., 1750-1773; Ep.

NICHOLAS JONES, K.B. for Va., 6 Dec. 1723; sett. Lynnhaven Par. (Princess Anne) Va., 2 Feb. 1726-18 Oct. 1728; sett. Suffolk Par. (Nansemond) Va., 1728-1731; Ep.

OWEN JONES, ord. Aug. 1703; K.B. for Va., 20 Aug. 1703; sett. St. Mary's Par. (Essex) Va., 1704-1724; Ep.

RICHARD JONES, owned 950 acres of land in Martin's Brandon Parish, 1650, and 1500 acres of land nearby, 1655; sett. Martin's Brandon Par. (Prince George) Va., 1650-1655; Ep.

RICHARD JONES, ord. Prince George co., Va., 30 Apr. 1727; sett. Burley (Isle of Wight) Va., 1727-1756; Bapt.; d. Va., after Dec. 1756.

ROLAND JONES, b. Swimbrook, Oxfordshire, Eng., 1643, son of Rev. Roland Jones of Kimbell, Bucks, Eng.; matric. Merton Coll., Oxford, 13 Nov. 1663, a. 19; sett. Bruton Par. (James City) Va., at Williamsburg, 1674-1688; sett. James City Par. (James City) Va., at Jamestown, 1680-1680; sett. Martin's Hundred Par. (James City) Va., 1680-1684; Ep.; d. Williamsburg, Va., 23 Apr. 1688, a. 45.

SAMUEL JONES, sett. James City Par. (James City) Va., at Jamestown, 1671; Ep.

WALTER JONES, b. ca. 1699, son of Hector Jones of Llanelly, co. Carnarvon, Wales; matric. Jesus Coll., Oxford, 9 Apr. 1717, a. 18; adm. Trinity Coll., Dublin, 3 May 1720; K.B. for Va., 17 Dec. 1724; sett. Cople Par. (Westmoreland) Va., 1725-1732; Ep.

ROBERT JORDON, b. Nansemond co., Va., 1668, son of Thomas and Margaret (Brasseur) Jordon; Quaker preacher at Chuckatuck, Middletown, Va., Friend; d. Nansemond co., Va., 1728.

SAMUEL JORDON, b. Nansemond co., Va., 1711, son of Rev. Robert and Mary (Belson) Jordon; Friend's preacher, Nansemond co., Va.; Quaker; d. Nansemond co., Va., 1767.

MARTIN KAUFMAN, sett. Mill Creek (Culpeper) Va., 1772-1774; sett. Whitehouse, Mill Run, Va., 1776-1805; Bapt.; d. Mill Run, Va., 1805.

MICHAEL KAUFFMAN, b. 21 June 1714; sett. Luray (Page) Va., 1733-1788; sett. Linville Creek (Rockingham) Va., 1733; Mennonite; d. Luray (Page) Va., 21 Dec. 1788.

WILLIAM KAY, b. Burnsall, Yorks, Eng., ca. 1721, son of John Kay; adm. sizar Trinity Coll., Camb., 18 May 1741 a. 20; Emmanuel Coll., Camb., 25 Jan. 1742/3; sett. Lunenburg Par. (Richmond) Va., 1745-1750; sett. Cumberland Par. (Lunenburg) Va., 1751-1755; Ep.; d. Cumberland Parish, Va., 1755.

GEORGE KEITH, b. ca. 1585; minister in Bermuda; came to Va., 1617; sett. Elizabeth City Par. (Elizabeth City) Va., 1624-1626; Kecoughtan Par. (Elizabeth City) Va., 1624-1626; in Eng., 1626-4 Mar. 1628; sett. Hampton Par. or Chishiack Par. (York) Va., 1628-1637; reputed a Puritan; Ep.

GEORGE KEITH (prob. the grandson of Rev. George Keith above); had been a Quaker; preached at Kecoughtan Chh., near James River, Elizabeth City Par. (Elizabeth City) Va., 20 May 1703; Ep. (See *C.C.N.E.*).

JAMES KEITH, b. Scotland, 1696, K.B. to Va., 4 Mar. 1728/9; sett. Henrico Par. (Henrico) Va., 1730-1733; sett. Hamilton Par. (Fauquier) Va., 1736-1757; he was grandfather of Chief Justice John Marshall; Ep.; d. Hamilton Par., Va., 1757.

ROGER KELLSALL (perhaps matric. Jesus Coll., Camb., 1698); sett. Elizabeth River Par. (Norfolk) Va., 1708-1709; Ep.; d. Elizabeth River Parish, Va., 1708/9.

RODHAM KENNER, SR., b. Northumberland co., Va.; educated at Glasgow Univ.; ord. deacon, 1729; ord. priest, 1731; sett. St. George's Par. (Spotsylvania) Va., 1729-1732; Ep.; d. 1734.

RODHAM KENNER, JR., William & Mary Coll., 1759-1760; ord. 1772; lic. for Hampshire Par., Va., 21 Sept. 1772; K.B. for Va., 10 Oct. 1772; sett. Hanover Par. (King George) Va., 1780-1785; res. Fauquier co., after 1785; Ep.

MR. KENYON, sett. Cople Par. (Westmoreland) Va., 1684 *et post;* Ep.

ISAAC KEY, A.B. (prob. matric. sizar St. Catharine's Coll., Camb., Easter, 1661, A.B., 1662); vicar of Margaretling, Essex, Eng., 1664-1672; Rector of Stanway Magna, 1671-1677; sett. Hungar's Par. (Northampton) Va., 1677 *et seq.*; Ep.

JOHN KING, sett. Christ Church Par. (Middlesex) Va., 1767; Ep.

PETER KIPPAX, A.B., b. Lancaster, Eng., 1671, son of John Kippax; matric. Brasenose Coll., Oxford, 28 June 1689, a. 18; A.B., 1693; K.B. for Va., 27 June 1699; ord. 1 Nov. 1699; sett. North Farnham Par. (Richmond) Va., 1702-1714; sett. Sittingbourne Par. (King George) Va., 1714-1715; Ep.

GEORGE SAMUEL KLUG, ord. St. Mary's Church, Danzig, 30 Aug. 1736 (Luth.); sett. Madison (Madison) Va., 1738-1761; sett. Winchester (Frederick) Va., Strasburg Lutheran Chh., 1738-1761; Luth.

SAMUEL KLUG, usher, William & Mary Coll., 1766; lic. for Va., 4 June 1768; K.B. Va., 21 June 1768; sett. Christ Church Par. (Middlesex) Va., 1768-1795; chairman, Middlesex County Committee of Safety, Am. Rev.; Ep.; d. Christ Church Parish, Va., 1795.

JOHN KOONES (or Koontz), ord. Mill Creek (Culpeper) Va., 1776; sett. Mill Creek, Va., 1774-1804; Bapt.; d. Mill Creek, Va., after 1809.

THOMAS LAKE, sett. Southwark Par. (Surry) Va., 1655; Ep.

THOMAS LANDRUM (prob. pens. Trinity Coll., Dublin, 31 Jan. 1759; A.B., 1763); adm. Attorney, in King George County Court, Va., 1758; ord. Eng., 1764, lic. for Va., 3 Apr. 1765; K.B. Va., 4 Apr. 1765; sett. Hanover Par. (King George) Va., 1765-1771; J.P., King George co., Va., 1767; Ep.; d. King George co., Va., 1771 (will probated, King George co., Va., 1771).

DUTTON LANE, b. near Baltimore, Md., 7 Nov. 1732; ord. Dan River (Pittsylvania) Va., 22 Oct. 1764; sett. Dan River, Va., Aug. 1760-1767; sett. Upper Spotsylvania, Va., 1767 et seq.; Bapt.

JOHN LANG (See C.C.Md.), ord. London, May 1725; K.B. for Va., 4 June 1725; sett. St. Peter's Par. (New Kent) Va., 1725-1727; sett. in Md., 1728-1748; Ep.; d. St. James's Parish, Md., 1748.

CHARLES LANGE (See C.C.Md.), b. Innsbruck, Tyrol, 1731; arriv. Am., 1766; sett. in Md., 1766-1768; sett. the following German Reformed Churches in Va.: Lower Church; Peaked Mountain (Rockingham); Potomac Mountain; South Branch or South Fork of Potomac, prob. in W.Va.; Strasburg (Shenandoah) at Staufferstown; Upper Church; Upper Tract; Woodstock (Shenandoah) at Millerstown; all 1766-May 1768; German Reformed; d. ca. 1770.

PETER LANSDALE, A.M., matric. sizar Clare Coll., Camb., 1620; A.B., Trinity Hall, Camb., 1623/4, A.M., 1627; preached before the General Assembly at Jamestown (James City) Va., 1658, 1660; Ep.

LEWIS LATANÉ, b. Jouan, Guyenne, France, 1672, son of Henry Latané; fled from France, Oct. 1685; matric. Queen's Coll., Oxford, 24 Nov. 1691, a. 19; ord. London, 2 Dec. 1700; sett. South Farnham Par. (Essex) Va., Upper Piscataway Chh., 1701-1737; Hug.-Ep.; d. South Farnham Parish, Va., 1737.

JOHN LAWRENCE, A.B., came from Bedfordshire, adm. sizar Emmanuel Coll., Camb., 10 June 1650; A.B., 1653/4; sett. Denbigh Par. (Warwick) Va., 1680-1684; sett. Mulberry Island Par. (Warwick) Va., 1680-1684; also preached in Md.; Ep.; d. Point Comfort, Va., 1684.

JOSHUA LAWRENCE, sett. Pungo (Princess Anne) Va., Jan. 1774-1810; Bapt.

SAMUEL LEAKE, A.B., Princeton, A.B., 1764; lic. Tinkling Spring (Augusta) Va., 18 Apr. 1766; ord. Cook's Creek (Rockingham) Va., 3 May 1770; sett. Rich Cove (Albemarle) Va., 1770-1775;

sett. North Garden (Albemarle) Va., 1772-1775; Presb.; d. Albemarle co., Va., 2 Dec. 1775.

MR. LECHARCEY, sett. St. Stephen's Par. (Northumberland) Va., 1724; Ep.

WILLIAM LEETE, came from Suffolk, Eng.; matric. sizar Corpus Christi Coll., Camb., Easter, 1604; Ep.; sett. in Va., 1622.

WILLIAM LEIGH, b. West Point, King & Queen co., Va., 1748, son of Ferdinand Leigh; William & Mary Coll., 1763-1769; Univ. of Edinburgh; ord. London, 1772; lic. for Shelburne Parish, Va., 16 Mar. 1772; K.B. Va., 28 Apr. 1772; sett. Manchester Par. (Chesterfield) Va., 1773-1776; sett. Dale Par. (Chesterfield) Va., 1775-1786; Ep.; d. Dale Parish, Va., 1787, a. 39.

JOHN LELAND, sett. Wicomico Par. (Northumberland) Va., 1746-1787; Ep.; father of Rev. John Leland, Jr.

JOHN LELAND, JR., son of Rev. John Leland; William & Mary Coll., 1772; ord. 1775; lic. for Wicomico Parish, Va., 11 Apr. 1775; K.B., Va., 25 Apr. 1775; sett. Wicomico Par. (Northumberland) Va., 1775-1791; Ep. (Dr. Brydon gives his years of settlement as 1778-1789).

JOHN LELAND (See *C.C.N.E.*), b. Grafton, Mass., 14 May 1754; began preaching there, 20 June 1774; lic. to preach, 1775; sett. Bellingham, Mass., 1775; missionary to Va., Oct. 1775-1791; ord. Culpeper, Va., as a Presb., Aug. 1776; ord. Va., June 1787 (as a Bapt.); sett. Orange co., Va., 1776 *et seq.*; sett. Cheshire, Mass., Feb. 1792-1841; Presb.-Bapt.; d. North Adams, Mass., 14 Jan. 1841, a. 86 years 8 mos.

WILLIAM LE NEVE, M.B. b. Lynn, ca. 1689, son of John Le Neve; adm. pens. St. John's Coll., Camb., 13 May 1707, a. 18; M.B., 1712; ord. (Bsp. of London), 29 Apr. 1722; K.B. for Providence Island, 21 May 1722; came from Eng. to Va., 1722; sett. James City Par. (James City) Va., at Jamestown, 1722-1737; sett. Mulberry Island Chh. (Warwick) Va., 1722-1737; lectured at Williamsburg, 1723; Ep.

ROBERT LESLIE, A.M., son of Rt. Rev. Henry Leslie, Bsp. of Down and Connor in Ireland; A.B., Trinity Coll., Dublin, 23 Mar. 1636/7; A.M., Aberdeen, 16 July 1638; A.M., Oxford and Camb., 1641; sett. Charles City, Va., 1654; ret. to Ireland before 1660; Archdeacon of Connor, 1660-1671; Bsp. of Dromore, 1660-1661; Bsp. of Raphoe, 1661-1671; Bsp. of Clogher, 1671-1672; Ep.; d. Ireland, 10 Aug. 1672.

IVESON LEWIS, b. King & Queen co., Va., 4 Mar. 1741, son of John Lewis; sett. Mathews (Mathews) Va., 1775-Dec. 1814; sett. Exol (King & Queen) Va., 1775-1814; Bapt.; d. King & Queen co., Va., 5 Jan. 1815.

MATTHEW LIDFORD, A.B., b. Eng., ca. 1663, son of Rev. James Lidford of Sandwich, Purbeck, Dorset, Eng.; matric. Magdalen Coll., Oxford, 27 Oct. 1682, a. 19; clerk, 1685-1686; A.B.,

1686; K.B. for Va., 20 Oct. 1690; sett. Christ Church Par. (Middlesex) Va., 1691-1692; Ep.; d. Christ Church Parish, Va., 22 Mar. 1692/3.

DAVID LINDSAY, b. South Leith, Scotland, 2 Jan. 1603, son of Sir Hierome Lindsay, Lord Lyon King of Arms; sett. Wicomico Par. (Northumberland) Va., 1655-1677; Ep.; d. Northumberland co., Va., 3 Apr. 1677.

THOMAS LLOYD, sett. Drysdale Par. (Caroline) Va., 1758; Ep.

JOHN LOCKE, sett. Kingston Par. (Mathews) Va., ca. 1750; Ep.

HENRY LOVEALL (*alias* Desolate Baker) (See *C.C.Md.*), b. 1694; sett. Newport, R.I., 1729-1730; ord. Piscataway, N.J., Chh. at Stilton, Raritan, 1730-1742; sett. Chestnut Ridge, Md., Sater's Chh., Fall's Road, 1742-1772; sett. Opequon (Berkeley) W.Va., Mill Creek Chh., 1746-1751; General Bapt.; living at Chestnut Ridge, Md., 1772, a. 78.

PATRICK LUNAN, lic. for Va., 23 Dec. 1759; K.B. Va., 29 Jan. 1760; sett. St. Andrew's Par. (Brunswick) Va., 1760-1760; sett. Upper Par. (Nansemond) Va., 1760-1774; Ep.

THOMAS LUNDIE, lic. for Va., 7 Dec. 1767, K.B. Va., 7 Jan. 1768; sett. St. Andrew's Par. (Brunswick) Va., 1769-1799; chairman, Committee of Safety for Brunswick County, Am. Rev.; Ep.; d. after 1799.

LEWIS LUNSFORD, b. Stafford co., Va., ca. 1753; began preaching as an itinerant preacher, Va., 1770-1774; sett. Northern Neck, Va., 1774-1778; sett. Moratico (Northumberland) Va., 1778-1793; Bapt.; d. Essex co., Va., 26 Oct. 1793, a. ca. 40.

JOHN LYFORD, A.M. (See *C.C.N.E.*), A.B., Magdalen Coll., Oxford, 1597, A.M., 1602; Ep. minister in Ireland; came to Plymouth, Mass., 1624; preached there 1624; at Hull, Mass., 1625; at Cape Anne, Mass., 1625; at Salem, Mass., 1626-1628; sett. Martin's Hundred Par. (James City) Va., 1628-1629; Ep.; d. in Va. before 10 Oct. 1634.

JOHN LYON, A.B. (See *C.C.N.E.* and *C.C.Del.*), A.B., Yale Coll., 1761; lic. for N.E., 29 June 1765; K.B. N.E., 11 July 1764; St. Thomas's Chh., Taunton, Mass., 1765-1769 (also chapels at Bridgewater and Middleborough, Mass.) sett. as S.P.G. missionary, Lewis, Indian River, Dagsboro, Cedar Creek Hundred and Broadkill, Del., 1769-1774; sett. St. George's Par. (Accomac) Va., 1774-1786; Ep.; d. Va. ca. 1796.

JOHN LYTH, A.B., b. Newton Pickering, Yorks, Eng.; adm. sizar Clare Coll., Camb., 30 Oct. 1751; A.B., 1756; lic. for Va., 10 Oct. 1763; K.B. Va., 8 Dec. 1763; sent to S.C., 1767; left S.C., 1767; Ep.

DANIEL McCALLA, D.D., b. Neshaminy, Pa., 1748; A.B., Princeton, 1766; D.D., Univ. of S.C., 1808; lic. 1772; ord. Nov. 1772; sett. Norriton, Charleston and Lower Providence, Pa., 1774-1776;

sett. Hanover (Hanover) Va., 1776-1788; sett. near Charleston, S.C., 1788-1809; chaplain, Am. Rev., 1775-1776; Presb.; Christ Church Parish, S.C., May 1809.

JAMES MACARTNEY (See *C.C.N.C.*), b. Ireland, sett. N.C., 1768-1772; sett. St. Patrick's Par. (Prince Edward) Va., 1773-1774; Ep.

SAMUEL SMITH McCROSKEY, lic. for Christ Chh. Par., Va., 21 Sept. 1772; K.B. Va., 16 Dec. 1772; sett. Hungar's Par. (Northampton) Va., 1774-1803; Chairman, Committee of Safety, Northampton co., Am. Rev.; Ep.; d. Hungar's Parish, Va., 1803.

RODERICK McCULLOCH, ord. Eng., 1730, K.B., for Va., 30 Oct. 1730; sett. Washington Par. (Westmoreland) Va., 1731-1745; sett. Hanover Par. (King George) Va., 1736-1747; Ep.; d. Va., ca. 1748.

DANIEL McDONALD, K.B. for Va., 20 Oct. 1731; sett. Brunswick Par. (Stafford) Va., 1732-1762; sett. Hanover Par. (King George) Va., 1732-1735; Ep.; d. Brunswick Parish, Va., 1762.

BISHOP ALEXANDER MACK, JR., b. Schwartzenau, Germany, 28 Jan. 1712, son of Rev. Alexander and Anna Margareta (Kling) Mack; arriv. Phila., Pa., 15 Sept. 1729; ord. (elder) 7 June 1748; ord. (bishop), Germantown, Pa., 10 June 1753; sett. Ephrata, Pa., 1739-1748; sett. Germantown, Pa., 1 June 1748-1803; left Ephrata Chloister, 4 Sept. 1745; went to Va., sett. Mahanaim, Va., 1745-1748; ret. to Ephrata, Pa., 1748; Tunker or German Bapt.; d. Germantown, Pa., 20 Mar. 1803, a. 91.

WILLIAM MacKAY, K.B. for Va., 8 Jan. 1735/6; sett. Hanover Par. (King George) Va., 1737-1747; sett. North Farnham Par. (Richmond) Va., 1754-1774; Ep.

FRANCIS MAKEMIE (See *C.C.Md.*), b. 1658; ord. Ireland, 1682; sett. Rehoboth and Snow Hill, Md., 1683-1688; sett. Accomac (Accomac) Va., 1688-1708; first Presb. minister in Am.; moderator of the first Presbytery in Am., Dec. 1706; Presb.; d. Matchatank (Accomac) Va., summer, 1708, a. 50.

WILLIAM McKENNAN, b. Delaware, ca. 1719; supply at North Mountain, South Mountain, Timber Grove, North River, Cook's Creek, John Hinson's, Va., 1752-1753; ord. White Clay Creek, Del., Dec. 1755; sett. White Clay, Red Clay Creek and Wilmington (1st Presb. Chh.), 1755-1809; Presb.; d. Red Clay Creek, Del., 5 May 1809, a. 90.

KENNETH McKENSIE (or Mackenzey), sett. Isle of Wight co., Va., 1746; sett. Suffolk Par. (Nansemond) Va., 1753-1754; Ep.; d. Suffolk Parish, Va., 1754.

JOSIAS MACKIE, b. prob. at St. Johnstone, Donegal, Ireland, son of Patrick Mackie; had been Ep., but was dismissed for nonconformity, 1692; became a Presb.; sett. Lynnhaven, on Elizabeth River, Va. (Presb. Chh.), 1692-1716; Great Neck (Princess Anne) Va., 1696-1716; also had preaching stations at Eastern Branch, Tanner's Creek, Western Branch and Southern Branch, 1696-1716;

Presb.; d. Lynnhaven, Va., 1716, unm. (will dated 7 Nov. 1716; proved 16 Nov. 1716).

JOHN McKNIGHT, D.D., b. near Carlisle, Pa., 1 Oct. 1754, son of Major McKnight; A.B., Princeton, 1773, A.M., 1786, D.D., Yale Coll., 1791; lic. 1775; sett. Elk Branch (Jefferson) W.Va., 1775-1783; sett. Lower Marsh Creek (Adams) Pa., 1783-1789; sett. N.Y.C., 2 Dec. 1789-1815; President, Dickinson Coll., 1815-1816; moderator, General Assembly, 1795; Presb.; d. Dickinson Coll., Pa., 21 Oct. 1823.

ROBERT McLAURINE, came from Scotland; lic. for Va., 24 Aug. 1750; K.B. Va., 5 Sept. 1750; sett. St. James-Southam Par. (Powhatan) Va., 1751-1772; Ep.; d. St. James-Southam Parish, Va., 1772.

JOHN McLEROY, b. Ireland; sett. Appomattox (Prince Edward) Va., 1773-1790; went to Ga., 1790; Bapt.

WILLIAM McMILLAN, lic. 22 Sept. 1724; supplied Rehoboth Chh., Pocomoke (Worcester) Md., 1724; and Northern Accomac co., Va., 1724; Presb.; d. prob. ca. 1724.

JAMES McMORRAN, K.B. for Md., 16 Mar. 1709/10; arriv. Va., 1710; sett. Elizabeth River Par. (Norfolk) Va., 1710-1720; Ep.

CHRISTOPHER MacRAE, b. Scotland; educated at Edinburgh; lic. for Va., 23 Dec. 1765; K.B. for Va., 2 Jan. 1766; sett. Southwark Par. (Surry) Va., 1766-1772; sett. Littleton Par. (Cumberland) Va., 1773-1787; Tory; Ep.; d. Powhatan co., Va., 22 Dec. 1808.

ARCHIBALD McROBERT (or McRoberts), b. Scotland, lic. for Va., 25 Feb. 1761; K.B. Va., 5 Mar. 1761; ord. London, 1762; sett. Dale Par. (Chesterfield) Va., 1773-1776; sett. St. Patrick's Par. (Prince Edward) Va., 1776-1779; left 1779; chairman, Committee of Safety for Chesterfield co., Am. Rev.; Ep.; became a Presb.

BISHOP JAMES MADISON, D.D., b. Port Republic, Rockingham co., Va., 27 Aug. 1749, son of John Madison and 2nd cousin of President James Madison; William & Mary Coll., 1768-1772; D.D., U. of Pa., 1785; lic. for Va., 1 Oct. 1775; ord. London, 1775; prof. natural phil. and math., William & Mary Coll., 1773-1777; President, William & Mary Coll., 1777-1812; sett. James City Par. (James City) Va., at Jamestown, 1785-1812; first Bishop of Va., 19 Sept. 1790-1812; chaplain, Va. House of Delegates, 1777; Ep.; d. Williamsburg, Va., 6 Mar. 1812, a. 63 (GS).

RICHARD MAJOR, b. near Pennsbury, Pa., 1722; brought up a Presb. but became a Bapt., 1744; ord. Little River (Loudoun) Va., 1768-1802; sett. Bull Run (Fairfax) Va., 1775-1802; sett. Popeshead (Fairfax) Va., 1775-1802; Bapt.; d. Fauquier co., Va., ca. 1802, ca. 80 years of age.

PHILIP MALLORY, A.M., bapt. 29 Apr. 1618, son of Rev. Thomas Mallory, Dean of Chester; matric. Corpus Christi Coll., Oxford, 28 May 1634, a. 17; A.B., St. Mary's Hall, 1637, A.M., 16 Jan. 1639/40; Vicar of Norton, Durham, England, 1641; sett. Lynnhaven Par. (Princess Anne) Va., 1657-1657; sett. James City Par. (James City) Va., at Jamestown, 1658-1661; and in York co., Va., 1658-1661; chaplain, General Assembly, 1658, 1659; Ep.; ret. to England, 1661; d. London, Eng., 1661.

GEORGE MANLEY, A.B., adm. pens. St. Catharine's Coll., Camb., 12 May 1707; A.B., 1710/11; K.B. for Va., 11 Nov. 1715; chaplain, Br. Navy, 1725-1728; J.P. for Bedfordshire; Ep.; d. 2 May 1738.

NATHANIEL MANNING, M.D., A.B., Princeton, 1762, A.M., M.D.; physician in N.J.; memb. of N.J. Medical Soc., 1767; lic. for Hampshire Par., Va., 16 Mar. 1772; K.B. Va., 20 Mar. 1772; sett. Hampshire Par. (Hampshire) Va., 1772-1774; Ep.

JOHN MARKS, came from Pa., to Va., ca. 1756; sett. Ketockton (Loudoun) Va., 1756-1786; Bapt.; d. Ketockton, Va., 1786.

RICHARD MARSDEN, A.M. (See C.C.Md.), sett. Md., 1696-1707; sett. S.C., 1707-1709; to Eng., 1709; came to Va. without a Bishop's certificate; sett. Lynnhaven Par. (Princess Anne) Va., 7 Jan. 1729-14 Nov. 1729; left Lynnhaven £400 in debt; sett. N.C., 1729-1742; Ep.; d. near Wilmington, N.C., 1742.

JOHN MARSHALL, sett. Blue Stone (Mecklenburg) Va., Dec. 1772-1786; Bapt.

MUNGO MARSHALL, K.B. for Va., 20 Sept. 1744; sett. St. Thomas's Par. (Orange) Va., 1754-1758; Ep.; d. St. Thomas's Parish, Va., 1758.

WILLIAM MARSHALL, b. Northern Neck, Va., 1735; itinerant minister in Fauquier and Shenandoah counties, Va.; sett. Happy Creek, Va.; removed to Ky., 1780; uncle of Chief Justice John Marshall; Bapt.; d. Shelby co., Ky., 1808, a. 72.

JOHN MARTIN, A.M., lic. (Hanover Presbytery), 25 Aug. 1756; sett. Albemarle, Va., 1756-1757; ord. Hanover (Hanover) Va., 3 June 1757, evidently for the church in Wappetaw, S.C.; missionary to the Cherokee Indians, 1757-1759; sett. Wappetaw (Cong. Chh.) at Wando Neck, S.C., 9 June 1757-1772; sett. Cainhoy, S.C., 1760-1770; sett. Wilton (Colleton) S.C., 1772-1774; first Presb. minister to be ordained in Va.; d. Wilton, S.C., June 1774.

LAZARUS MARTIN, sett. Henrico City Par. (Henrico) Va., 1629 et post; Ep.

THOMAS MARTIN, lic. for Va., 24 June 1767; K.B. Va., 8 July 1767; sett. St. Thomas's Par. (Orange) Va., 1768-1769; Ep.; d. St. Thomas's Parish, Va., 1769. (Note: Thomas Martin, A.B., Princeton, d. 1770).

JAMES MARYE, Sr., b. Rouen, Normandy, France; educated for the Roman Catholic priesthood; ord. in Eng. as an Ep., 1726; came to Va., 1729; sett. St. James's Par. (Goochland) Va., 1730-1732; sett. King William Par. (Powhatan) Va., at Manakintown, 1730-1732; sett. St. George's Par. (Spotsylvania) Va., Oct. 1735-1767; Hug.-Ep.; d. St. George's Parish, Va., 1767.

JAMES MARYE, Jr., b. Goochland co., Va., 1731, son of the

Rev. James and Letitia (Staige) Marye; William & Mary Coll., 1754; lic. for Va., 27 Dec. 1755; K.B., Va., 30 Dec. 1755; sett. St. Thomas's Par. (Orange) Va., 1761-1768; sett. St. George's Par. (Spotsylvania) Va., 1768-1780; Ep.; d. St. George's Parish, Va., 1780.

LEE MASSEY, b. King George's co., Va., 1728; ord. London, 1766; lic. for Va., 21 Sept. 1766; K.B. Va., 21 Oct. 1766; sett. Truro Par. (Fairfax) Va., 1767-1801; member, Fairfax co. Committee of Safety, Am. Rev.; Ep.; d. "Bradley," Occoquan River, Truro Parish, Va., 1814, a. 86.

JOHN MATTHEWS, b. Gloucester co., Va., 1739, son of John and Dorothy Matthews; William & Mary Coll., 1754; lic. for Va., 29 June 1764; K.B. Va., 12 July 1764; sett. St. Anne's Par. (Essex) Va., 1774-1792; sett. St. Bride's Par. (Norfolk) Va., 1795-1799; Ep.

JAMES MAURY, brought up in Va., son of Strother and Anne (Fontaine) Maury; William & Mary Coll.; went to Eng. for ordination, Feb. 1741/2; ord. London, 1742; K.B. Va., 29 June 1742; sett. Fredericksville Par. (Albemarle) Va., 1754-1770; Hug.-Ep.; d. Fredericksville, Va., 1770.

MATTHEW MAURY, son of Rev. James Maury; William & Mary Coll., 1768; ord. 1769; lic. for Va., 24 Aug. 1769; K.B. Va., 8 Sept. 1769; sett. Fredericksville Par. (Albemarle) Va., 1770-1808; Ep.; d. Fredericksville, Va., 1808.

SAMUEL MAYCOCKE, son of Roger Maycocke of Yelverstoft, Nhants, Eng.; adm. sizar Jesus Coll., Camb., 18 May 1611; Caius Coll., Camb., 15 May 1612; came to Va., 1618; appointed to the Council, 1619; Ep.; killed by the Indians in the great massacre of 22 Mar. 1622.

WILLIAM MEASE (or Mays), came to Va., ca. 1610; sett. Upper Par. (Elizabeth City) Va., 1610-1620; sett. Kecoughtan Par. (Elizabeth City) Va., 1610-1620; Ep.; prob. ret. to Eng., 1620 or 1623.

JOHN MEGLAMRE, b. Md., 7 June 1730; began preaching in N.C., ca. 1765; ord. Fishing Creek (Halifax) N.C., Feb. 1767; sett. Kehukee Chh. (Halifax) N.C., 1765-2 May 1772; sett. Raccoon Swamp (Sussex) Va., 1772-1799; moderator, Kehukee Assn., 1773-1774; Bapt.; d. Sussex co., Va., 13 Dec. 1799, a. 69.

WILLIAM MELDRUM, lic. for Va., 13 June 1756; K.B. Va., 23 June 1756; sett. Frederick Par. (Frederick) Va., ante 1765; Ep.

ADAM MENZIES, ord. 1750; lic. for Va., 28 Dec. 1750; K.B. Va., 10 Jan. 1750/1; sett. Bromfield Par. (Culpeper) Va., 1751-1755; sett. St. Stephen's Par. (Northumberland) Va., 1758-1767; Ep.

JOSEPH MESSENGER (See C.C.Md.), b. Eng., ca. 1747; ord. 1772; lic. for Stafford co., Va., 7 May 1772; K.B. Va., 19 May 1772; sett. Overwharton Par. (Stafford) Va., 1772-1774; sett. in Md., 1775-1806; Ep.; d. St. John's Parish (Prince George) Md., 1810, a. ca. 63.

ALEXANDER MILLER, came from Ardstraw, Ireland, 1753;

had been a minister in the Presbytery of Letterkenny, Ireland; preached in Orange co., N.C., 1756; expelled from Highco Presb. for improper conduct 1757; installed, Cook's Creek (Rockingham) Va., 1757-1769; sett. Peaked Mountain, Harrisonburg (Rockingham) Va., 1757-1769; deposed 3 May 1765; Presb.

FRANCIS MILNE (Mylne), ord. for Va., 3 Nov. 1707; K.B. for Md., 27 Oct. 1707; sett. Kingston Par. (Mathews) Va., 1714; member of the Va. convention, 1719, parish not given; Ep.

JOHN MILNER, A.B., b. Westchester co., N.Y., 1738, son of Nathaniel Milner; A.B., Princeton, 1758; ord. Eng., 1761; lic. for N.Y., 25 Feb. 1761; arriv. N.Y., 13 May 1761; Rector, Westchester, N.Y., 12 June 1761-1766; St. Paul's Chh., East Chester, N.Y., 1761-1766; St. John's Chh., Yonkers, N.Y., 1761-1764; sett. Warwisqueake Par. (Isle of Wight) Va., 1766-1775; Ep.; d. Newport Parish, Va., 1775.

CASPER MINTZ, ord. Prince George co., Va., 30 Apr. 1727; sett. Burley (Isle of Wight) Va., 1727-1756; Bapt.; d. Burley, after Dec. 1756.

ANDERSON MOFFET, sett. Mill Creek (Culpeper) Va., 1772-1774; sett. Smith's Creek (Shenandoah) Va., 1776-1809; Bapt.

JOHN MONCURE, b. Scotland; sett. Overwharton Par. (Stafford) Va., 1738-1764; Ep.; d. Overwharton Parish, Va., 1764.

ALEXANDER MONRO, son of Rev. John Monro; came to Va., 1696; sett. Newport Par. (Isle of Wight) Va., 1700-1719; Ep.

JEREMIAH MOORE, b. Prince William co., Va., 7 June 1746; sett. Difficult (Fairfax) Va., 1775-1795; sett. Centerville, Va.; Bapt.; d. Va., 24 Feb. 1815.

NICHOLAS MOREAU, sett. St. Peter's Par. (New Kent) Va., 1696-1697; Ep.; ret. to Eng.

RICHARD MORRIS (possibly matric. All Souls' Coll., Oxford, 18 Mar. 1657/8; A.B., Magdalen Coll., Oxford, 7 Feb. 1661/2); sett. Christ Church Par. (Middlesex) Va., 1663-1666; sett. Lancaster Par. (Middlesex) Va., 1663-1666; sett. Pianketank Par. (Middlesex) Va., 1663-1666; Ep.

ANDREW MORTON (or Moreton), lic. for N.J., 17 Mar. 1760; K.B. N.J., 18 Mar. 1760; S.P.G. missionary at St. Thomas's Chh., Alexandria, N.J., 1760-1765; S.P.G. missionary at St. Andrew's Chh., Amwell, N.J., 1760-1765; S.P.G. missionary to St. George's Par. (Northampton) N.C. and Mecklenburg co., N.C., 1766-1766; left in 1766 on account of ill health; sett. Drysdale Par. (Caroline) Va., 1774-1775; Ep.

DAVID MORTLAND, K.B. for Md., 1 Sept. 1733; sett. Lunenburg Par. (Richmond) Va., 1745; ret. to Eng., 1745-1748; sett. St. Stephen's Par. (Northumberland) Va., 1748-1754; Ep.

DAVID MOSSOM (See C.C.N.E.), b. London, Eng., 25 Mar. 1690 (GS); St. John's Coll., Camb.; K.B. for Va., 18 Aug. 1718; S.P.G. missionary at Marblehead, Mass., 1718-1726; sett. St. Peter's

Par. (New Kent) Va., 1727-1767; sett. King William Par. (Powhatan) Va., 1727-1728; Ep.; d. St. Peter's Par. (New Kent) Va., 4 Jan. 1767 (GS).

BRIG.-GEN. JOHN PETER GABRIEL MUHLENBERG, b. Trappe, Pa., 1 Oct. 1746, son of Rev. Henry Melchior and Anna Maria (Weiser) Muhlenberg; U. of Pa., 1763; U. Halle, 1763; ord. (Lutheran) 1768; sett. New Germantown, N.J. (Zion's Chh.), 12 May 1768-1772; sett. Bedminster, N.J. (St. Paul's Chh.), 12 May 1768-1772; sett. Greenwich, N.J. (St. James's Chh.), 1769-1772; ord. Ep. (Bsp. of London) 23 Apr. 1772; K.B. for Va., 7 May 1772; sett. Beckford Par. (Shenandoah) Va., 1772-1775; sett. Madison (Madison) Va., Old Hebron (Lutheran) Chh., 1772-1775; sett. Woodstock, Lutheran Chh. (Shenandoah) Va., 1772-1775; member, Va. House of Burgesses, 1774; Gen. in Rev. war; at Battle of Sullivan's Island, June 1776; Brig.-Gen., 21 Feb. 1777; in command at Battles of Brandywine, Monmouth, Stony Point and Yorktown; Maj.-Gen., 1800-1807; member of Congress, 1789-1801; Senator, 1802; collector of the Port of Philadelphia, 1802-1807; Luth.-Ep.; d. Philadelphia, Pa., 1 Oct. 1807, a. 60.

WILLIAM MULLIN, sett. Glebe Landing (Essex) Va., 1772-1792; Bapt.; d. Glebe Landing, Va., 1792.

JOHN MUNRO, came to Va., ca. 1650, from Scotland; sett. Stratton-Major Par. (King & Queen) Va., 1650-1655; Pamunkey Chapel, later St. John's Par. (King William) Va.; brother of Andrew Monroe, ancestor of President James Munroe; Ep.

JOHN MONROE, JR., son of Rev. John Munro; sett. Hungar's Par. (Northampton) Va., 1692-1695; sett. St. John's Par. (King William) Va., 1695-1723; Ep.; d. St. John's Parish, Va., 1723.

WILLIAM MURDAUGH, sett. St. James's Par. (Goochland) Va., 1725-1727; sett. King William Par. (Powhatan) Va., at Manakintown, 1727; Ep.

WILLIAM MURPHY, b. Spotsylvania, Va., 1732, son of William Murphy, ord. Holston-Staunton, Va., 1763; missionary in S.W. Va.; sett. Holston (Washington) Va., 1763-1780; sett. Staunton (Augusta) Va., 1763-1780; went to Tenn., 1780; installed Cherokee (Washington) Tenn., 2 Apr. 1783; brother of the Rev. Joseph Murphy; Bapt.; d. Eastern Tennessee, ca. 1800.

ALEXANDER MURRAY, a Royalist with King Charles at the Battle of Worcester, 1652; came to Va.; sett. Ware Par. (Gloucester) Va., 1653-1672; Ep.; d. between 1672 and 1703.

MR. MYNNARD, sett. Martin's Hundred Par. (James City) Va., ante 1628; Ep.

WILLIAM NAIRN, Elizabeth River Par. (Norfolk) Va., 1680; Ep.

WILLIAM NAIRN (perhaps the same), K.B. for Bermuda, 8 May 1722; sett. King William's Par. (Powhatan) Va., at Manakintown, 1727-1728; sett. Henrico Par. (Henrico) Va., 1727-1728; ret. to a parish in Wiltshire, 1728; Hug.-Ep.

JOHN NAVISON, lic. for Va., 25 Feb. 1752; K.B. Va., 5 Mar. 1752; sett. Meherrin Par. (Greensville) Va., 1754-1758; Ep.

JOSHUA NELSON, sett. Wicomico Par. (Northumberland) Va., 1740-1744; Ep.

WILLIAM NELSON, A.M., b. Harkham, Suffolk, Eng., 17 Oct. 1698, son of the Rev. George Nelson; adm. sizar Magdalene Coll., Camb., 5 June 1716; adm. scholar, Trinity Hall, Camb., 22 Dec. 1718; A.B., 1720/1; sett. St. John's Par. (King William) Va., 1724 *et seq.*; Ep.

T. NOEL, sett. Upper Essex (Essex) Va., 1773-1810; Bapt.; liv. Upper Essex, Va., 1810.

ROBERT NORDIN, b. Eng.; ord. London, Eng., May 1714; sett. Burley (Isle of Wight) Va., 1714-1725; Bapt.; d. Burley, Isle of Wight co., Va., 1 Dec. 1725.

JAMES OGILVIE, lic. for Hampshire Parish, Va., 22 Sept. 1771; K.B. Va., 5 Oct. 1771; ord. London, 1771; sett. Westover Par. (Charles City) Va., 1776-1786; member, Committee of Safety, Charles City co., Am. Rev.; Ep.

GRONOW (or Goronwy) OWEN, b. Llanfair, Mathafarn, Wales, ca. 1723, son of Owen Owen; matric. Jesus Coll., Oxford, 3 June 1742, a. 19; lic. for Va., 21 Oct. 1757; K.B. for Jamaica, 3 Nov. 1757; master, Grammar School, William & Mary Coll., 1758-1759; sett. St. Andrew's Par. (Brunswick) Va., 1760-1769; "Premier poet of Wales"; Ep.; d. St. Andrew's Parish, Va., 1770.

JOHN OWENS, sett. Wicomico Par. (Northumberland) Va., *ante* 1673-1675; Ep.; d. Wicomico Parish, Va., 1675.

JOHN PAGE, prob. matric. Brasenose Coll., Oxford, 11 Apr. 1660, A.B., 1663, A.M., 1669; rector, Wood Walton, Hunts, 1669; sett. Elizabeth City Par. (Elizabeth City) Va., 1677-1687; sett. St. Peter's Par. (New Kent) Va., 1687-1688; Ep.; d. St. Peter's Parish, Va., 1688.

SAMUEL PALMER, sett. Hungar's Par. (Northampton) Va., 1695-1702; Ep.

THOMAS PALMER, sett. Hungar's Par. (Northampton) Va., 1647-1648; Ep.

ANTHONY PANTON, inducted, York Par. (York) Va., Jan. 1637/8-1640 (banished, 8 Oct. 1638; restored); sett. Chiskiack Par., later Hampton Par. (York) Va., 1637-1640; Ep.

WILLIAM PARIS, sett. Washington Par. (Westmoreland) Va., 1682-1686; Ep.

HENRY PARKE, b. 1648 (ae. 30 yrs. in 1678); sett. Accomac Par. (Accomac) Va., Aug. 1678-1687; sett. St. George's Par. (Accomac) Va., 1666-1687; Ep.; d. Accomac Parish, Va., ca. 1687.

ROBERT PARKE, came to Va., ca. 1675; sett. Warwisqueake Par. (Isle of Wight) Va., 1680; Ep.

JAMES PASTEUR, b. Williamsburg, Va.; schoolmaster at Norfolk, Va., 1739; lic. for Va., 23 Dec. 1753; K.B. Va., 16 Jan. 1754; lecturer in Norfolk, Va., 1754; sett. Bath Par. (Dinwiddie)

Va., 1755-1756; sett. St. Bride's Par. (Norfolk) Va., 1773-1774; Ep.; d. St. Bride's Parish, Va., 1774.

HENRY PATILLO, A.M., b. Scotland, 1726; came to Am., 1735; A.M., Hampton Sidney Coll. (Hon.), 1787; lic. Cub Creek, 29 Sept. 1757; ord. Cumberland co., Va., 12 July 1758; sett. Willis Creek (Cumberland) Va., 1758-1762; sett. Byrd (Fluvanna) Va., 1758-1762; sett. Buck Island (Cumberland) Va., 1758-1762; dism. from these three charges, 7 Oct. 1762; sett. Deep Creek (Cumberland) Va., May 1763-1765; sett. Harris Creek (Amherst) Va., 1763-1765; sett. Farmville (Cumberland) Va., 1763-1765; sett. Hawfields (Alamance) N.C., inst. 2 Oct. 1765-1774; sett. Eno (Orange) N.C., 1765-1774; sett. Little River (Durham) N.C., 1765-1774; sett. Nutbush, N.C., 1780-1801; sett. Grassy Creek, N.C., 1780-1801; deputy, 1st Prov. Cong. of N.C., 1775, from Bute co.; Presb.; d. Dinwiddie co., Va., 1801, a. 75.

DAVID PATTERSON, sett. Totier (Albemarle) Va., 1773-1774; sett. Providence (Buckingham) Va., 1774-1780; Bapt.

ROBERT PAULETT, came to Va., 1619; sett. Martin's Brandon Par. (Prince George) Va., 1619-1621; sett. Martin's Hundred Par. (James City) Va., 1619-1621; sett. Weyanoke Parish at Berkeley Hundred (Charles City) Va., 1621-1622; physician and surgeon; Ep.

ROBERT PAXTON, ord. for Va., 21 Oct. 1709; K.B. Va., 20 Oct. 1709; invited to officiate in Bruton Parish, Va., 1710; no record of his service; Ep.; prob. d. soon.

DUELL PEAD, A.B. (See C.C.Md.), bapt. 1663, A.B., Trinity Coll., Camb.; ord. (Bsp. of London) 17 May 1668; sett. Christ Church Par. (Middlesex) Va., 1683-1690; ret. to Eng.; author; Ep.; d. 12 Jan. 1726/7, buried at Clerkenwell.

THOMAS PEADOR, sett. Elizabeth City Par. (Elizabeth City) Va., 1727-1731; Ep.

FRANCIS PEART, b. ca. 1700, son of Francis Peart of St. John's, Worcester, Eng.; matric. Magdalen Hall, Oxford, 30 Oct. 1719, a. 19; K.B. for Va., 19 Nov. 1730; sett. St. Stephen's Par. (Northumberland) Va., 1731-1742; also officiated at St. George's Par. (Spotsylvania) Va., 1730, and at St. Mark's Par. (Culpeper) Va., ca. 1732; supply, Wicomico Par. (Northumberland) Va., 1734; Ep.

WILLIAM PEASELEY, A.M. (or Peazley), b. Dublin, 1714, pens. Trinity Coll., Dublin, 23 June 1732, a. 18, A.B., 1737; K.B. for Newfoundland, 8 Mar. 1742/3; S.P.G. missionary at Bonavista, Newfoundland, 1742-1743; at St. John's, Newfoundland, 1744-1745; S.P.G. missionary in South Carolina, 1751; sett. St. Helena's Par. (Beaufort) S.C., 1751-12 Mar. 1756; resigned because of ill health and left S.C., 1756; sett. Tillotson Par. (Buckingham) Va., 1773-1787; preacher, 6th annual meeting of the clergy, S.C., 1754; Ep.

MR. PEDIER, sett. Newport Par. (Isle of Wight) Va., ca. 1770; Ep.

JAMES PEDIN, sett. Nottoway Par. (Nottoway) Va., 1742 *et seq.*; Ep.

NATHANIEL PENDLETON, A.B., b. St. Peter, Mancroft, Norwich, Eng., son of Henry Pendleton; adm. sizar Corpus Christi Coll., Camb., 1669; matric., Easter, 1671; A.B., 1672/3; ord. deacon (Bsp. of Norwich) Sept. 1673; came to Va., 1674; d. soon after; Ep.

THOMAS PERKINS, sett. Sittingbourne Par. (King George) Va., ca. 1684; Ep.

THOMAS PHILLIPS (See *C.C.Md.*), K.B. for Va., 9 Aug. 1715; sett. in a "Parish of Potomac River," 1716 (prob. Overwharton Par. (Stafford) Va.); sett. in Md., 1719-1731; Ep.

WILLIAM PHILLIPS, b. ca. 1708, son of Rev. William Phillips of St. Michael's Chh., Worcester, Eng.; matric. Merton Coll., Oxford, 1 July 1724, a. 16; K.B. for Va., 8 Jan. 1735/6; sett. South Farnham Par. (Essex) Va., 1739-1744; Ep.

JOHN PHIPPS (possibly b. Dublin, 1704, son of Charles (schoolmaster); pens. Trinity Coll., Dublin, 16 Feb. 1724/5, a. 17; A.B., 1730); officiated at a baptism in Overwharton Par. (Stafford) Va., 1747; Ep.

JOHN PICKETT, b. King George co., Va., 14 Jan. 1744; ord. Carter's Run (Fauquier) Va., 27 May 1772-1803; sett. Battle Run (Culpeper) Va., 1773-1803; sett. Firey Run (Culpeper) Va., 1771-1803; Bapt.; d. Carter's Run, Va., June 1803.

REUBEN PICKETT, b. Fauquier co., Va., 1752; ord. Reedy Bottom (Halifax) Va., 1772-1774; sett. Mayo (Halifax) Va., 1774-1828; Bapt.; living at Mayo Creek, Va., 19 Oct. 1823.

YOUNG PITTS, sett. Upper King and Queen (King & Queen) Va., 1774-1780; Bapt.

GEORGE PLUMMER, sett. Pungo (Princess Anne) Va., 1766-1773; Bapt.

MR. POOLE, preached in Jamestown (James City) Va., 19 May 1611; Ep.

GREVILLE POOLEY, came to Va., 1622; sett. Flowerdew Hundred, Weyanoke Par. (Charles City) Va., 1622-1629; sett. Martin's Brandon Par. (Prince George) Va., 1622-1629; Ep.; d. Va., ca. 1629.

JAMES PORTER, came from Ireland; sett. Lynnhaven Par. (Princess Anne) Va., 1678-1683; Ep.; d. Lynnhaven Parish, Va., Aug. 1683.

EDWARD PORTLOCK, came to Am., 1698; preached at Perth Amboy, N.J., 22 Feb. 1698-1699; and at Woodbridge, N.J., 1698-1699; sett. Christ Chh., Philadelphia, Pa., 1699-29 Nov. 1700; sett. Stratton-Major Par. (King & Queen) Va., 1702-1705; Ep.

WILLIAM POW, K.B. for N.C., 31 Jan. 1748/9; sett. St. Andrew's Par. (Brunswick) Va., 1750-1750; sett. Bath Par., at Petersburg (Dinwiddie) Va., 1752-1754; Ep.; ret. to Eng. as chaplain on H.M.S. "Triton," 1754.

ROBERT POWIS, sett. Southern Shore Par. (Norfolk) Va., ca. 1640-1645; sett. Lynnhaven Par. (Princess Anne) Va., 1645-1652 (inducted, 1648); lawyer; Ep.; d. Lynnhaven Parish, Va., 1652.

WILLIAM PRESTON, A.M., b. 1719/20, son of Rev. William Preston of Broughton, Westmoreland, Eng.; matric. Queen's Coll., Oxford, 22 Feb. 1736/7, a. 16; A.B., 1741, A.M., 24 Nov. 1744; Prof. of Moral Phil., William & Mary Coll., 1744-1757; sett. James City Par. (James City) Va., at Jamestown, 1755-1757; ret. to Eng., 1757; Ep.; d. 1775.

HENRY PRETTY, A.B., b. ca. 1656, son of Rev. George Pretty, of Edwardstone, Suffolk, Eng.; adm. sizar Jesus Coll., Camb., 6 July 1674, a. 18; A.B., 1677/8; ord. June 1680; Rector of Hargham, Norfolk, Eng., 1681-1689; in Virginia, 1696; Ep.

THOMAS PRICE, from Hanover co., Va.; William & Mary Coll., 1754; lic. for Va., 23 Dec. 1759; K.B. Va., 23 Jan. 1760; sett. Abingdon Par. (Gloucester) Va., 1773-1778; sett. Petsworth Par. (Gloucester) Va., ca. 1782; preached before the Va. convention, 1774; chaplain, Va. convention, 1775; Ep.

JOHN PRINCE, A.B., Camb., 1709; ord. 16 June 1717; K.B. for Bermuda, 10 July 1717; sett. Hanover Par. (King George) Va., 1717-1726; Ep., d. Hanover Parish, Va., 1726.

WILLIAM PROCTOR, a Scotsman; formerly a Presb.; lic. for Va., 1 July 1745; K.B. Va., 21 Aug. 1745; sett. Nottoway Par. (Nottoway) Va., 1754-1758; Tutor and librarian at Westover, Va.; Ep.

GEORGE PURDIE, sett. Cumberland Par. (Lunenburg) Va., 1749-1750; sett. St. Andrew's Par. (Brunswick) Va., 1751-Apr. 1760; dismissed; Ep.

GILES RAINSFORD, A.M. (See C.C.Md.), b. 1679; ord. 1702; sett. East or Lower Par. (Nansemond) Va., 1714-1716; sett. St. Anne's Par. (Essex) Va., 1717-1718; Culpeper co., Va., 1718-1720; Ep.

JOHN RAMSAY, lic. for Va., 12 July 1751; K.B. Va., 25 Sept. 1751; sett. St. Anne's Par. (Albemarle) Va., 1754-1758; Ep.

JOHN READE, b. Gloucester co., Va., great-grandson of Rev. John Gwynn (q.v.); ord. Eng., 1737; K.B. for Va., 13 June 1737; sett. Stratton-Major Par. (King & Queen) Va., 1737-1743; sett. Petsworth Par. (Gloucester) Va., as supply, 1739; Ep.

JOSEPH REDDING, b. Fauquier co., Va., 1750; began preaching ca. 1771; preached in Va., 1771-1773; in S.C., 1773-1779; sett. Ky., 1779; Bapt.; d. Ky., Dec. 1815.

JOHN REID, lic. for N.C., 1 Apr. 1745; K.B. Va., 4 Apr. 1745; sett. Newport Par. (Isle of Wight) Va., 1746-1755; Ep.

JOHN RHODES, sett. Luray (Page) Va., before 1766; Mennonite; killed by the Indians, Page co., Va., Aug. 1766.

ALEXANDER RHONALD, lic. for Va., 25 Aug. 1759; K.B. for Va., 14 May 1760; Master, Eaton School, Hampton, Va.; sett. Elizabeth River Par. (Norfolk) Va., 1762-1772; Ep.

DAVID RICE, A.B., b. Hanover co., Va., 20 Dec. 1733, son of Thomas Rice; A.B., Princeton, 1761; lic. Cub Creek, Va., Oct. 1763; ord. Hanover (Hanover) Va., Dec. 1763-1768; sett. Concord (Bedford) Va., 1770-1777; sett. Hat Creek (Campbell) Va., 1770-1777; sett. The Peaks, Peaks of Otter (Bedford) Va., 1770-1780; sett. Cane Run (Lincoln) Ky., Oct. 1783-1816; The Forks (Lincoln) Ky., 1783-1816; Concord (Lincoln) Ky., 1783-1816; the first grammar school in Ky. was opened in his house, 1784; Founder and Trustee, Transylvania Univ., 1785-1816; President of the Board, 1783-1787; Presb.; d. Green co., Ky., 18 June 1816, a. 82.

JOHN RICHARDS, b. Eng., 1689; K.B. for Va., 13 Aug. 1724; Rector, Nettlestead, Kent, Eng.; Vicar, Teston, Kent, Eng.; sett. Ware Par. (Gloucester) Va., 1724-1735; Ep.; d. Ware Parish, Va., 12 Nov. 1735, a. 46.

DANIEL RICHARDSON, not epis. ordained; sett. Hungar's Par. (Northampton) Va., before 1676; Independent.

JOHN ROBERTS, dism. from a parish in Va., 1740; Ep.

ELEAZER ROBERTSON, sett. Bristol Par. (Dinwiddie) Va., 1748-1753; Ep.; d. 1753.

GEORGE ROBERTSON, schoolmaster; chaplain of a man-of-war, 1692; sett. Bristol Par. (Dinwiddie) Va., 1693-1739; patented 2000 acres of land in Prince George co., Va., 1728; Ep.; d. Revelans, Bristol Parish, Va., 1740.

JAMES ROBERTSON (See C.C.Md.), K.B. for Va., 15 Jan. 1717/8; attended convocation in Williamsburg, Va., 1719; sett. Westover Par. (Charles City) Va., 1718-1720; went to Md.; Ep.

JOHN ROBERTSON, lic. for Va., 21 Jan. 1745/6; K.B. Va., 4 Feb. 1745/6; sett. St. James-Southam Par. (Powhatan) Va., 1746-1751; sett. St. James-Northam (Goochland) Va., 1746-1751; sett. St. John's Par. (King William) Va., 1752-1758; Ep.

MOSES ROBERTSON, K.B. for Va., 4 Mar. 1728/9; sett. St. Stephen's Par. (Northumberland) Va., 1743-1748; Ep.

FRANCIS ROBINSON, clergyman; usher, grammar school, William & Mary Coll.; Ep.; d. before 11 Aug. 1741.

WILLIAM ROBINSON (See C.C.Del.), b. Eng., ca. 1700; ord. New Brunswick, N.J., 4 Aug. 1741; sett. Round Oak, Cub Creek (Charlotte) Va., 1742-1743; itinerant missionary in Va. and the Carolinas; first known Presb. minister to preach in N.C.; sett. Del.; Presb.; d. St. George's, Del., 1 Aug. 1746.

COMMISSARY WILLIAM ROBINSON, A.B., b. Middlesex co., Va., 1717, son of Christopher Robinson; matric. Oriel Coll., Oxford, 2 Apr. 1737; A.B., 1740; ord. London, June 1743; K.B. Va., 25 Sept. 1746; sett. Stratton-Major Par. (King & Queen) Va., Nov. 1744-1768; Bishop's Commissary for Va., 1761-1768; Ep.; d. Stratton-Major Parish, Va., 1768.

JOHN RODGERS, sett. Hungar's Par. (Northampton) Va., 1664; Ep.

CHARLES ROSE (brother of Rev. Robert Rose), b. Scotland;

K.B. for Va., 15 Mar. 1736/7; sett. Cople Par. (Westmoreland) Va., 1739-1761; Ep.

ROBERT ROSE, b. Scotland, 1704; sett. St. Anne's Par. (Essex) Va., 1725-1746; sett. St. Anne's Par. (Albemarle) Va., 1747-1751; large landowner in Amherst co., Va.; Ep.; d. St. Anne's Parish (Albemarle) Va., 30 June 1751, a. 47; bur. at Richmond.

JOHN ROSIER, A.M., b. London, Eng., ca. 1704, son of Robert Rosier; adm. sizar Caius Coll., Camb., 9 Feb. 1619/20, a. 15; A.B., 1623/4, A.M., 1627; sett. Hampton Par. (York) Va. 1640; sett. York Par. (York) Va., 1640; sett. Hungar's Par. (Northampton) Va., 1644; sett. Cople Par. (Westmoreland) Va., 1653-1660; Ep.; d. before 24 June 1663, when his wife is named as his widow.

JACOB ROWE, A.M., b. ca. 1730, son of Isaac Rowe of Cornwall; adm. pens. Trinity Coll., Camb., 28 Apr. 1748, a. 18; A.B., 1752; A.M., 1755; ord. (Bsp. of London) 23 Dec. 1754; perhaps a chaplain in the Navy, 1756; lic. for Va., 13 Feb. 1758; K.B. Va., 14 Feb. 1758; Prof. of Morality at William & Mary Coll., 1758-1760; Ep.

WILLIAM RUDD, ord. Eng., 12 Aug. 1699; K.B. Va., 31 Aug. 1699; sett. Elizabeth River Par. (Norfolk) Va., 1700-1702; sett. West Par. (Nansemond) Va., 1703 ff.; Ep.

SAMUEL SANDFORD, A.M., b. ca. 1669, son of Samuel Sandford of Whitechurch, Shropshire, Eng.; matric. Pembroke Coll., Oxford, 17 Dec. 1686, a. 17; A.B., All Souls Coll., 1690; A.M., 1694; sett. St. George's Par. (Accomac) Va., 1694-1702; Rector, Presteign, Radnor, Wales, 1702; Ep.; by will made at London, 27 Mar. 1710, he bequeaths 3,420 acres of land in Accomac co., Va., for the education of poor children.

GEORGE SANDYS, A.M. (prob. A.B., Corpus Christi Coll., Oxford, 1594; A.M., 1597; Rector of Moorlinch, Somersetshire, Eng., 1604); came to Va., 1620; sett. Hog Island (Surrey) Va., 1620; Ep.

HEINRICH SANGMEISTER, b. Hornburg, near Wolfenbuettel, Prussia, 9 Aug. 1723, son of Stephen Heinrich and Anna Margaretha Sangmeister; came to Philadelphia, 1743; sett. Strasburg (Shenandoah) Va., 1750-1764; Dunkard or Germ. Bapt.; d. Ephrata, Pa., 30 Dec. 1784.

RICHARD SANKEY, b. Ireland, son of Jacob and Abigail Sankey; lic. 13 Oct. 1736; ord. East Hanover, Pa., Hanover Chh., Manada Creek, 31 Aug. 1738; sett. East Hanover, Pa., 1737-1760; sett. Carlisle, Pa., 1738-1755; sett. Buffalo Creek (Prince Edward) Va., 1760-1790; sett. Walker's Church (Prince Edward) Va., 1760-1790; Presb.; d. Prince Edward co., Va., 1790.

JOHN HYDE SAUNDERS, of Cumberland co., Va.; William & Mary Coll., 1762-1763; ord. London, for James City Par., Va., 1772; lic. for James City, Va., 21 Sept. 1772; K.B. Va., 10 Oct. 1772; sett. St. James-Southam Par. (Powhatan) Va., Nov. 1773-1801 *et post;* member, Cumberland co. Committee of Safety, Rev. war; Ep.; d. after 1801.

JONATHAN SAUNDERS (came to Md., 1681 with allowance for passage); sett. Lynnhaven Par. (Princess Anne) Va., 1695-1700; Ep.; d. Lynnhaven Parish, Va., before 1701.

NATHANIEL SAUNDERS, ord. Mountain Run (Orange) Va., 1768-1782; sett. Mount Poney (Culpeper) Va., 1774-1777; Bapt.; d. 1808.

THOMAS SAX, sett. Lancaster Par. (Middlesex) Va., prior to 1654; Ep.

JOHANNES SCHWARZBACH, b. 8 Mar. 1719; sett. Elizabeth (Lancaster) Pa., Emmanuel Lutheran Chh., 1775-1776; sett. Upper Hanover (Montgomery) Pa., New Goshenhoppen Chh., 1775-1776; sett. Madison (Madison) Va., Old Hebron Luth. Chh., 1775-1776; Luth.; d. Bensalem, Pa., (31 Aug.) 1800.

JAMES SCLATER, A.M., b. Oxford, Eng., 1657, son of John Sclater; matric. St. Edmund's Hall, Oxford, 14 Nov. 1673, a. 16; A.B., 1677; A.M., 1680; sett. Bruton Par. (James City) Va., 1688-1688; sett. Charles Par. (York) Va., 1688-1723; sett. Mulberry Island Par. (Warwick) Va., 1714-1723; held two livings in Eng. *in absentia;* Ep.; d. Charles Parish, Va., 1723.

ALEXANDER SCOTT, A.M., b. Scotland, 20 July 1686; K.B. for Va., 10 Oct. 1710; sett. Overwharton Par. (Stafford) Va., 1711-1738; sett. St. Paul's Par. (King & Queen) Va., 1711 *et post;* Ep.; d. Dipple, Stafford co., Va., 1 Apr. 1738, a. 53.

JAMES SCOTT, son of Rev. Alexander Scott; ord. Eng., 1741; sett. Dettingen Par. (Prince William) Va., 1745-1782, as the first minister; Ep.; d. Dettingen Parish, Va., 1782.

JOHN SCRIMGEOUR, sett. Cople Par. (Westmoreland) Va., 1687-1691; Ep.; d. Cople Parish, Va., before 1693.

GEORGE SEAGOOD, A.M., b. London, Eng., 1681, son of George Seagood; matric. Christ Church Coll., Oxford, 31 Mar. 1696, a. 15; A.B., 1702, A.M., 1704/5; K.B. for Va., 12 Dec. 1716; sett. Sittingbourne Par. (Richmond) Va., 1717-1724; Ep.; d. Sittingbourne Parish, Va., ca. 1724.

BENJAMIN SEBASTIAN, b. Va., ca. 1739; lic. for Va., 21 Sept. 1766; K.B. Va., 2 Oct. 1766; ord. for Frederick Par., Va., 1766; sett. Frederick Par. (Frederick) Va., 1766-1767; sett. St. Stephen's Par. (Northumberland) Va., 1767-1777; sett. Christ Church Par. (Calvert) Md., 1782-1785; sett. William & Mary Par. (St. Mary's) Md., 1785-1788; remov. to Ky., 1788; Judge of Court of Appeals; Ep.; d. Ky., 1832, a. 93.

MILES SELDEN, b. Va., son of Joseph Selden; lic. for Va., 15 Jan. 1752; K.B. Va., 21 Jan. 1752; sett. Henrico Par. (Henrico) Va., 1752-1785; chaplain, Convention, 1775; chaplain, House of Delegates, 1780; Ep.; d. Henrico Parish, Va., 1785.

WILLIAM SELDEN, b. Northern Neck, Va., 1741, son of John and Grace (Rosewell) Selden; William & Mary Coll., 1752-

1755; lawyer; ord. London, 1771; lic. for Va., 14 Mar. 1771; K.B. Va., 14 Mar. 1771; sett. Elizabeth City Par. (Elizabeth City) Va., 1771-1783; Ep.; d. Elizabeth City co. Va., soon after 1783.

WILLIAM SELLAKE, A.B., b. ca. 1617, son of John Sellake of Tiverton, Devon; matric. Balliol Coll., Oxford, 13 May 1635, a. 18; A.B., Pembroke Coll., 12 May 1636; sett. St. Peter's Par. (New Kent) Va., 1680-1682; Ep.

JAMES SEMPLE, lic. for Va., 30 Sept. 1760; sett. St. Peter's Par. (New Kent) Va., 1767-1789; Ep.

WILLIAM SEMPLE, Commissary of the Bsp. of London in Va., before 1689, but without definite authority; Ep.

JOHN SHACKLEFORD, b. Caroline co., Va., 1750; ord. 1778; sett. Spotsylvania (Spotsylvania) Va., 1772-1776; sett. Tuckahoe (Caroline) Va., 1776-1792; sett. Ky., 1792-1829; Bapt.; d. Ky., 1829, a. 79.

THOMAS SHARPE, ord. for Va., 2 Oct. 1699; K.B. Va., 31 Aug. 1699; sett. Warwisqueake Par. (Isle of Wight) Va., 1702-1708; sett. St. Paul's Par. (Hanover) Va., 1708-1720; officiated at St. Peter's Par. (New Kent) Va., 1720; Ep.

JAMES SHELBURNE, b. James City co., Va., 29 Nov. 1738; ord. Reedy Creek (Lunenburg) Va., June 1775-1820; Bapt.; d. Reedy Creek, Va., 6 Mar. 1820, a. 82.

JOHN SHEPHARD (b. Eng. 1644, son of Nicholas Shephard of Modbury, Dorset; matric. Wadham Coll., Oxford, 12 July 1661, a. 16); sett. Christ Church Par. (Middlesex) Va., 1668-1682; Ep.; d. Christ Church Parish, Va., ca. 1683.

SAMUEL SHIELD, came from York co., Va.; William & Mary Coll., 1769; lic. for Drysdale Par., Va., 21 Dec. 1774; K.B. Va., 18 Jan. 1775; sett. Drysdale Par. (Caroline) Va., 1776-1778; sett. St. Asaph's Par. (Caroline) Va., 1779-1785; sett. Yorkhampton Par. (York) Va., 1786-1792; sett. Charles Par. (York) Va., 1791-1792; president, Convention of the Clergy, 1784; Ep.; d. Charles Parish, Va., 1793.

SAINT JOHN SHROPSHIRE, A.B., b. Marlborough, Wilts, ca. 1666, son of Oliver Shropshire; matric. Magdalen Hall, Oxford, 9 Apr. 1685, a. 19; A.B., Queen's Coll., Oxford, 1688; sett. lower Va., 1704; sett. Washington Par. (Westmoreland) Va., 1703-1718; Ep.; d. Washington Parish, Va., 1718.

JOSEPH SIMPSON, D.D., b. Redmayne, Cumberland, Eng., 1710, son of John Simpson; matric. Queen's Coll., Oxford, 8 Apr. 1728, a. 18; A.B., 1 Feb. 1732/3; Fellow; A.M., 1736; B.D. and D.D., 1761; lic. for Va., 2 June 1746; lived in King & Queen co., at Leedstown, 1748; sett. Hanover Par. (King George) Va., 1747-1751; sett. Lunenburg Par. (Richmond) Va., 1754-1755; Rector, Weyhill, Hants, 1756-1763; Rector, Garsden, Wilts, 1763-1796; Ep.; d. Garsden, Wilts, 17 Aug. 1796.

JOHN SKAIFE, ord. for Va., 9 Sept. 1708; K.B. Va., 13 Sept.

1708; came to Va., ca. 1710; sett. Stratton-Major Par. (King & Queen) Va., 1710-1736; Ep.

WILLIAM SKELTON (or Skelson), K.B. for Antigua, 8 Apr. 1724; sett. Wicomico Par. (Northumberland) Va., 1734-1738; "Clerke, late of Virginia in America," will probated in England, 1739; Ep.; d. 1738/9.

HENRY SKYRING (or Skyren), b. White Haven, Eng., 1729; lic. as a curate (Bsp. of Lincoln) 2 June 1760, at Wymondley, Hertfordshire, Eng., 1760-1763; lic. for Va., 10 Oct. 1763; K.B. Va., 19 Oct. 1763; sett. St. John's Par. (King William) Va., 1764-1787; sett. Elizabeth City Par. (Elizabeth City), Va., 1787-1795; Ep.; d. Hampton, Va., 1795.

JOHN SMELT, b. Eng., educated at Oxford (but not in Foster); lic. for Va., 28 Mar. 1748; sett. St. Anne's Par. (Essex) Va., 1749-1758; Ep.

ADAM SMITH, sett. Augusta Par. (Augusta) Va., 1772-1773; went to S.C., 1773 and returned from S.C., 1773; sett. Botetourt Par. (Botetourt) Va., 1774-1776; served in the Va. militia; Ep.

AUGUSTINE SMITH, sett. Cople Par. (Westmoreland) Va., ca. 1770; Ep.

CHARLES SMITH, sett. Wicomico Par. (Northumberland) Va., 1727-1733; Ep.

CHARLES SMITH (poss. same as above), b. 1711; K.B. for Va., 28 Oct. 1740; sett. Elizabeth River Par. (Norfolk) Va., 1743-1761; sett. Portsmouth Par. (Norfolk) Va., 1761-1773; Ep.; d. Portsmouth, Va., 11 Jan. 1773, a. 61.

CHARLES JEFFRY SMITH, A.M., b. St. George's Manor, Brooklyn, L.I., N.Y., 1740, son of Henry and Ruth (Smith) Smith; A.B., Yale, 1757, A.M., 1761; ord. Lebanon, Conn., 30 June 1763; Indian missionary in N.Y. state; preached extensively in Va. and elsewhere in the south; Presb.; d. Brooklyn, N.Y., 10 Aug. 1770.

GUY SMITH, b. Ely, Cambridge co., Eng.; adm. sizar Corpus Christi Coll., Camb., 1683; matric. 1683/4; sett. Abingdon Par. (Gloucester) Va., 1702-1719; Ep.; d. Abingdon Parish, Va., ca. 1720.

JAMES SMITH, K.B. for Va., 12 Jan. 1702/3; sett. Wicomico Par. (Northumberland) Va., 1703-1705; sett. St. Andrew's Par. (Essex) Va., 1704 et post; performed a bapt. in Surry co., 1742; Ep.

JOSEPH SMITH, K.B. for Va., 21 Sept. 1727; had a parish in Va. and lectured at Jamestown; Ep.; d. Va., 1738.

PATRICK SMITH, sett. Southwark Par. (Surry) Va., 1690; Ep.

SAMUEL STANHOPE SMITH, D.D., LL.D., b. Pequea, Pa., 16 Mar. 1750, son of Rev. Dr. Robert and Elizabeth (Blair) Smith; A.B., Princeton, 1769; A.M.; Tutor, 1770-1773; D.D., Princeton, 1783; D.D., Yale, 1783; LL.D., Harvard, 1810; ord. Rockfish (Nelson) Va., 27 Oct. 1775; missionary to the western counties of Va.; inst. Cumberland and Prince Edward counties, Va., 9 Nov.

48     THE COLONIAL CLERGY OF VIRGINIA

1775; sett. as minister in Cumberland and Prince Edward counties, Va., 1775-28 Oct. 1779; President, Hampden-Sidney Coll., Va., 1775-1779; Prof. of Moral Phil., Princeton, 1779-1812; Pres. of Princeton Coll., 1795-1812; member, Am. Phil. Soc., 1785; Presb.; d. Princeton, N.J., 21 Aug. 1819.

THOMAS SMITH, K.B. for Va., 11 Oct. 1752; lic. for Va., 2 Feb. 1753; sett. St. Stephen's Par. (Northumberland) Va., 1754-1755; sett. Cople Par. (Westmoreland) Va., 1774-1789; chairman, Committee of Safety, Westmoreland co., Am. Rev.; father of Rev. John Augustine Smith, President of William & Mary Coll.; Ep.; d. Cople Parish, Va., 1789.

WILLIAM SMITH, K.B. for Va., 24 Sept. 1729; Ep.; d. 1734.

JOHN SPAN, b. ca. 1686, son of Cuthbert Span of Va.; matric. Queen's Coll., Oxford, 20 Mar. 1704/5, a. 18; K.B. for Va., 25 Oct. 1710; sett. St. Stephen's Par. (Northumberland) Va., 20 Mar. 1712-1722; Ep.

RICHARD SQUIRE (possibly b. 1661, son of Richard Squire of Blackford, co. Somerset, Eng., matric. New Inn Hall, 8 July 1679, a. 18); ord. Oct. 1702; K.B. for Va., 20 Nov. 1702; sett. St. Peter's Par. (New Kent) Va., 1703-1707; Ep.; d. St. Peter's Parish, Va., 1707.

THEODOSIUS STAIGE, b. Eng.; K.B. for Va., 4 June 1725; sett. St. George's Par. (Spotsylvania) Va., 1726-1728; sett. Charles Par. (York) Va., 1728-1747; Ep.

MR. STAUFFER, sett. Woodstock (Shenandoah) Va., 1754; Mennonite.

SHUBAEL STEARNS (See C.C.N.E.), b. Boston, Mass., 28 Jan. 1705/6, son of Shubal and Rebecca (Larriford) Stearns; ord. Tolland, Conn., 20 Mar. 1751; sett. Opequon Creek (Berkeley) W.Va., 1754-1755 till Braddock's defeat; sett. Sandy Creek (Randolf) N.C., 1754-1771; Bapt.; d. Sandy Creek, N.C., 20 Nov. 1771, a. 66.

JOHN CONRAD STEINER, SR. (See C.C.Md.), b. Switzerland, 1 Jan. 1707; came to Pa., 25 Sept. 1749; sett. Winchester (Frederick) Va., German Reformed Chh., 1756-1759; Germ. Ref.; d. Philadelphia, Pa., 6 July 1762, a. 55 (GS).

JAMES STEPHENSON, lic. for Va., 29 Sept. 1768; K.B. Va., 11 Oct. 1768; ord. London, 1768; sett. Camden Par. (Pittsylvania) Va., 1769; sett. Berkeley Par. (Spotsylvania) Va., 1769-1780; sett. St. Mark's Par. (Culpeper) Va., Apr. 1780-1794; sett. St. George's Par. (Spotsylvania) Va., 1794-1805; Ep.; d. 1809.

HUGH STEVENSON (See C.C.Del.), sett. Potomac Chh., Northumberland co., Va., 1733; Presb.; d. Philadelphia, Pa., May 1744.

WILLIAM STITH, A.M., b. Charles City co., Va., 1707, son of Captain John and Mary (Randolph) Stith; William & Mary Coll.; matric. Queen's Coll., Oxford, 21 May 1724, a. 17, A.B., 27 Feb. 1727/8; A.M., 1730; K.B. for Va., 12 Apr. 1731; master, grammar school, William & Mary Coll., 1731; sett. Henrico Par. (Henrico) Va., 1736-1752; Pres., William & Mary Coll., 1752-1755; author of a *History of Virginia;* Ep.; d. Williamsburg, Va., 19 Sept. 1755.

JONAS STOCKTON, b. ca. 1589, of Warwickshire, Eng., gent.; matric. Brasenose Coll., Oxford, 21 Feb. 1605/6, a. 17; came to Va., 1621; sett. Henrico Par. (Henrico) Va., 1621-1627; sett. Elizabeth City Par. (Elizabeth City) Va., 1621-1627; sett. Kecoughton Par. (Elizabeth City) Va., 1627 *et post;* Ep.

ROBERT STOCKTON, b. Albemarle co., Va., 12 Dec. 1743; sett. Leather Wood (Henry) Va., 1772-1800; sett. Ky., 1800-1825; Bapt.; d. Ky., 1825.

JOHN CASPAR STOEVER, Sr., b. Frankenberg, Hesse, 1685; arriv. Pa., 11 Sept. 1728; sett. Madison (Madison) Va., Old Hebron Luth. Chh. at White Oak Run, 1728-1734; sett. Winchester (Frederick) Va., Strasburg Chh., 1728-1734; sett. Woodstock (Shenandoah) Va., 1730-1734; sett. Md. and Pa., 1728-1734; went to Germany to obtain funds; resided in Germany, 1734-1738; Luth.; d. at sea en route to Va., 1738/9.

JACOB STRICKLER, son of Abraham Strickler; came from Lancaster co., Pa., to Va., 1729; sett. Luray (Page) Va., 1731-1784; Mennonite; d. Luray (Page) Va., 1784.

JOHN STRITCHLEY, b. 1699; Ep.; tomb at St. Mary's White Chapel Parish (Lancaster) Va.

DAVID STUART, from Scotland, 1715; sett. St. Paul's Par. (King George) Va., 1722-1749; Ep.; d. St. Paul's Parish, Va., 1749.

WILLIAM STUART, son of the Rev. David Stuart; lic. for Va., 26 Sept. 1746; K.B. Va., 8 Oct. 1746; sett. St. Paul's Par. (King George) Va., 1746-1796; Ep.; d. St. Paul's Parish, Va., 1796.

DANIEL STURGES, lic. for Norborne Par., Va., 11 Nov. 1771; K.B. Va., 28 Nov. 1771; sett. Norborne Par. (Berkeley) W.Va., 1771-1785; Ep.

WILLIAM SWIFT, K.B. for Bermuda, 8 May 1722; came to Va., 1728; sett. St. Martin's Par. (Hanover) Va., 1728-1734; sett. King William Par. (Powhatan) Va., at Manakintown, 1728-1729; Ep.; d. St. Martin's Parish, Va., 1734.

DANIEL TAYLOR, Sr., sett. Blissland Par. (New Kent & James City) Va., 1704-1729; Ep.

DANIEL TAYLOR, Jr., b. Va., son of Rev. Daniel Taylor; K.B. for Va., 30 May 1727; ord. 1727; sett. St. John's Par. (King William) Va., 1729-1742; Ep.; d. St. John's Parish, Va., 29 Sept. 1742.

JEREMIAH TAYLOR, sett. Elizabeth City Par. (Elizabeth City) Va., 1667 and after; Ep.

JOHN TAYLOR, sett. Fairfield Par. (Northumberland) Va., 1668-1670; sett. Chicacone Par. (Northumberland) Va., 1668-1670; Ep.

JOHN TAYLOR, b. Fauquier co. Va., 1752, son of Lazarus

and Anne (Bradford) Taylor; lic. 1770; ord. South River (Rockingham) Va., 1774, as an itinerant; preached in Va. and Ky.; sett. Cedar Creek, Ky., 1785-1795; sett. Black Run, Ky., 1816-1833; Bapt.; d. Black Run, Ky., 1833, a. 81.

THOMAS TAYLOR, sett. Blissland Par. (New Kent) Va., 1680 *et post;* Ep.

THOMAS TEACKLE, b. Gloucestershire, Eng., 1624; came to Va., 1656; sett. Nassawadox Par. (Northampton) Va., 1656-1696; sett. St. George's Par. (Accomac) Va., 1662-1694; sett. Hungar's Par. (Northampton) Va., 1680-1694; Ep.; d. Craddock, Accomac co., Va., 1694/6 (Mason gives 1696).

PETER TEMPLE, sett. York Par. (York) Va., *ante* 1686 *et post;* Ep.

JAMES TEMPLETON, A.M., A.B., Princeton, 1772, A.M., 1787; lic. Rockfish (Nelson) Va., 26 Oct. 1775; sett. S.C.; Presb.

JAMES TENNANT, ord. for Va., 25 May 1708; K.B. Va. 28 May 1708; sett. Lynnhaven Par. (Princess Anne) Va., 1714-1726; Ep.

CHICHELY THACKER, A.B., b. Middlesex co., Va., 1704, son of Henry Thacker of Christchurch, St. Croix, Virgin Islands, gent.; matric. Oriel Coll., Oxford, 21 May 1724, a. 20; A.B., 23 Jan. 1727/8; sett. Blissland Par. (New Kent) Va., 1729-1763; Ep.

DAVID THOMAS, A.M., b. London Tract, Pa., 16 Aug. 1732; educated at Hopewell, N.J., under Rev. Isaac Eaton; A.M., Brown U., 1769; ord. 1750; missionary to Va., 1751-1788; sett. Broad Run (Fauquier) Va., 1762-1788; sett. Occoquan (King William) Va., 1774-1788; sett. Mill Creek, Opequon (Berkeley) W.Va., 1788-1796; sett. Washington (Mason) Ky., 1796; res. East Hickman, Ky.; Bapt.; d. ca. 1815.

AMOS THOMPSON, A.M., A.B., Princeton, 1760; A.M.; sett. Leesburgh (Loudoun) Va., 1774-1776; chaplain, Stephenson's Maryland and Virginia Riflemen, 1776; Presb.; d. 1801.

ANDREW THOMPSON, b. Stone Hills, Scotland, 1674; K.B. for Va., 24 July 1712; sett. Elizabeth City Par. (Elizabeth City) Va., 1712-1719; Ep.; d. Elizabeth City Parish, Va., 1719.

DAVID THOMPSON, member, Separatist Bapt. Assn., N.C., 1772; sett. Thomson's (Louisa) Va., Goldmine Chh., 1774-1776; Bapt.

JAMES THOMPSON (or Thomson), b. near Glasgow, Scotland, 1739; son of James and Rosalie Thomson (A.B., Princeton, 1769); lic. for Va., 28 Feb. 1769; K.B. Va., 7 Mar. 1769; sett. Leed's Par. (Fauquier) Va., 1769-1812; tutor to Ch.Just. John Marshall; preached at Taylor's Chh., Old Bull Run Chh., Goose Creek Chh., and Piper's Chh., all near Salem, Va.; Ep.; d. near Salem, Leed's Parish, Va., 12 Feb. 1812.

JOHN THOMPSON, A.M., b. Scotland; A.B., A.M., Edinburgh U.; ord. London, 4 Nov. 1739; K.B. for Md., 8 Nov. 1739;

sett. St. Mark's Par. (Culpeper) Va., 1740-1772; Ep.; d. St. Mark's Parish, Va., 1772.

JOHN THOMSON (See C.C.Del.), b. Scotland, Sept. 1690; ord. Lewes (Sussex) Del., Apr. 1717-1729; sett. Pa. (q.v.), 1730-1744; sett. Opequon Creek (Frederick) Va., near Winchester, 1739-1739; sett. Cub Creek (Charlotte) Va., Round Oak Chh., 1744-1753; Buffalo (Prince Edward) Va., 1744-1753; Concord (Bedford) Va., 1744-1753; made missionary visits to N.C., 1744, 1751, 1753; Presb.; d. Centre, N.C., 1753.

THOMAS THOMSON, A.M. (See C.C.S.C.), sett. Chester and Concord, Pa., 1750-1756; sett. Antrim Par. (Halifax) Va., 1762-1763, as an old man; Ep.

ZACHARIAS THOMPSON, SR. (or Thomson), sett. Reedy Creek (Brunswick) Va., 1773-1787; Bapt.

WILLIAM THORN, b. Chestnut Level, Pa., 1750, son of Rev. David and Mary Thorn (possibly A.B., U. Pa., 1769, A.M., 1773); sett. Alexandria (Fairfax) Va., 15 Oct. 1772-1773, as first minister; Presb.; d. Alexandria, Va., 8 Aug. 1773 (GS).

WILLIAM THRIFT, came from Great Valley, Pa., sett. New Valley (Loudoun) Va., 1765-1778; Bapt.

COLONEL CHARLES MYNN THURSTON, b. Gloucester co., Va.; William & Mary Coll., 1754; lic. for Va., 13 Aug. 1765; K.B. Va., 15 Aug. 1765; sett. Petsworth Par. (Gloucester) Va., 1765-1768; sett. Frederick Par. (Frederick) Va., 1768-1777; Col. in Rev. army; chairman, Committee of Safety, Frederick County, Va.; sett. Mount Zion (Frederick) Va., and later at New Orleans, La.; Ep.

ARTHUR TILLYARD, A.M., b. Oxford, Eng., ca. 1673, son of Arthur Tillyard; matric. All Soul's Coll., Oxford, 1689, a. 16; A.B., 1693, A.M., St. Alban's Hall, 1697; ord. for Va., 23 June 1702; K.B. Va., 15 June 1702; was in Va., 1705; sett. Martin's Hundred Par. (James City) Va., 1704-1712; sett. York Par. (York) Va., 1704-1712; received aid from S.P.G., 1702; invited to officiate at Bruton Par. (James City) Va., 1710; Ep.; d. York co., Va., 1712.

DAVID TINSLEY, sett. Totier (Albemarle) Va., 1770-1775; sett. Powhatan (Powhatan) Va., 1771-1775; Bapt.

CHRISTOPHER TODD, William & Mary Coll., 1768-1770; lic. for Brunswick Par., Va., 26 Apr. 1775; K.B. Va., 9 May 1775; sett. Brunswick Par. (Stafford) Va., 1775; Ep.

JOHN TODD, A.M., b. co. Armagh, Ireland, 1719, son of Robert Todd; A.B., Princeton, 1749; A.M.; lic. 7 May 1750; ord. Hanover Presbytery, Va., 27 May 1751; installed Hanover (Hanover) Va. (as minister to seven congregations), 29 Nov. 1750-1792; inst. Providence (Louisa) Va., 12 Nov. 1752-1793; Presb.; d. Va. 27 July 1793.

WILLIAM TOMPSON, A.B. (See C.C.N.E., p. 205; C.C.Md., p. 66), sett. Nansemond, Va. and Upper Norfolk, Va., 1642-13 Oct. 1743; Cong.

WILLIAM TOMPSON, A.B. (See *C.C.N.E.*, p. 205, but he was prob. *not* son of the William Tompson above); A.B., Harvard Coll., 1653; sett. Springfield, Mass., 1654-1656 (as a Congregationalist); sett. New London, Conn., 1657-1661, as an Indian preacher for the "Soc. for Propagating the Gospel in New England" (not to be confused with the Anglican S.P.G.); sett. Mystic, Conn., 1659; sett. New London, Conn., 1659-1662; became an Ep.; sett. Southwark Par. (Surry) Va., 1662-1675; sett. Lawne's Creek Par. (Surry) Va., 1662-1675; sett. Washington Par. (Westmoreland) Va., 1688-1699; d. prob. in Va., after 1699.

JACOB TOWNSEND, in Va., without a cure, 1754; Ep.

HENRY TRENDALL, K.B. for Md., 31 Mar. 1767; sett. Durham Par. (Charles) Va., before 1775; Ep. (Also called Fendall).

JOHN URQHART, sett. Wicomico Par. (Northumberland) Va., 1702; Ep.

HUGH VANCE, A.B., Princeton, A.B., 1767; sett. Tuscarora, Va., 1774-1774; Presb.; d. 1791.

PHILIP CHARLES VAN GEMUENDEN, in Va., 1762-1764; Germ.Reformed.

WILLIAM VERE, lic. for Va., 22 Sept. 1771; K.B. Va., 5 Oct. 1771; sett. Accomac Par. (Accomac) Va., 1774-1786; sett. St. George's Par. (Accomac) Va., 1790-1792; Ep.; living as Rector of St. George's Parish, Va., 1792.

THOMAS VICARIS, in Va., 1665-1666; sett. Petsworth Par. (Gloucester) Va., 1677-1697; Ep.; d. Petsworth Parish, Va., 1697.

JAMES WADDELL, D.D., b. Newry, Ulster co., Ireland, July 1739; instructor, Pequea Academy, ca. 1760; D.D., Dickinson Coll., Carlisle, Pa., 1792; ord. Harris Creek (Prince Edward) Va., 16 June 1762; sett. Potomac Chh. (Lancaster and Northumberland) Va., 7 Oct. 1762-1776; sett. Tinkling Spring (Augusta) Va., 1 May 1776-1778; sett. Spring Hill, near Waynesborough, Va., 1778-1785; sett. Hopewell (Louisa) Va., 1785-1805; Presb.; d. Belle Grove, Louisa co., Va., 17 Sept. 1805.

JAMES WADDING, A.M., Oxford U., A.M., 20 Dec. 1670; sett. James City Par. (James City) Va., at Jamestown, 1672 *et post;* sett. Petsworth Par. (Gloucester) Va., 1672 *et post;* Ep.

ALEXANDER WALKER (possibly b. 1667, son of Rev. William Walker of Barbadoes; matric. Trinity Coll., Oxford, 12 Nov. 1684, a. 17; student in Middle Temple, 1685); K.B. for Va., 31 Aug. 1699; ord. Sept. 1699; in Va., 1700; sett. Southwark Par. (Surry) Va., 1702 *et post;* Ep.

JEREMIAH WALKER, b. Bute, Warren co., N.C., ca. 1747; sett. Nottoway (Nottoway) Va., 1769-1774; sett. Harper's (Dinwiddie) Va., 1774-1785; went to Ga., 1785; Bapt.; d. Ga., 20 Sept. 1792.

CALEB WALLACE, A.B., Princeton, A.B., 1770; trustee, Hampden-Sidney Coll., 1775; trustee, Washington & Lee Coll.,

1782; ord. Cub Creek, Va., 3 Oct. 1774; sett. Cub Creek (Charlotte) Va., Round Oak Chh., 1774-1779; sett. Little Falling River (Prince Edward) Va., 1774-1779; sett. Botetourt co., Va., 1779-1783; removed to Ky., 1783; member, Constitutional Convention, Ky., 1785-1799; Judge, Ky. Supreme Ct., 1792-1814; Presb.; d. Ky., 1814.

JAMES WALLACE, sett. Elizabeth City Par. (Elizabeth City) Va., 1691-1712; Ep.; d. Elizabeth City Parish, Va., 1712.

JOHN WALLER, b. Spotsylvania, Va., 23 Dec. 1741; ord. Waller's or Lower Spotsylvania Chh. (Prince Edward) Va., 2 June 1770-1793; sett. Burrus's (Caroline) Va., 1773-1793; sett. Abbeville, S.C., 1793-1802; Bapt.; d. Abbeville, S.C., 4 July 1802, a. 61.

SAMUEL WALLIS, ord. for Va., 8 Aug. 1709; K.B. Va., 8 Sept. 1709; sett. West Par. (Nansemond) Va., 1714; Ep.

JAMES WARDEN, came from Scotland; K.B. for Va., 27 Mar. 1712; officiated at James City Par. (James City) Va., Jamestown, 1712; sett. Weyanoke Par. (Charles City) Va., 1712-1716; sett. Martin's Brandon Par. (Prince George) Va., 1712-1716; sett. Lawne's Creek Par. (Surry) Va., 1717-1725; Ep.

JACOB WARE, K.B. for Va., 11 Nov. 1689; sett. St. Peter's Par. (New Kent) Va., 1690-1695; sett. Henrico Par. (Henrico) Va., 1690-1709; Ep.; d. Henrico co., Va., 1709.

ROBERT WARE, ord. Lower King & Queen (King & Queen) Va., 11 Feb. 1773; sett. Lower King & Queen, Va., 1772-1804; Bapt.; d. Lower King & Queen, Va., 1804.

THOMAS WARRINGTON, lic. for Va., 21 Sept. 1747; K.B. Va., 14 Oct. 1747; sett. Charles Par. (York) Va., 1749-1756; sett. Elizabeth City Par. (Elizabeth City) Va., 1756-1770; Ep.; d. Elizabeth City Parish, Va., 1770.

RALPH WATSON, A.B., b. Derbyshire, Eng., ca. 1602; matric. Brasenose Coll., Oxford, 28 Jan. 1619/20, a. 17; A.B., 22 Nov. 1621; Rector, Trusley, co. Derby, Eng., 1629; sett., parish not known, York co., Va., before 1645; Ep.; d. York co., Va., 1645.

ABNER WAUGH, b. Orange co., Va., son of Alexander Waugh and grandson of Rev. John Waugh (q.v.); William & Marv Coll., 1765-1768; lic. for St. Mary's Parish, Va., 11 Mar. 1771; K.B. Va., 14 Mar. 1771; sett. St. Mary's Par. (Caroline) Va., 1773-1806; sett. St. George's Par. (Spotsylvania) Va., 1806; chaplain, Continental regiment, Am. Rev.; chaplain, Va. Convention, 1788; Ep.; d. St. George's Parish, Va., ca. 1806.

JOHN WAUGH, b. Northern England; sett. Cople Par. (Westmoreland) Va., 1673-1677; sett. Potomac Par. (Stafford) Va., 1667-1680; sett. Overwharton Par. (Stafford) Va., 1680-1700; sett. St. Paul's Par. (Stafford) Va., 1680-1700; Ep.; d. Stafford co., Va., 1706.

JOHN WAYRE (or Woyre); sett. Lawne's Creek Par. (Surry) Va., 1680; Ep.

JOHN WEATHERFORD, b. Charlotte co., Va., ca. 1740; ord.

1761, as an evangelist; sett. Cub Creek (Charlotte) Va., ca. 1771; sett. Lower Fallings (Campbell) Va.; sett. Halifax co., Va., 1813-1823; Bapt.; d. Pittsylvania co., Va., 23 Jan. 1833.

WILLIAM WEBB (possibly b. 1713, son of Randolph Webb of Bath, co. Somerset, Eng., gent.; matric. St. Mary's Hall, Oxford, 18 July 1730, a. 17); lic. for Va., 16 Mar. 1746/7; K.B. Va., 7 Apr. 1747; sett. Upper Par. (Nansemond) Va., 1747-1760; master of the grammar school, William & Mary Coll., 1760-1762; Ep.

WILLIAM WEBBER, b. 15 Aug. 1747; ord. ca. 1771; sett. Dover (Goochland) Va., 1774-1808; Bapt.; d. Dover, Va., 29 Feb. 1808.

WILLIAM WERN, sett. Elizabeth River Par. (Norfolk) Va., 1680 et post; Ep.

SOLOMON WHEATLEY (or Whately), ord. Oct. 1699; came to Va., via Md., 1700; sett. Lynnhaven Par. (Princess Anne) Va., 1701-1702; sett. Bruton Par. (James City) Va., 1702-1710; chaplain, House of Burgesses, 1705; Ep.; d. Williamsburg, Va., 1710.

ALEXANDER WHITAKER, A.M., son of Rev. William Whitaker, D.D., Regius Prof. of Divinity at Cambridge, Eng., Puritan and Calvinist; came to Va., with his friend, Sir Thomas Dale, May 1611; sett. Henrico Par. (Henrico) Va., 1611-1617; "The Apostle of Virginia"; lived at Rock Dale, Va.; Ep.; d. (drowned) James River, Va., 1617.

ALEXANDER WHITE, ord. 1745; lic. for Va., 10 June 1745; K.B. Va., 12 June 1745; sett. St. David's Par. (King William) Va., 1754-1775; Ep.; d. St. David's Parish, Va., ca. 1775.

GEORGE WHITE, b. Gloucestershire, Eng., ca. 1601; matric. Broadgates Hall, Oxford, 12 June 1618, a. 17; sett. Denbigh Par. (Warwick) Va., ca. 1635; Ep.

THOMAS WHITE (A.B., Brasenose Coll., Oxford, 13 Dec. 1615; A.M., 17 Oct. 1618); sett. Elizabeth City Par. (Elizabeth City) Va., 1622-1624; Ep.; d. Va., before 1624.

WILLIAM WHITE, sett. York Par. (York) Va., before 1658; sett. St. Mary's White Chapel Par. (Lancaster) Va., 1658; Ep.; d. York co. Va., before Sept. 1658.

WILLIAM WICKHAM (possibly b. Somersetshire, 1570; matric. Merton Coll., Oxford, 15 June 1588, a. 18); sett. Henrico Par. (Henrico) Va., as curate, 1616-1622; Ep.

WILLIAM WILKERSON (possibly b. 1612, son of Rev. Gabriel Wilkerson of Bishop Coborne, Bucks; matric. Magdalen Hall, Oxford, 9 June 1626, a. 14; A.B., 3 Feb. 1629/30; A.M., 25 Oct. 1632); sett. Lynnhaven Par. (Princess Anne) Va., 1635-1637; Ep.

THOMAS WILKINSON, lic. for Va., 31 July 1753; K.B. Va., 8 Aug. 1753; sett. Bristol Par. (Dinwiddie) Va., Apr. 1753-1762; sett. Nottoway Par. (Nottoway) Va., 1773-1776; Ep.

JOHN WILLIAMS, b. Hanover co., Va., 1747; Sheriff of Lunenburg co., Va., 1769; ord. Meherrin (Lunenburg) Va., Dec.

1772; sett. Allen's Creek (Mecklenburg) Va., 1770-1790; sett. Meherrin (Lunenburg) Va., 1771-1785; sett. Sandy Creek (Charlotte) Va., 1785-1795; sett. Blue Stone Chh. (Mecklenburg) Va., 1786-1794; Bapt.; d. Sandy Creek, Va., 30 Apr. 1795.

PAUL WILLIAMS, sett. Weyanoke Par. (Charles City) Va., ca. 1680; sett. Martin's Brandon Par. (Prince George) Va., ca. 1680; Ep.

ROBERT WILLIAMS, sett. Norfolk (Norfolk) Va., 1774-1775; Meth.; d. near Norfolk, Va., 26 Sept. 1775.

WILLIAM WILLIAMS, b. 1657, son of John Williams of Cwmdu, Breconshire; matric. Hart Hall, Oxford, 22 Mar. 1677/8, a. 20; sett. St. Stephen's Par. (King & Queen) Va., 1680 et post; sett. St. Peter's Par. (New Kent) Va., 1689-1690; was in Va. as late as 1705; Ep.

WILLIAM WILLIE, sett. Albemarle Par. (Sussex) Va., 1753-1776; Ep.

FRANCIS WILSON, lic. for Drysdale Par., Va., 24 Aug. 1772; K.B. Va., 4 Feb. 1773; sett. Washington Par. (Westmoreland) Va., 1782-1787; Ep.

JOHN WILSON, sett. Elizabeth River Par. (Norfolk) Va., 1637-1640; Ep.; d. Elizabeth River Parish, Va., 1640.

JOHN WINGATE, lic. for Dale Par., Va., 22 Sept. 1771; K.B. Va., 5 Oct. 1771; sett. St. Thomas's Par. (Orange) Va., 1774, and perhaps longer; Ep.

THOMAS WINTER, sett. Wicomico Par. (Northumberland) Va., 1739; Ep.

JOHN WISHART, lic. for Va., 29 June 1764; K.B. Va., 11 July 1764; sett. Brunswick Par. (Stafford) Va., 1764-1774; Ep.; d. Brunswick Parish, Va., 1774.

JOHN WOOD (son of a clergyman; matric. Magdalen Hall, Oxford, 22 July 1658); sett. Upper Par. (Nansemond) Va., 1684 et post; Ep.

WILLIAM WOODS, sett. Albemarle (Albemarle) Va., 1767-1809; Bapt.; living, Albemarle, Va., 1809.

JOHN WRIGHT, sett. New Pocuoson Par. (York) Va., 1680; Ep.

JOHN WRIGHT, K.B. for Md., 25 Mar. 1729/30; sett. Northern Neck, Va., 1731; Ep.

JOHN WRIGHT, A.B., b. Scotland; A.B., Princeton, 1752; ord. (New Castle Presbytery) June 1753; installed, Farmville (Cumberland) Va., July 1755; sett. Farmville, Oct. 1754-1762; Presb.; d. after 1763.

RICHARD WRIGHT, lic. 1770; came to Am., 1772; itinerant minister in Md. and Va.; sett. Norfolk (Norfolk) Va., 1773-1774; Meth.

HAWTE WYATT, b. Boxley, Kent, Eng., ca. 1594, son of George Wyatt; matric. Queen's Coll., Oxford, 25 Oct. 1611, a. 17; student at Gray's Inn, 1611; came to Va. with his brother, Gov.

Francis Wyatt, Oct. 1621; sett. James City Par. (James City) Va., at Jamestown, 1621-1625; ret. to Eng.; sett. Marston, Kent, Eng., 1630; Vicar of Boxley, Kent, 1632; Ep.; d. Boxley, Kent, Eng., 31 July 1638.

JOHN WYATT, A.M., b. Drayton, Berks, Eng., 1650, son of Richard Wyatt; matric. New Coll., Oxford, 1666, a. 16; A.B., 1670, A.M., 1673; Rector, Hatherope, Gloucestershire, Eng., 1680; in Va., 1705; Ep.

RICHARD WYATT, b. Marlborough, Wilts, Eng., 1643, son of Richard Wyatt; matric. Exeter Coll., Oxford, 1661, a. 18; vicar of Upham, Wilts, 1666; in Va., 1705; Ep.

WILLIAM WYE, A.B. (See C.C.Md.), b. Ireland, 1684; sett. Wicomico Par. (Northumberland) Va., 1727 as supply; sett. St. Stephen's Par. (Northumberland) Va., 1727-1731; Ep.; d. North Elk Parish, Md., 16 Nov. 1744.

ROBERT YANCEY, lic. for Va., 25 July 1768; K.B. Va., 28 July 1768; sett. Trinity Par. (Louisa) Va., 1774; Ep.

BARTHOLOMEW YATES, Sr., A.B., b. 1677, son of William Yates of Shropshire, Eng., and brother of Rev. Robert Yates, Sr., whom he succeeded; matric. Brasenose Coll., Oxford, 10 Mar. 1694/5; A.B., 1698; ord. 10 Sept. 1700; K.B. Va., 18 Sept. 1700; came to Va., Feb. 1700/1; sett. Sittingbourne Par. (King George) Va., 1702; sett. North Side of St. Mary's Par. (Richmond) Va., 1702; sett. Kingston Par. (Gloucester) Va., 1702-1703; sett. Christ Church Par. (Middlesex) Va., Mar. 1703-1734; Prof. of Divinity, William & Mary Coll., 1729; Ep.; d. Christ Church Parish, Va., 26 July 1734, a. 57.

BARTHOLOMEW YATES, Jr., A.B., b. Christ Church Parish, Va., 1712, son of Rev. Bartholomew and Sarah (Mickleborough) Yates; matric. Oriel Coll., Oxford, 29 Feb. 1731/2, a. 18; A.B., 1735; K.B. for Va., 13 June 1737; sett. Christ Church Par. (Middlesex), 1737-1767; Ep.

ROBERT YATES, Sr., A.B., b. ca. 1674, son of William Yates of Shropshire, Eng.; matric. Brasenose Coll., Oxford, 22 June 1692, a. 18; A.B., 1696; K.B. for Va., 3 Jan. 1698/9; sett. Christ Church Par. (Middlesex) Va., 1699-1703; ret. to Eng.; Rector, Wickham Bishops, Essex, Eng., 1706; Ep.

ROBERT YATES, Jr., A.B., b. 1715, son of Rev. Bartholomew and Sarah (Mickleborough) Yates; matric. Oriel Coll., Oxford, 12 July 1733, a. 18; A.B., 1737; K.B. for Va., 6 July 1741; sett. Petsworth Par. (Gloucester) Va., 1741-1761; Ep.; d. Petsworth Parish, Va., 1761.

WILLIAM YATES, b. Christ Church Parish, Va., 1720, son of Rev. Bartholomew Yates; William & Mary Coll.; lic. for Va., 1 Apr. 1745; K.B. Va., 23 Apr. 1745; sett. Abingdon Par. (Gloucester) Va., 1750-1759; sett. Bruton Par. (James City) Va., 1759-1764; Pres., William & Mary Coll., 1759-1764; Ep.; d. Williamsburg, Va., 1764.

GEORGE YOUNG, ord. 13 Oct. 1699; sett. Petsworth Par. (Gloucester) Va., 5 Feb. 1699/1700-Oct. 1700; Ep.

JOHN YOUNG, b. Caroline co., Va., 11 Jan. 1739; ord. 1773; sett. Read's (Caroline) Va., 1773-1799; sett. Mt. Moriah, Buffalo, Va., 1799-1817; Bapt.; d. Read's, Caroline co., Va., 16 Apr. 1817.

W. GEORGE YOUNG, sett. Washington Par. (Westmoreland) Va., 1776-*et seq.*; Ep.

JACOB CHRISTOPHER ZOLLICOFFER, b. St. Gall, Switzerland; sett. Germanna (Orange) Va., Massanutton Chh., before 1730; Luth.-Ep.

MICHAEL ZYPERNE (or Zyperus), came from Curacoa, Aug. 1659, to N.Y.C. as a candidate; joined the Dutch Reformed Chh. as a student of divinity in Jan. 1660; went to Va., 1664; conformed to the Church of England; sett. Kingston Par. (Mathews) Va., 1680-1687; D.R.-Ep.

\*     \*     \*     \*     \*

Summary: Baptists, 86; Congregationalists, 6; Episcopalians, 489; Friends, 4; German Reformed, 5; Lutherans, 5; Mennonites, 5; Methodists, 2; Moravians, 2; Presbyterians, 44. Total: 648.

# THE COLONIAL CLERGY OF NORTH CAROLINA
## 1708-1776

JAMES ABBINGTON, ord. Sandy Run (Bertie) N.C., 1764-1772; Bapt.; d. Sandy Run, Feb. 1772.

HENRY ABBOT, sett. Tar River (Granville) N.C., 1761; member Kehukee Assn., 1765; sett. Shiloh Chh. (Camden), 1765-1791; member, N.C. state convention, 7 times; member, Provincial Congress; Bapt.; d. Camden, N.C., May 1791.

JAMES ADAMS, Curate, Castlemore, Ireland, 1702-1707; K.B., N.C., 26 July 1707; came to Va., Apr. 1708; sett. St. John's Par. (Pasquotank) N.C., 1708-1710; sett. Currituck Par. (Currituck) N.C., 1708-1710; Ep.; S.P.G.; d. N.C., 30 Oct. 1710.

JOSEPH ALEXANDER, D.D. (See *C.C. South Carolina*), ord. Buffalo (Guilford) N.C., 4 Mar. 1768; Presb.; sett. Sugar Creek (Mecklenburg) N.C., May 1768-1774.

ROBERT ARCHIBALD, A.B., Princeton, A.B., 1772; lic. (Orange Presb.) Fall, 1775; ord. Rocky River Center (Mecklenburg) N.C., 7 Oct. 1778; sett. Rocky River, 1778-1792; Poplar Tent (Mecklenburg) N.C., 1778-1792; Presb.; became a Univarsalist; physician; d. after 1797.

JOHANN GOTTFRIED ARNDS, came from Germany, 1773; schoolmaster, 1773-1775; ord. Charleston, S.C., 1775; sett. Salisbury (Rowan) N.C., St. John's Luth. Chh., 1775-1786; sett. Organ Church (Rowan) N.C., Zion Chh., 1775-1785; sett. St. Paul's Chh. (Alamance) N.C., Frieden's Chh., Gibsonville (Guilford) N.C., Lows' Chh. (Guilford) N.C., 1775-1789; sett. St. Paul's Chh. (Catawba) N.C., Philadelphia Chh. (Gaston) N.C., and Daniel's Chh., Lincolnton (Lincoln) N.C., 1785-1807; Luth., d. N.C., 1807.

LUDWIG GOTTLIEB BACHHOF, was in N.C., 4 Nov. 1775; sett. Bethania (Forsyth) N.C., 1761-1770; inst. Friedberg, N.C., 18 Feb. 1770-1776; Morav.

LAWRENCE BAGGE, arriv. America, 16 Nov. 1754; sett. Bethabara, N.C., at Wacovia, 1764-1769; 1773-1784; Moravian.

TRAUGOTT BAGGE, came to N.C., 1768; Moravian; d. Salem, N.C., 1800.

HEZEKIAH JAMES BALCH, A.M., b. Deer Creek (Harford) Md., 1746; A.B., Princeton, 1766, A.M.; lic. (Donegall Presb.), 1768; ord. (same Presb.), 1770; sett. Poplar Tent (Mechlenburg) N.C., 1770-1776; sett. Rocky River Center (Mecklenburg) N.C., 1770-1776; on the committee to prepare the Resolves and a Signer of the Mechlenburg Declaration, 20 May 1775; Capt. of a Md. co., Cont. Army; Presb.; d. Poplar Tent, N.C., before 4 July 1776.

JOHN BARNETT, lic. for N.C., 2 May 1765, K.B., N.C., 10 May 1765; S.P.G. missionary in N.C., Oct. 1765-1770; sett. St.

James's Par., Wilmington (New Hanover) N.C., 1765-1766; sett. St. Philip's Par. (Brunswick) N.C., 1767-1768; sett. St. George's Par. (Northampton) N.C., 1769-1770; sett. St. Thomas's Par. (Orange) Va., 1771-1774; Ep.

THOMAS BAYLEY (See *C.C.Md.* and *C.C.Va.*); itinerant minister in N.C.; Ep.

CHRISTIAN THOMAS BENZIEN, arr., N.Y., 15 Apr. 1754; in N.C., 28 Apr. 1755; Moravian.

BISHOP JOHN DAVID BISCHOFF, Steward of the First Sea Congregation; arr. Philadelphia, Pa., 7 June 1742; ord. Bethlehem, Pa., 1749; sett. Warwick (Lancaster) Pa., St. James's Chh. at Litiz, 1756-1756; in N.C., 12 Sept. 1756; sett. Bethabara, N.C., at Wacovia, 1756-1760; sett. Bethania (Forsyth) N.C., 1760-1763; Indian missionary and minister of rural churches; Moravian; d. Bethania, N.C., Sept. 1763.

JOHN BLAIR, K.B., N.C., 17 Apr. 1703; arr. in N.C., Jan. 1704; ret. to England same year; Ep.

PETER BLINN, lic. (Bsp. of London), 29 Sept. 1769; K.B., N.C., 5 Oct. 1769; itinerant S.P.G. missionary in N.C., 1769-1771; Ep.

NATHANIEL BLOUNT, b. Beaufort co., N.C.; ord. (Bsp. of London); lic. 21 Sept. 1773; K.B., N.C., 27 Aug. 1773; miss. S.P.G., 1773-1774; sett. Beaufort Par. (Beaufort) N.C., 1773-1774; sett. Trinity Church, Chocowinity (Beaufort) N.C., 1773-1774; Ep.

JOHN BOYD, ed. Glascow U.; physician in Va.; miss. S.P.G., N.C., 1732-1738; sett. Bertie Par. (Albemarle) N.C., 1732-1738; Ep.; d. Bertie Parish, N.C., 19 May 1738.

JAMES BREED (lay preacher); sett. Little River (Durham) N.C., 1760-1765; Presb.

DANIEL BRETT, K.B. Carolina, 7 June 1700; came to N.C., 1701/2; first Chh. of England missionary in N.C.; Ep.

HOBART BRIGGS, lic. (Bsp. of London), 5 Apr. 1768; K.B., N.C., 14 Apr. 1768; sett. St. Gabriel's Par. (Dublin) N.C., 1769-1770; S.P.G.; Ep.

EDWARD BROWN, sett. Great Cohara (Sampson) N.C., 1749-1776; Bapt.

HENRY JOHN BURGES (See *C.C.Va.*), b. Va., 28 Nov. 1744, son of Rev. Thomas Burges of Va.; S.P.G. missionary in N.C.; sett. St. Mary's Par. (Edgecomb) N.C., 1769-1770; ret. to Va.; Ep.; d. Nottoway Parish, Va., 1797.

JOHN BURGES, b. Shiloh, N.C., 1725, son of Rev. William Burges; ord. Shiloh (Camden) N.C., 20 Jan. 1758-1763; Bapt.; d. Shiloh, N.C., 13 July 1763, ae. 36.

THOMAS BURGES, Sr. (See *C.C.Va.*), b. Staffordshire, England, 6 Sept. 1712; K.B., N.C., 2 Oct. 1741; sett. Va., 1754-1758; sett. St. Mary's Parish at Tarboro (Edgecomb) N.C., 1759-1779; kept school in both Va. and N.C.; Ep.; d. Edgecombe co., N.C., 1779.

THOMAS BURGES, JR., son of Rev. Thomas Burges, q.v.; sett. St. Mary's Par. (Edgecomb) N.C., 1769 *et post;* Ep.

ELDER WILLIAM BURGESS, sett. Shiloh (Camden) N.C., 1729-1750; J.P., 1746, 1750; Bapt.; d. Shiloh, N.C., after 1750.

WILLIAM BURGESS, JR., b. Pasquotank, N.C., 24 Dec. 1721, son of Elder William Burgess; ord. Kehukee (Halifax) N.C., 2 May 1772-1775; Bapt.; d. Kehukee, N.C., after 1775.

LEMUEL BURKITT, b. Yoppin near Edenton (Chowan) N.C., 26 Apr. 1750, son of Thomas and Mary Burkitt; ord. Sandy Run Church (Bertie) N.C., Nov. 1773; sett. Sandy Run, 1772-1807; delegate to the constitutional convention, 1788; Bapt.; d. Meherrin, N.C., Nov. 1807, a. 57.

DAVID CALDWELL, D.D., M.D., b. Lancaster co., Pa., 22 Mar. 1725, son of Andrew and Ann (Stewart) Caldwell; A.B., Princeton, 1761; D.D., Univ. of N.C., 1810; M.D.; Trustee, U. of N.C., 1777-1824; missionary to N.C., 1764; lic. Trenton, N.J. (New Brunswick Presb.), 8 June 1763; ord. by same, 5 July 1765; inst. Buffalo Chh., near Greensborough (Guilford) N.C., 3 Mar. 1768; sett. Buffalo (Guilford) and Alamance (Guilford) N.C., 1765-1824; Capt. of vols., Cont. Army; kept a classical school (among his pupils were 5 who became governors and 50 who became clergymen); member, Constitutional Conventions of N.C., 1776, 1788; physician; Presb.; d. Buffalo, N.C., 25 Oct. 1824, a. 99 y. 5 m.

JAMES CAMPBELL, b. Campbellton-on-Kintyre, Argyleshire, Scotland; came to America, 1730; lic. 1735; ord. 3 Aug. 1742; sett. Tinicum (Bucks) Pa., 1738-1749 (inst. 24 May 1744); Tohickon (Bucks) Pa., 1739-1749; Newtown (Bucks) Pa., 1739-1749; Durham (Bucks) Pa., 1742-1749; Forks of the Delaware, Pa., 1742-1749; Greenwich (Warren) N.J., 1742-1749; Oxford (Warren) N.J., 1742-1749; Rocky Spring Chh., Letterkenney (Franklin) Pa., 1749-1757; Conococheague or Falling Spring Chh., Guilford (Franklin) Pa., 1749-1757; Welsh Run Chh., Montgomery (Franklin) Pa., 1749-1757; in 1757 he removed to N.C.; sett. Bluff Chh., Cape Fear River, near Fayetteville (Columbia) N.C., 1757-1774; and at Barbecue and Long Street, N.C., 1765-1770, and preached in English and Gaelic in all three churches; (Crosscreek became Campbellton, now Fayetteville); meanwhile he also preached as an itinerant in the following N.C. counties: Moore, Anson, Richmond, Robeson, Bladen, Sampson and Cumberland, 1757-1772; to these labors he added in S.C.: Bullock's Creek, S.C., 1773-1774; Bull Run (Chester) S.C., 1773-1774; and Catholic Congregation, at Rocky Creek, S.C., 1776-1780; he was a member of the Presb. of S.C., 1757-1773, and of the Orange Presb., 1773-1781; Presb.; d. Cape Fear, N.C., 1781.

NICHOLAS CHRISTIAN, lic. (Bsp. of London), 13 Aug. 1773; K.B., N.C., 27 Aug. 1773; sett. St. Philip's Par. (Brunswick) N.C., 1773-1774; sett. Wacamaw, N.C., 1773-1774; S.P.G.; Ep.

WILLIAM COOK, sett. Dutchman's Creek (Davie) N.C., 1772-1778; Tory; Bapt.

ALEXANDER CRAIGHEAD (See *C.C.N.E.* and *C.C.Va.*); third Presb. minister to settle in N.C.; only minister, 1758-1766, between the Yadkin and Catawba rivers; sett. Sugar Creek (Mecklenburg) N.C., inst. 27 Sept. 1758-1766; sett. Rocky River Center (Mecklenburg) N.C., 1758-1766; had seven congregations in the Sugar Creek area: Steel Creek, Providence, Hopewell, Center, Rocky River and Poplar Tent, all in Mecklenburg except Center which was in Iredell co.; author of a pamphlet on political independence, 1743; Presb.; d. Rocky Creek, N.C., Mar. 1766.

JOHN CRAMP, K.B., N.C., 9 Oct. 1767; sett. N.C., 1767-1768, as S.P.G. missionary; sett. St. Philip's Par. (Brunswick) N.C., 1769-1770, S.P.G.; Ep.

JAMES CRESWELL, b. Ireland; lic. Tinkling Spring, Va., 2 May 1764; ord. Lower Hico, N.C., 6 Oct. 1765; sett. Little River, S.C., 1764-1776; Grassy Creek (Granville) N.C., 1765-1766; Nutbush (Granville) N.C., 1765-1766; Duncan's Creek, S.C., 1766-1776; Fairforest, S.C., 1771-1776; Rocky Creek, now Rock Creek Chh. (Abbeville) S.C., 1772-1776; Ninety-Six, at New Cambridge (Abbeville) S.C., 1775-1776; Presb.; d. Little River, S.C., 1776.

CHARLES CUPPLES (or Crupples), K.B., N.C., 13 June 1766; sett. St. John's Par. (Bute) N.C., 1767-1768; S.P.G.; Ep.

CHARLES DANIEL, b. near Richmond, Va., Jan. 1731; ord. Fishing Creek (Halifax) N.C., 16 Aug. 1753-1772; suspended, 1773; Bapt.

THOMAS DANIEL, sett. Fishing Creek (Halifax) N.C., 1773-1775 *et post;* Bapt.

ELNATHAN DAVIS, b. Baltimore county, Md., 9 Nov. 1735; bred a Seventh Day Bapt.; came to Haw River, N.C., 1757; ord. Sandy Creek, N.C., 13 Nov. 1770; sett., Haw River (Chatham) N.C., 1764-1798; sett. S.C., 1798-1813; liv. Saluda Association, S.C., 1813; Bapt.

JEREMIAH DARGAN, sett. High Hills of Santee, Statesburg, S.C., 1769-1771; sett. Cashie (Bertie) N.C., 1771-1776; Bapt.

JOHN DeBOW, A.B., Princeton, 1772; lic. 1775; ord. 1775; inst. Upper Mount Bethel (Northampton) Pa., 19 May 1775-1775; Oxford (Warren) N.J., 1775-1775; sett. Hawfields (Alamance) N.C., 1775-1783; Eno (Orange) N.C., 1775-1783; Little River (Durham) N.C., 1775-1783; Presb.; d. Hawfields, N.C., Sept. 1783.

FREDERICK WILLIAM de MARSCHALL, b. Stolpen, near Dresden, 5 Feb. 1721, son of the commander of the great fortress of Koenigstein on the Elbe; law student at Lindheim, 1744, a. 23; arriv. N.Y.C., 19 Oct. 1761; sett. Salem, N.C., 1763-1802; sett. Bethabara, N.C., 1763-1802; General Supt. of the Moravian Church in N.C., 1768; Senior Civilis, 1771-1802; Morav.; d. Salem, N.C., 11 Feb. 1802.

CLAUDE PHILIPPE de RICHEBOURGE (See *C.C.Va.* and *C.C.S.C.*), came to Va., 1700; sett. King William Par., Va., 1700-1707; sett. Trent River, N.C., (Hug. Chh.), 1708-1711, until the

Indian massacre of 11 Sept. 1711; sett. Jamestown, St. James's Parish, Santee, French Santee, S.C., 1712-1719; sett. Charleston, S.C., Hug. Chh., 1717-1719; sett. Western Branch of Cooper River (F.R., 1699), S.C. (later St. John's Colleton), 1712-1719; French Reformed—Huguenot; d. St. James's Santee (will made 15 Jan. 1718/9).

THEODORUS SWAINE DRAGE, lic. (Bsp. of London), 29 May 1769; K.B., N.C., 8 June 1769; sett. St. Luke's Par. (Rowan) N.C., 1769-1771; S.P.G.; Ep.

MR. DuPERT, preached in N.C., 1764; Germ. Ref.

DANIEL EARLE, K.B., N.C., 23 Sept. 1756; sett. St. Paul's Chh., Edenton (Chowan) N.C., 1759-1783; S.P.G.; Ep.

HENRY EASTERLING, b. Neuse River, N.C., 24 May 1733; ord. Hitchcock's Creek (Richmond) N.C., 28 Mar. 1772; sett. Hitchcock's, 1770-1785; sett. Beauty Spot Chh., S.C., 1785-1792; Bapt.

JOHN JACOB ERNST, sett. Bethania (Forsyth) N.C., 1770-1784; Salem, N.C., 1784-1802; Friedland, N.C., 1791-1800; Germ. Ref.-Morav. (One of this name b. 22 Feb. 1744; d. Berlin, Pa., 30 Aug. 1804, but perhaps not the same).

BISHOP JOHN ETTWEIN, b. Trendenstadt, Wurtemberg, 29 June 1721; ord. Deacon, 1746; arr. N.Y.C., 15 Apr. 1754; sett. N.Y.C., Moravian Chh., 1754-1755; missionary among the Indians; was in N.C., 22 July 1758; sett. Bethabara, N.C., 1759-1766 (at Wacovia); sett. Bethlehem, Pa., 20 Sept. 1766-1802, as senior pastor; sett. Hope (Warren) N.J., 1769-1770; "traveled thousands of miles, often on foot, and preached in eleven of the thirteen original colonies"; consecrated Bishop, 25 June 1784-1801, retired 1801; founder of "Soc. for Prop. the Gospel among the Heathen . . . 1787"; d. Bethlehem, Pa., 2 Jan. 1802.

SAMUEL FISKE, lic. 1 Sept. 1768; K.B., N.C., 12 Sept. 1766; sett. St. John's Par. (Pasquotank) N.C., 1768-1769; Ep.

DANIEL FOGG, JR., A.M. (See *C.C.N.E.*, p. 86); K.B., Mass. Bay, 3 Sept. 1770; missionary, Bath (Beaufort) N.C., St. Thomas's Chh., 1771-1772; Ep.

JOHN JACOB FRIES, had a university education; arr. N.Y.C., 9 Sept. 1753; in N.C., 15 Apr. 1754; sett. Bethabara, N.C., at Wacovia, 1754-1755; chaplain at Bethlehem, Pa., May 1777-1793; Moravian; d. Bethlehem, Pa., 1793.

WILLIAM FULSHER, sett. Pungo (Beaufort) N.C., 1755-1772; Bapt.

JAMES GAMEWELL, sett. Pasquotank and Currituck counties, N.C., 1769-1772; at Three Creeks (Johnston) N.C., ca. 1772; sett. Cowenjack (Curritick) N.C., 1775-1781; Bapt.

GAMMERN, see van Gammern.

JOHN GANO, b. Hopewell, N.J., 22 July 1727, son of Daniel and Sarah (Britton) Gano; ord. 29 May 1754; missionary in the South, 1754; sett. Morristown (Morris) N.J., 1754-25 Sept. 1757; sett. Jersey Settlements (Davidson) N.C., 1758-1760; commissioned a Captain in N.C., 1758-1760; sett. N.Y.C., N.Y. (1st Bapt. Chh.),

1762-1788; sett. Town Fork Chh., near Lexington, Ky., 1788-1798; Chaplain, Am. Rev.; Bapt.; d. Frankfort, Ky., Aug. 1804, a. 77 (GS).

JOHN GARZIA (See *C.C.Va.*), missionary, S.P.G., from Va. to N.C., 1739-1744; sett. Bath (Beaufort) N.C., St. Thomas's Chh., 1739-1744; Ep.; d. Bath, N.C., 29 Nov. 1744.

WILLIAM GORDON, A.M., K.B., N.C., 26 Sept. 1707; sett. Edenton (Chowan) N.C., St. Paul's Chh., 1707-1708; sett. Perquimans Par. (Perquimans) N.C., 1708-1708; Ep.

BISHOP JOHN MICHAEL GRAFF, Univ. of Jena, 1738; Univ. of Koenigsberg; ord. in Europe; arriv. N.Y.C., 24 Sept. 1751; consecrated Bishop, 1773; sett. Nazareth, Pa., 1755-1762; went to N.C., 20 Apr. 1762; Bethabara, N.C., 1762-1773; Salem, N.C., 1774-1782; hymn writer; Moravian; d. Salem, N.C., 29 Aug. 1782.

GEORGE GRAHAM, sett. Bear Creek (Lenoir) N.C., 1756-1772; retired, 1772, an old man past laboring; Bapt.

BEVIL GRANVILLE, sett. Edenton (Chowan) N.C., St. Thomas's Chh., 1732-1732; Bath (Beaufort) N.C., 1732-1732; had to leave because he was not paid; Ep.

BERNARD ADAM GRUBE, b. near Erfurth, Germany, 1715; grad. Univ. of Jena; arriv. Bethlehem, Pa., 26 June 1746; Indian missionary in Monroe co., Pa., 1752; sett. Bethabara, N.C. (at Wacovia), Oct. 1753-1754, as the first Moravian minister in N.C.; sett. Kent, Conn., 1758-Oct. 1760; sett. Province Island, Nov. 1763-Mar. 1765; sett. Warwick (Lancaster) Pa., St. James's Chh. at Lititz, 1765-1780; sett. Bethlehem, Pa., May 1787-1808; sett. Hope (Warren) N.J., 1791-1793; sett. Emaus (Lehigh) Pa., 1791-1808; Moravian; his wife Sarah was his assistant; d. Bethlehem, Pa., 20 Mar. 1808, a. 93.

JOSEPH HABERLAND, sett. N.C., 1753; Morav.

CLEMENT HALL, b. Eng.; sett. Perquimans co., N.C.; lay reader and J.P.; ord. in England, 1743; appointed a minister to four northern counties of N.C., 14 Jan. 1744; sett. Edenton (Chowan) N.C., St. Paul's Chh., 14 Jan. 1744-1759, S.P.G.; Perquimans Par. (Perquimans) N.C., 1744-1759; St. John's Par. (Pasquotank) N.C., 1744-1759; Currituck Par. (Currituck) N.C., 1744-1759; Ep.; d. Edenton, N.C., Jan. 1759.

JAMES HALL, D.D., b. Carlisle, Pa., 22 Aug. 1744, of Scotch-Irish parents; A.B., Princeton, 1774; D.D., Princeton, 1803; D.D., Univ. of N.C., 1810; lic. Fall, 1775; Chaplain and Captain in vol. cavalry, N.C., 1778-1782; inst. Fourth Creek (Iredell) N.C., 8 Apr. 1778-1790; Concord (Iredell) N.C., 1778-1790; Bethany (Iredell) N.C., 1778-1826 (all near Statesville); moderator, General Assembly, N.C., 1803; Presb.; d. Bethany, N.C., 25 July 1826, a. 82.

DR. JOSIAH HART, first mentioned in a court record, 1733; sett. Reedy Creek (Warren) N.C., 1750-ca. 1770; prob. a physician; d. Reedy Creek, N.C., before 1770; Bapt.

ROBERT HENRY, A.M. (See *C.C.Va.*), b. Scotland; A.B., Princeton, 1751, A.M.; ord. (Presb. of N.Y.), 1753; sett. New

Providence (Mecklenburg) N.C., 1766-1767; sett. Steel Creek (Mecklenburg) N.C., 1766-1767; Presb.; d. Cub Creek (Charlotte) Va., 8 May 1767.

JOSHUA HERRING, b. Lenoir co., N.C., 23 Nov. 1723, son of John and Catherine Herring; ord. Bear Creek (Lenoir) N.C., 1772-1776; J.P., 1776; Bapt.; d. Bear Creek, N.C., 1801.

GREEN HILL, a Methodist minister from Bute co., N.C., who was a delegate to the First Provincial Congress in N.C., 1775.

WILLIAM HILL, a Bapt. minister, delegate from Surry co., N.C., to the First Provincial Congress of N.C., 1775.

JOHN GOTTLOB HOFFMAN, arr. N.Y.C., 12 June 1748; in N.C., 4 Nov. 1755; sett. Bethabara, N.C., 1755-1764; Moravian.

STEPHEN HOLLINGSWORTH, came to N.C., 1735; ord. 1750; sett. Bladen and Robeson counties, N.C., Jan. 1756-1772; Bapt.

EZEKIEL HUNTER, prob. son of Nicholas Hunter of Carteret, N.C.; ord. New River (Onslow) N.C., 1759-1773; sett. Lockwood's Folly (Brunswick) N.C., 1762-1773; sett. Neus River, S.C., ca. 1760; member of the General Assembly from Onslow co., Jan.-Mar. 1773; Bapt.; d. New River, N.C., ca. 1773.

FRANCIS JOHNSTON, lic. (Bsp. of London), 29 Sept. 1768; K.B., N.C., 18 Oct. 1768; sett. Society Par. (Bertie) N.C., 1770 et post; Ep.

GOTTLOB KOENIGSDERFER, arr. N.Y.C., 9 Sept. 1753; arriv. N.C., 1753; returned to Bethlehem, Pa.; Moravian.

TIDENCE LANE, b. near Baltimore, Md., 31 Aug. 1724, son of Richard and Sarah Lane; ord. before 1772; sett. St. Clair Bottom, Tenn., 1776-1778; sett. Buffalo Ridge Bapt. Chh. (Washington) Tenn., 1778-Aug. 1784; became a farmer; Bapt.; d. Bent Creek (Hamblen) Tenn., 30 Jan. 1806.

JOHN de LA PIERRE, A.B. (See C.C.S.C.), b. France, 1769, son of Charles de La Pierre, gent.; pens. Trinity Coll., Dublin, Ireland, 8 Aug. 1701, ae. 22 yrs.; A.B., 1706; ord. (Bsp. of London) 1708; K.B., S.C., 23 Feb. 1707/8; sett. St. Dennis Par., Orange Quarter (Berkeley) S.C., 1711-1728; Fr. Prot. Chh., Charleston, S.C., 1712-1713; 1728-1728; sett. St. James's Chh., Wilmington (New Hanover) N.C., 1729-1735; sett. St. Philip's Chh., Brunswick, N.C., 1729-1735; Hug.-Ep.

JACOB LASH, came to N.C., 1753; sett. Bethabara, N.C., 1735-1769; Morav.

HENRY LEDBETTER, b. Prince George co., Va., 25 Feb. 1721; ord. Reedy Creek (Warren) N.C., 28 June 1750; sett. Lynch's Creek (Craven) S.C., 1755-1761; sett. Tar River (Granville) N.C., 1761-1777; Bapt.

HUGH McADEN, A.M., b. Pa., A.B., Princeton, 1753, A.M.; lic. 1755; ord. (New Castle Presb.), 1757; was the first Presbyterian preacher in N.C., 3 June 1755-6 May 1756; became a member of Rockfish Presbytery, 18 July 1759; his papers were destroyed by British soldiers in Jan. 1781; sett. Grove Chh., Goshen (Duplin)

N.C., 18 July 1759-1769; Wilmington (New Hanover) N.C., 1759-1769; sett. Red House, Middle Hyco (Caswell) N.C., 1769-1781; sett. Greer's, Upper Hyco, Hico, County Line Creek, Dan River (Caswell) N.C., 1769-1781; sett. Pittsylvania Court House, Va., 1769-1781; New Side Presb.; d. Red House, near Milton (Caswell) N.C., 20 Jan. 1781.

JAMES MACARTNEY (See *C.C.Va.*), b. Ireland; school-master in N.C.; went to England of Holy Orders; lic. (Bsp. of London) 25 July 1768, for N.C.; K.B., N.C., 1 Sept. 1768; missionary, S.P.G., in N.C., 1768-1769; sett. Granville Par. (Granville) N.C., 1768-1772; sett. St. Patrick's Par. (Prince Edward) Va., 1773-1774; asst. Master, New Bern Acad., New Bern, N.C.; Ep.

THOMAS HARRIS McCAULE, A.B., Princeton, A.B., 1774; ord. Center (Guilford) N.C., 1776-1783; chaplain, Cont. Army; Trustee, Univ. N.C., 1777-1780; Pres., Mt. Zion College, Winnsboro, S.C., 1783-1796; Presb.; d. South Carolina, 1796.

SAMUEL EUSEBIUS McCORKLE, D.D., b. near Harris's Ferry (Lancaster co.), Pa., 23 Aug. 1746; A.B., Princeton, 1772; D.D., Dickinson Coll., 1792; lic. 1774; ord. 2 Aug. 1777; sett. Thyatira (Rowan) N.C., 1774-1811; Trustee, N.C. Univ., 1789-1801; Prof. of Moral and Polit. Phil., N.C.U., 1795-1811; Presb.; d. Thyatira, N.C., 21 Jan. 1811.

JAMES McDANIEL, son of Thomas McDaniel of Craven co., N.C., sett. Trent (Jones) N.C., 1761-1776; Bapt.; d. Trent, N.C., prob. during Rev. war.

JOHN MacDOWELL, K.B., N.C., 8 Aug. 1753; arriv. N.C., Jan. 1754; sett. St. James's Par. (New Hanover) N.C., Jan. 1754-May 1757; sett. St. Philip's Par. (Brunswick) N.C., Mar. 1757-1763; Ep.; d. Brunswick, N.C., Nov. 1763.

JOHN McLEOD, came from Scotland, 1770, to N.C.; sett. Bluff Church, near Fayetteville (Columbia) N.C., 1770-1773; Long Street (Columbia) N.C., 1770-1773; Barbecue (Columbia) N.C., 1770-1773; Upper Little Rivers (Cumberland) N.C., 1770-1773; Lower Little Rivers (Cumberland) N.C., 1770-1773; Presb.; left N.C.; never heard of again; prob. d. at sea.

NEILL McNEILL, came from Argyleshire, Scotland, 1747, to Cape Fear, N.C.; sett. Fayetteville (Columbia) N.C., 1747 *et post;* Presb.

CHARLES MARKLAND, ord. prob. Oct. 1762; sett. South-west (Lenoir) N.C., 1760-1776; Rev. soldier; member, Board of Trustees, Dobbs Academy at Kingston, 1785; Bapt.

MARSCHALL, see de Marschall.

RICHARD MARSDEN (See *C.C.Md.*), sett St. James's Par. (New Hanover) N.C., 1729-1742; Ep.

DANIEL MARSHALL (See *C.C.S.C.* and *C.C.Ga.*), b. Windsor, Conn., 1706; Deacon in the Cong. Chh. at Windsor, 20 yrs. and missionary to the Indians at Onnaquaggy, N.Y., 1753-1754; ord. (as a Bapt.) at Abbot's Creek (Davidson) N.C., 1757-1760; in S.C., 1760-

1771 and Ga., 1771-1784; supply, Shallow Fords (Yadkin) N.C., ca. 1772; Bapt.; d. Ga., 2 Nov. 1784.

JOHN NICHOLAS MARTIN (See *C.C.S.C.* and *C.C.Ga.*), b. Zweibrucken, Lorraine, France; ord. by the Salzburgers at Ebenezer, Ga.; sett. Waxhaw (Union) N.C., 1750-1763; in. S.C., 1760-1795; Luth.; d. Charleston, S.C., 1795.

JOHN MEGLAMRE (See *C.C.Va.*), b. Md., 7 June 1730; ord. Fishing Creek (Halifax) N.C., Feb. 1767; sett. Kehukee Chh. (Halifax) N.C., 1765-1772; sett. Raccoon Swamp (Sussex) Va., 1772-1799; Bapt.; d. Sussex co., Va., 13 Dec. 1799.

BISHOP GEORGE MEIKLEJOHN, lic. for N.C., 12 Mar. 1766; K.B., N.C., 29 Mar. 1766; ord. London, 1766; missionary, S.P.G., Rowan co., N.C., 1766; sett. St. Matthew's Par. (Orange) N.C., 1766-1784; loyalist; sett. St. James's Chh., Mechlenburg, 1784-1817; Bishop of N.C., ca. 1817; Ep.

SILAS MERCER, b. Currituck Bay, N.C., Feb. 1745; began preaching in Ga., 1775; sett. Halifax co., N.C., 1775-1781, as an itinerant during which time he preached more than 2000 sermons; Bapt.; d. Ga., 1796, a. 51 yrs.

BENJAMIN MILLER, b. Scotch Plains, N.J., 1716; ord. Scotch Plains (Fanwood) N.J., 13 Feb. 1748-1781; sett. Jersey Settlements (Davidson) N.C., 1754-1756; Bapt. d. Fanwood, N. J., 14 Nov. 1781, a. 65 (GS).

WILLIAM MILLER, lic. (Bsp. of London), 31 Mar. 1775, for N.C.; sett. St. Patrick's Par. (Dobbs) N.C., 1770 *et seq.*; Ep.

JAMES MOIR, from N.C.; K.B., N.C., 1739; sett. St. James's Par., Wilmington (New Hanover) N.C., 1740-1747; sett. St. Philip's Par. (Brunswick) N.C., 1742-1747; sett. St. Mary's Chapel, Tarboro (Edgecombe) N.C., 1747-1765; S.P.G.; Ep.; d. Edgecombe co., N.C., Feb. 1767.

JOHN MOORE, SR., b. Nansemond co., Va., 13 Aug. 1717; came to N.C., ca. 1740; ord. Falls of Tar River (Nash) 30 Oct. 1748-1780; member, Kehukee Assn., 1765; Bapt.

JOHN MOORE, JR., son of Rev. John Moore; sett. Swift Creek (Wake) N.C., 1757-1793; Bapt.; d. after 1793.

ANDREW MORTON (or Moreton) (see *C.C.Va.*), missionary, S.P.G., to St. George's Par. (Northampton) N.C. and Mecklenburg co., N.C., 1766-1766; Ep.

PHILIP MULKY, b. near Halifax, N.C., 14 May 1732, son of Philip Mulky; ord. Deep River (Chatham) N.C., Oct. 1757-1760; sett. Trent (Jones) N.C., 1757-1760; sett. S.C. (q.v.), 1760-1790; Bapt.

JOSEPH MURPHY (brother of William Murphy), b. Spotsylvania, Va., 1 Apr. 1734; ord. Deep River, N.C., 1760, as a missionary to south-western Va.; sett. Little River of Pee Dee (Montgomery) N.C., 1759-1768; Shallow Ford (Yadkin) N.C., 1769-1780; Deep Creek (Surry) N.C., 1790-1803; Bapt.; d. Surry co., N.C., after 1803.

THOMAS NEWMAN, K.B., N.C., 19 Oct. 1721; arriv. N.C., 10 Apr. 1722; sett. St. Paul's Chh., Edenton (Chowan) N.C., 1722-1723; S.P.G.; Ep.; d. Edenton, N.C., 1723.

JOHN NEWTON, b. Kent co., Pa., 7 Aug. 1732; ord. Black River (Harnett) N.C., 7 Mar. 1757-1765; ord. Congaree, S.C., Feb. 1768-1768; removed to Ga.; Bapt.; d. Ga., 1791.

SAMUEL NEWTON, sett. Bull Tail (Pender) N.C., 1756-1776; Bapt.; d. Bull Tail, N.C., ca. 1776 (during Rev. war).

TOEGE NISSEN, inst. Friedland, N.C., 18 Feb. 1775-1780; Moravian.

ROBERT NIXON, sett. New River (Onslow) N.C., 1773-1793; sett. Lockwood's Folly (Brunswick) N.C., 1773-1793; Bapt.; d. New River, N.C., 4 Dec. 1794.

JOHN NOBLES, organized the church at Bear Marsh, 25 Feb. 1763; sett. Bear Marsh (Duplin) N.C., 1763 et seq.; Bapt.

ADOLPHUS NUESSMAN, b. Germany, Aug. 1739; educated at Univ. of Goettingen; arriv. as a missionary in America, 1773; sett. St. John's Chh., Salisbury (Rowan) N.C., 1773-1774; Zion's Chh., Organ Chh. (Rowan) N.C., 1773-1774; Lower Chh. (German Reformed) (Rowan) N.C., 1773-1774; sett. Dutch Buffalo Creek, N.C., St. John's Lutheran Chh., 1774-1794; Luth.; sett. St. Paul's Chh. (Alamance), Frieden's Chh. (Guilford) and Lows' Chh. (Guilford) N.C., 1774-1789; d. Dutch Buffalo Creek (Cabarrus) N.C., 3 Nov. 1794, a. 55 y.

PAUL PALMER, b. in Md.; bapt. at Welsh Tract, Del; came to N.C., 1720; was qualified for Perquimans, 1738, where he was a large landowner; ord. (it is said) in Conn.; sett. N.J. and Md. before 1727; at Chestnut Ridge, Md., ca. 1742; visited N.E., 1730; Piscatawy, N.J.; sett. Perquimans, 1727-1754; Bapt.; d. Perquimans, N.C., ca. 1754.

JOSEPH PARKER, b. N.C., ca. 1705, son of Joseph Parker; sett. Chowan (Chowan), 1727-1730; Meherrin (Hartford) N.C., 1730-1742; Falls of Tar River (Nash) N.C., 1744-1748; Fishing Creek (Halifax) N.C., 1748-1753; Great Contentnea (Greene) N.C., 1761-1772; Wheat Swamp (south of Tar River) N.C., 1773-1791; Bapt.; d. Wheat Swamp, N.C., 1791.

WILLIAM PARKER, son of William Parker; sett. Meherrin (Hartford) N.C., 1742-1794; Bapt.

HENRY PATILLO, A.M. (See C.C.Va.), b. Scotland, 1726; ord. Cumberland, Va., 12 July 1758; in Va., 1758-1765; inst., Hawfields (Alamance) N.C., 2 Oct. 1765-1774; sett. Eno (Orange) N.C., 1765-1774; Little River (Durham) N.C., 1765-1774; Nutbush, N.C., 1780-1801; Grassy Creek, N.C., 1780-1801; Presb.; d. Dinwiddie co., Va., 1801, a. 75.

BISHOP CHARLES PETTIGREW, b. Pa., after 1740, son of James Pettigrew; lic. (Bsp. of London), 1 Mar. 1775; K.B., N.C., 7 Mar. 1775; ord. London, 1775; missionary, S.P.G. at Edenton, N.C., 1775-1776; sett. Edenton (Chowan) N.C., 20 May 1775-1794; Bishop of N.C., May 1794; overseer and founder of the Univ. of N.C., 1790-1793; sett. Bonarva and Begrod, 1794-1807; Ep.; d. Bonarva Plantation (Tyrrel) N.C., 7 Apr. 1807.

THOMAS POPE, b. VA., 1728; ord. 1751; sett. Kehukee (Halifax) N.C., 1755-1762; sett. Reedy Creek (Warren) N.C., 1754-1762; Bapt.; d. Kehukee. N.C., 1 Mar. 1762.

EVAN PUGH (See C.C.S.C.), ord. Head of Yadkin, N.C., 22 Nov. 1764; sett. Head of Yadkin, N.C., 1762-1765; Bapt.

GILES RAINSFORD, A.M., (See C.C.Md.), missionary, S.P.G., at St. Paul's Chh., Edenton (Chowan) N.C., 1712-1714; Ep.

CHRISTIAN HENRY RAUCH (See C.C.N.Y. and C.C.Pa.), sett. Bethabara, N.C., 4 Nov. 1755-1756; Germ.-Ref.; Moravian.

JAMES READ, b. Edgecombe co., N.C., ca. 1726; ord. Grassy Creek (Granville) N.C., 1762; sett. Grassy Creek, N.C., 1757-1779; excommunicated 21 Nov. 1770; restored, Nov. 1772; missionary in Culpeper co., Va., 1766-1798; Bapt.; d. Grassy Creek, N.C., 1798, a. 71.

JESSE READ, ord. Rocky Swamp (Halifax) N.C., 1775-1791; Bapt.

JAMES REED, sett. Christ Church Parish (Craven) N.C., 1757-1777, S.P.G.; discharged, 1775; Ep.; d. Craven Town, N.C., May 1777.

JEREMIAH RHAME, sett. Catfish, near Latta (Dillon), S.C., 1752-1758; sett. Red Banks (Pitt) N.C., 1758-1772; sett. Catfish, Little Peedee Chh., and Cashaway Neck, S.C., 1772-1805; Bapt.; d. S.C., 1805.

RICHEBOURGE, see de Richebourge.

JACOB ROGERS, arriv. America, 17 May 1752; sett. Staten Island, N.Y., 1756-1756; sett. Bethabara, N.C., 22 July 1758-1762; was the English minister of Dobbs Parish; Moravian; returned to Europe, 1 July 1762.

JOHN MICHAEL SAUTER, arriv. N.Y.C., 22 June 1749; sett. Bethabara, N.C., 1757-1760; Moravian.

MATTHEW SCHROPP, came for Kaufbeuren, Swabia; arriv. N.Y.C., 26 Nov. 1743; ord. Deacon, 1748; sett. Nazareth, Pa., 25 June 1747; sett. Bethabara, N.C., 1766-1767; Moravian; d. Bethabara, N.C., 1767.

CHRISTIAN SEIDEL, sett. Wyoming, Pa., 1755; was in N.C., 22 Aug. 1756; sett. Bethabara, N.C., 1756-1759, as the "German minister"; Moravian.

JAMES SMART, b. Prince George co., Va., 13 Oct. 1714; ord. Fishing Creek (Bute) N.C., 28 June 1750-1755; sett. Reedy Creek (Warren) N.C., 1750-1752; sett. Lynch's Creek, S.C., 1755-1759; sett. Coosawhatchie (Jasper) S.C., 1759-1788; Bapt.; d. Coosawhatchie, S.C., ca. 1788.

MICHAEL SMITH, A.M. (See C.C.S.C.), sett. St. James's Parish, Wilmington (New Hanover) N.C., 1759-1760; Ep.

WILLIAM SOJOURNER, b. Va., 1706; came to N.C. from

Burleigh, Isle of Wight, Va.; sett. Kehukee (Halifax) N.C., 1742-1750; Bapt.; d. Kehukee, N.C., 18 Feb. 1749/1750, ae. 43 y. 7 m.

SHUBAEL STEARNS (See *C.C.Va.*), b. 1705/6; sett. Sandy Creek (Randolph) N.C., 1754-1771; Bapt.; d. Sandy Creek, N.C., 20 Nov. 1771.

ALEXANDER STEWART, K.B., 27 June 1753; sett. St. Thomas's Chh., Bath (Beaufort) N.C., 1753-1770; S.P.G.; sett. Beaufort Par. (Beaufort) N.C., 1767-1770; Ep.; d. Beaufort co., N.C., Spring of 1771.

SAMUEL SUTHER, b. Switzerland, 18 May 1772; arriv. S.C., 5 Jan. 1738/9; school teacher in Virginia, Carolina, Georgia, Pennsylvania and Maryland, 1739-1768; taught in the German-Reformed School, Philadelphia, 1749; ord. Philadelphia; sett. as itinerant preacher in Mechlenburg co., N.C., June 1768-25 Oct. 1771; in Guilford and Orange counties, N.C., 1771-7 Jan. 1782; sett. Orangeburg District, S.C., 1786-1788; sett. Cold Water Luth. Chh., Concord (Cabarrus) N.C., 1768-1775; Germ.-Ref.; d. Orangeburg District, S.C., 28 Sept. 1788.

JOHN TANNER, sett. Falls of Tar River (Nash) N.C., 1772-1776; sett. Swift's Creek (Edgecombe) N.C., 1777-1779; went to Ky., 1781; Bapt.

JOSEPH TATE (See *C.C.Pa.*), b. 1711; ord. East Donegal, Pa., 23 Nov. 1748; in Pa., 1748-1768; visited Fairforest, S.C., 1754; sett. Wilmington (New Hanover) N.C., 1770-1774; kept a classical school at Wilmington; Old Side Presb.; d. Wilmington, N.C., 11 Oct. 1771, a. 63.

CHARLES EDWARD TAYLOR, lic. (Bsp. of London), 1 Jan. 1771; K.B., N.C., 8 Jan. 1771; sett. St. George's Par. (Northampton) N.C., 1770-1773; S.P.G.; chaplain, First Provincial Congress of N.C., 1775; Ep.

EBENEZER TAYLOR, K.B., S.C., 13 Nov. 1711; sett. St. Andrew's Parish, Ashley River, S.C., 1711-1717; left S.C., 1717; sett. Bertie Parish (Albemarle) N.C., 1716-1720; Perquimans Par. (Perquimans) N.C., 1716-1720; St. Thomas's Chh., Bath (Beaufort) N.C., 1716-1720; S.P.G.; Ep.; d. N.C., Feb. 1720, probably murdered.

JOHN THOMAS (See *C.C.Del.; C.C.Va.*), made missionary visits to N.C., 1744, 1751, 1753; Presb.; d. Center, N.C., 1753.

JOHN THOMAS, J.P., Esq., sett. Toisnot (Edgecombe) N.C., 1748-1758; J.P., Edgecombe co., 1749; Bapt.

JOHN THOMAS, Jr., son of Rev. John Thomas, sett. Toisnot (Edgecombe) N.C., 1758-1777; moderator, Kehukee Assn., 1777; Bapt.

JONATHAN THOMAS, son of Rev. John Thomas, ord. Dec. 1758; sett. Toisnot (Edgecombe) N.C., 1759-1774; sett. Flat Swamp (Pitt) N.C., 1766-1774; moderator, Kehukee Assn., 1769-1772; Bapt.; d. Toisnot, N.C., Feb. 1774.

PAUL TIERSCH, arriv. N.Y.C., 21 Oct. 1763; schoolmaster at

Nazareth, Pa., 1763-1771; ord. 1771; sett. Salem, N.C., 1771-1774; Moravian.

THOMAS TULLY, received a grant of 300 acres of land in Edgecombe co., N.C., 25 Sept. 1741; preached in Bute co., 1755; sett. Three Creeks (Johnston) N.C., 1757-1772; Bapt.

JAMES TURNER, sett. Lockwood's Folly (Brunswick) N.C., 1762-1773; Bapt.; d. Lockwood's Folly, N.C., ca. 1773.

JOHN URMSTONE (See *C.C.Md.*), S.P.G. missionary at North Shore of N.C.; sett. St. John's Par. (Pasquotank) N.C., 1709-1720; sett. St. Paul's Chh., Edenton (Chowan) N.C., 1709-1720; Ep.; "Burned to death in N.C.," 1732.

RICHARD UTLEY (See *C.C.Del.*), b. Yorkshire, Eng., 22 Feb. 1720; sett. Bethabara, N.C., 1766-1770; sett. Salem, N.C., 1772-1775; Moravian; d. Salem, N.C., 9 Oct. 1775.

ABRAHAM van GAMMERN, arr. N.Y.C., 19 Oct. 1761; sett. Bethabara, N.C., 8 June 1762-1765; Moravian.

SAUNDERS WALKER, b. Prince William co., Va., 17 Mar. 1740, brother of Jeremiah Walker; began preaching in S.C., 1767; sett. Bute co., N.C., 1771-1782; sett. Ga., 1782; Bapt.; d. Ga., 1805, a. 65 y.

WILLIAM WALKER, b. New Kent co., Va., 24 Jan. 1717; ord. Reedy Creek (Warren) N.C., 1748-1752; 1763-1784; sett. Sandy Creek (Franklin) N.C., 1772-1784; Bapt.; d. Reedy Creek, N.C., 1784.

WILLIAM WALLACE, member Kehukee Assn., N.C., 1765; Bapt.

WILLIAM WASHINGTON, b. Va.; ord. Va., ca. 1746; sett. Reedy Creek (Warren) N.C., prob. before 1750; sett. Tar River (Granville) N.C., 1756-1761; General Bapt.

JAMES WILLIS, sett. Swift Creek (Craven) N.C., 1774-1780; Bapt.

JOSEPH WILLIS, sett. Swift Creek (Craven) N.C., 1756-1780; Bapt.

JOHN WILLS, K.B., N.C., 9 Feb. 1769; S.P.G., N.C., 1768-1769; sett. St. James's Parish, Wilmington (New Hanover) N.C., 1770-1777; Ep.

JOHN WINFIELD, sett. Pungo (Beaufort) N.C., 1755-1755; sett. Bear River, N.C., 1772-1772; Bapt.

BARTHOLOMEW ZAUBERBÜHLER, Sr., sett. New Windsor, N.C., 1736-1738; sett. Purysburg (Jasper) S.C., 1738-1738; German-Reformed.

* * * * *

Summary: Baptists, 51; Episcopalians, 42; German Reformed, 3; Huguenots, 1; Lutherans, 3; Methodists, 1; Moravians, 24; Presbyterians, 19. Total: 155.

# THE COLONIAL CLERGY OF SOUTH CAROLINA
## 1681-1776

HUGH ADAMS, A.M. (See *C.C.N.E.*), b. 7 May 1676; Harvard, 1697; sett. Independent-Cong.-Presb. Chh., Charleston, S.C., 1698-1699; sett. Wappetaw, S.C., Chh., at Wando River, 1699-1703; sett. South Edisto River, S.C., 1703-1705; Cong.; d. Oct. 1748.

JOSEPH ALEXANDER, D.D., b. Pa.; A.B., Princeton, 1760, A.M.; D.D., Coll. of S.C., 1807; lic. by New Castle Presb., 1767; ord. Buffalo (Guilford) N.C., 4 Mar. 1768; sett. Union Chh., Brown's Creek (Union) S.C., 1765-1765; sett. Sugar Creek (Mecklenburg) N.C., May 1768-1774; sett. Bullock's Creek (Union) S.C., 1774-1801; sett. Nazareth, at Spartanburg (Spartanburg) S.C., 1774-1776; Thicketty Creek (Union) S.C., 1775-1775; sett. Beersheba, S.C., 1775-1780; founder of Queen's Coll., N.C.; Alexandria Coll. was named for him, 1797; Presb.; d. Bullock's Creek, S.C., 30 July 1809.

HUGH ALISON, A.B., b. Pa.; A.B., Princeton, 1762; Chaplain of Penna. forces at Fort Pitt, 1760; teacher in Charleston, S.C.; sett. Williamsburg, S.C., Dec. 1761-1766; James Island (Charleston) S.C., 1768-1781; Salem (Sumpter Dist.) S.C., 1769-1770; Presb.; d. Charleston, S.C., 1781.

JOHN ALISON, b. 1730; inst. Wilton (Colleton) S.C., 1 May 1759-1761; sett. Altamaha, Ga., 1761-1766; sett. James Island (Charleston) S.C., 1765-1766; Presb.; d. James Island, S.C., 17 Oct. 1766, a. 36.

MOSES ALLEN, A.B., b. Northampton, Mass., 14 Sept. 1748; A.B., Princeton, 1772; lic. 1 Feb. 1774; ord. Christ Chh. Par., S.C., 16 Mar. 1775; inst. Wappetaw, Wando Neck (Berkeley) S.C., 1775-8 June 1777; sett. Midway, Ga., 1777-1779; chaplain, Ga. brigade, Am. Rev., 1778-1779; Presb.; d. (drowned escaping from a British prison), 8 Feb. 1779, a. 30.

ISAAC AMORY, A.M., b. England; came to S.C., 1764; sett. St. John's Par. (Colleton) S.C., 19 Nov. 1764-13 Sept. 1765; left S.C., 1766; sett. Newark-upon-Trent, Eng., 1766-1793; Ep.; d. Newark-upon-Trent, Eng., 1793, s.p.

GEORGE ANDERSON, b. Scotland; arriv. S.C., 25 Dec. 1750; inst. Walterborough (Colleton) at Pon Pon, S.C., Mar. 1750/1-1751; Presb.; d. Walterborough, S.C., 20 Nov. 1751.

JOHN ANDREWS, B.C.L., b. 1730, son of John Andrews of Berkeley, co. Gloucester, Eng.; matric. Trinity Coll., Oxford, 30 Mar. 1748, a. 18; B.C.L., St. Mary's Hall, Oxford, 9 July 1759; ord. (Bsp. of Oxford), 24 Dec. 1752; K.B., S.C., 8 Aug. 1753; arriv. S.C., 1753; sett. St. Philip's Chh., Charleston, S.C., 1753-9 Nov.

1756; left S.C., 1756; sett. Stinchcombe (Glouc.) Eng.; Vicar, Marden (Kent) Eng.; Ep.

HEZEKIAH BALCH, D.D. (See *C.C.Md.*), b. Deer Creek, Md., 1741; Princeton, 1766; ord. Va., 8 Mar. 1770; sett. Bethel, S.C., 1770-1774; sett. Bethesda, S.C., 1770-1774; Presb.; d. Greenville, Tenn., Apr. 1810.

ALEXANDER BARON, A.B., b. Aberdeen, Scotland; Marischal Coll., 1741; A.B., Univ. of Aberdeen, 1745; came to S.C., 1748 as Schoolmaster of a Man-of-War; headmaster of the Free School, Charleston; ord. (Bsp. of London), 17 June 1753; sett. St. Paul's Par. (Colleton) S.C., 1754-1758; sett. St. Helena's Par., Port Royal Island (Beaufort) S.C., 1758-1759; Ep.; d. St. Helena's Parish, S.C., 1759.

ROBERT BARON, A.M., ord. (Bsp. of London) 29 Sept. 1752; lic. S.C., 2 Feb. 1753; K.B., S.C., 14 Feb. 1753; arriv. 1 June 1753 as S.P.G. missionary, S.C.; sett. St. Bartholomew's Par. (Colleton) S.C., 7 June 1753-1764; Ep.; d. St. Bartholomew's Parish, S.C., Apr. 1764.

THOMAS BARRET, sett. Independent-Congregational-Presbyterian Chh., Charleston, S.C., 1684-1685; Presb.

NATHAN BASSETT, A.M., b. Chilmark, Martha's Vineyard, Mass., 14 Feb. 1701/2, son of Nathan and Mary (Huckins) Bassett; A.B., Harvard, 1719, A.M.; ord. Brattle Street Chh., Boston, Mass., 14 Apr. 1724; sett. Independent Chh., Charleston, S.C., 1724-1738; Presb.-Cong.; d. Charleston, S.C., 26 June 1738, of small pox, a. 37 (GS).

JOHN BAXTER, sett. Cainhoy, S.C., Jan. 1733/4-1744; Presb.

NICHOLAS BEDGEGOOD, b. Thornbury, Gloucestershire, Eng.; came to Am., 1751; well educated; had studied law; Ep.; sett. Orphan House, Ga., 1757-1759; ord. (as a Baptist) 1759; sett. Welsh Neck Chh., Society Hill (Darlington) S.C., 1759-2 Mar. 1765; 12 Apr. 1767-1774; Bapt.; d. Welsh Creek, S.C., ca. 1 Feb. 1774.

THOMAS BELL, sett. James Island (Charleston) S.C., 1750-1755; Presb.; elderly and sick, 1755.

ANDREW BENNETT, b. England; sett. Philadelphia, Pa., First Presb. Chh., 22 May 1758-Sept. 1758; sett. Charleston, S.C. (Independent-Cong.-Presb. Chh.), 1761-1763; sett. Barbadoes, 1763-1804; bequeathed $2000 to the Independent Chh. of Charleston; Cong.-Presb.; d. Barbadoes, 1804.

ROBERT BETHAM, A.M., b. Westmoreland, 1717, son of Robert of Woodfoot; matric. Queen's Coll., Oxford, 13 Mar. 1734/5, a. 18, A.B., 1739, A.M.; Curate at Ware, Hertfordshire; K.B., S.C., 16 Oct. 1745; came S.C., 1746; asst. min., St. Philip's Chh., Charleston, S.C., 25 Jan. 1745/6-1747; Ep.; d. Charleston, S.C., 31 May 1747.

BENJAMIN BLACKBURN, K.B., Bermuda, 7 Jan. 1774; came to S.C., 1775; sett. St. John's Par. (Colleton) S.C., 7 Aug. 1775-1775; Ep.; d. St. John's Parish, S.C., 1775.

THOMAS BLOUNT, sett. Dog Bluff Chh., S.C., 1768-1772; Bapt.

BISHOP JOHN PETER BOEHLER (See *C.C.Del.*), b. 31 Dec. 1712; sett. Purysburg (Jasper) S.C., 1738-1739; Moravian; d. 27 Apr. 1775.

JAMES BOISSEAU, sett. Charleston, S.C., Huguenot Chh., 1712-1712; Hug.

CHARLES BOSCHI, had formerly been a Franciscan friar; lic. for S.C., 12 Dec. 1744; K.B., S.C., 20 Dec. 1744, as S.P.G. missionary; sett. St. Bartholomew's Par. (Colleton) S.C., 25 Feb. 1744/5-1749; preacher at the 17th visitation in 1747; was preparing to become chaplain at Ruatan, Bay of Honduras; Ep.; d. St. Bartholomew's Parish, S.C., 1749.

MR. BOUTITON (brother-in-law of Mr. Gibert, q.v.); sett. New Bordeaux, Hillsboro, S.C., 1772-1772; Hug.

JOHN BROWN, b. near Burlington, N.J., 20 Aug. 1714; came to Welsh Neck, 1737; ord. Welsh Neck Chh., Society Hill (Chesterfield-Darlington) S.C., 7 May 1750-1754; sett. Cashaway Neck, at Mt. Pleasant (Charleston) S.C., 1760-1762; Bapt.; d. after 1790.

JOSEPH BUEGNION, b. Switzerland; ord. (Bsp. of St. David's) 27 July 1732; sett. Purysburg (Jasper) S.C., Swiss Colony, St. Peter's Parish, German-Reformed, 1732-1735; sett. St. James's Par., Santee, S.C., at Jamestown, 1733-1735; naturalized, Feb. 1733; left S.C., 1739; Germ.-Ref., became Ep., Feb. 1746.

COMMISSARY WILLIAM TREDWELL BULL, A.M., b. ca. 1684, son of George Bull of Warnton, Oxon, gent.; matric. Wadham Coll., Oxford, 20 Mar. 1698/9, a. 15; A.B., 1702, A.M., 1705; S.P.G. missionary to S.C., 1712; K.B., S.C., 1 July 1712; Rector, St. Paul's Parish (Colleton) S.C., 1712-1723; Commissary, S.C., 1716-1723; Ep.; left S.C. for England, 1723.

JOHN BULLMAN, A.M., came to S.C., ca. 1770; sett. St. Michael's Chh., Charleston, S.C., as asst., 10 Dec. 1770-18 Aug. 1774; Ep.; dismissed as a Tory; sailed for England, 21 Mar. 1775.

JAMES CAMPBELL (See *C.C.N.C.*), sett. Bullock's Creek, S.C., 1773-1774; Bull Run (Chester) S.C., 1773-1774; Catholic Congregation, at Rocky Creek, S.C., 1776-1780; Presb.

ISAAC CHANLER, b. Bristol, England, 1701; came to Ashley, S.C., 1733; sett. Ashley River, S.C., 1733-1749; sett. Charleston, S.C., supply, 1744-1749; Bapt.; d. Ashley River, S.C., 30 Nov. 1749, a. 49.

HENRY CHIFFELLE, b. Switzerland; ord. (Bsp. of London), 21 July 1734; S.P.G. missionary to S.C.; arriv. Nov. 1734; sett. St. Peter's Parish, Purysburg (Jasper) S.C., 1744-1758; Fr.-Ref.-Ep.; d. Purysburg, S.C., 1758.

MOSES CLARK, K.B., N.E., 17 Nov. 1720; came to S.C., 1720; sett. St. John's Par. (Berkeley) S.C., 1720-1720; Ep.; d. St. John's Parish, S.C., 1720.

RICHARD CLARKE, A.M., b. 1723, son of Henry Clarke of

Winchester; matric. Univ. Coll., 17 Dec. 1741, a. 18; K.B., S.C., 15 Aug. 1753; ord. (Bsp. of Bangor), 23 Sept. 1750; sett. as Rector, St. Philip's Chh., Charleston, S.C., 1753-9 Feb. 1759; preacher 10th annual meeting of the clergy of S.C., 1758; ret. to England; sett. Stoke-Newington and St. James's Aldgate, London, 1759-1768; curate, Cheshunt, Herts., 1768-1780; Ep.; d. England, after 1780.

MR. CLAYTON, sett. Tuckaseeking, Ga., 1759-1764; sett. Edisto, S.C., 1764 ff.; 7th Day Bapt.

DAVID COLLADON, K.B., S.C., 6 Apr. 1733; sett. St. James's Parish, Santee, S.C., 1733-1733; Hug.-Ep.; d. St. James's Parish, S.C., 1733.

ROBERT COOPER, A.B., b. Wales, 1731, son of Ellis Cooper of Knighton, Radnor, Wales; matric. Jesus Coll., Oxford, 5 July 1748, a. 17; A.B., 1752; K.B., S.C., 11 May 1758; arriv. S.C., 1758; Rector, Prince William's Parish, S.C., 1758-1759; sett. St. Philip's Chh., Charleston, S.C., 10 Dec. 1759-1761; Rector, St. Michael's Chh., Charleston, S.C., Feb. 1761-June 1776; ret. to England; curate, St. Andrew's Chh., Holborn, London and Rector, St. Michael's Church, Cornhill, London, 1776-1812; Ep.; d. London, England, 1812 or 1813.

WILLIAM CORBIN, b. 1658, son of Luke Corbin, of Totnes, Devon; matric. New Inn Hall, Oxford, 19 Oct. 1679, a. 21; served the Chapel of Bromley St. Leonard, Middlesex, Eng.; came to S.C., 1700; sett. Goose Creek Chh., St. James's Par. (Berkeley) S.C., 1700-1703; left S.C., 1703; Ep.

JONATHAN COPP, A.B. (See C.C.Ga.), bapt. Montville, Conn., 1 Aug. 1725, son of Jonathan and Margaret Copp; A.B., Y.C., 1744; sett. St. John's Par. (Colleton) S.C., 28 Jan. 1756-1762; preacher at the 9th annual meeting of the clergy of S.C., 1757; Ep.; d. St. John's Par. (Colleton) S.C., 4 Jan. 1762, a. 36.

JOHN COSSON, sett. Bethel, S.C., ca. 1769-1770; Presb.; was a missionary sent over from England by Lady Huntingdon.

WILLIAM COTES, ord. (Bsp. of Hereford), 1 Feb. 1746/7; came to S.C., 1748; sett. St. George's Parish, Dorchester (Dorchester) S.C., 1748-1752; preacher at 1st annual meeting of the clergy of S.C., 1749; Ep.; d. St. George's Parish, Dorchester, S.C., 19 July 1752.

JOHN COTTON, JR., A.M. (See C.C.N.E.), b. Boston, 15 Mar. 1639/40; A.B., Harvard College, 1657; sett. Plymouth, Mass., 1669-1697; inst. Independent Chh., Charleston, S.C., 15 Mar. 1698/9-1699; Cong.; d. Charleston, S.C., 18 Sept. 1699, a. 59; buried at Plymouth.

STEPHEN COULET, b. France; ord. for the Church of Rome; lic. for S.C., 9 Aug. 1731; K.B., S.C., 3 Aug. 1731; arriv. S.C., 9 Dec. 1731; sett. St. James's Parish, Santee, S.C., Dec. 1731-1733; R.C.-Hug.-Ep.; d. St. James's, Santee, S.C., 1733.

JAMES CRALLAN, A.M., b. Manchester, co., Lancaster, England, 1740, son of James Crallan; matric. Brasenose Coll., Oxford,

2 Mar. 1756, a. 16; A.B., 1759, A.M.; came to S.C., 1765; ass't., St. Philip's Chh., Charleston, S.C., 14 Oct. 1767-25 Apr. 1768; deranged in mind; Ep.; d. (suicide) on way to England, 1768.

JAMES CRESWELL (See *C.C.N.C.*), sett. Little River, S.C., 1764-1776; Duncan's Creek, S.C., 1766-1776; Fairforest, S.C., 1771-1776; Rocky Creek, now Rock Chh. (Abbeville) S.C., 1772-1776; Ninety-Six (Abbeville) S.C., at New Cambridge, 1775-1776; Presb.; d. Little River, S.C., 1776.

ROBERT CUMMING, A.M. (ed. in Scotland); K.B., N.C., 31 Jan. 1748/9; ord. (Bsp. of Peterborough), 28 Dec. 1748; arriv. S.C., 18 Nov. 1749; sett. St. John's Par. (Berkeley) S.C., 1749-1750; Ep.; d. St. John's Parish, S.C., 26 July 1750.

JEREMIAH DARGAN, sett. High Hills of Santee, S.C., at Statesburg, 1769-1771; sett. Cashie (Bertie) N.C., 1771-1776; Bapt.

FREDERICK DASER, A.M., came from Wuerttemberg, Germany; ord. Charleston, S.C. (Lutheran Chh.), 1770-1774; ord. England (Episcopalian), 1774; sett. Charleston, S.C. (Lutheran Chh.), 1781-Aug. 1786; sett. Orangeburg, S.C., St. Matthew's Chh., 1786-1788; Luth.-Ep.; d. after 1788.

MR. DAVIS, sett. St. Mark's Parish, S.C., 1773-1774; Ep.; d. St. Mark's Parish, S.C., 1774.

WILLIAM DAWSON, A.M., b. East Lothian, Scotland, 1718; ed. at St. Andrew's Coll., Edinburgh; ord. (Bsp. of Coventry) as deacon, 6 May 1764; lic. for S.C., 2 July 1764; arriv. S.C., Aug. 1765; sett. St. John's Par. (Colleton) S.C., Aug. 1765-1767; Ep.; d. John's Island, S.C., 19 Jan. 1767.

DAVID DELESCURE, sett. Charleston, S.C. (Hug. Chh.), 1735-1737; Hug.

CLAUDE PHILIPPE de RICHEBOURGE (See *C.C.N.C.*), sett. St. James's Santee, at Jamestown, French Santee, 1712-1719; Charleston, S.C. (Hug. Chh.), 1717-1719; Western Branch of Cooper River (French Reformed, 1699, later St. John's Parish (Colleton), Ep.), 1712-1719; Hug.-Ep.; d. St. James's Santee, S.C. (will made 15 Jan. 1718/9).

DANIEL DOBEL, son of the Rev. Philip Dobel; sett. Stono, S.C., 1772-1774; Bapt.; d. Charleston, S.C., 24 Aug. 1774.

PHILIP DOBEIL, sett. Stono, 1772-1774; Bapt.; d. Charleston, S.C., 20 Aug. 1774.

WILLIAM DONALDSON (See *C.C.Md.*), ord. Pa., 1755; sett. Waccamaw (Horry District) S.C., at Conwaysboro, 1752 and 1756; Presb.

SAMUEL DRAKE, came to S.C., 1762; left S.C., 1766; preacher at the 15th annual meeting, 1763, and at the 17 annual meeting, 1765, S.C. clergy; Ep.

JOHN DUNDASS, A.M., K.B., S.C., 11 June 1773; arriv. S.C., 1774; sett. St. John's Par. (Colleton) S.C., Apr. 4, 1774-1774; Ep.; d. St. John's Par. (Colleton) S.C., May 1774 (buried at St. Michael's, Charleston).

WILLIAM DUNLOP, son of the Rev. Alexander Dunlop of Paisley, Scotland; sett. Stuart's Town, Port Royal (Beaufort) S.C., 1683-1686; Deputy, 1687; Presb.

WILLIAM DUNN (See *C.C.Va.*), b. ca. 1677; from Clogher, Ireland; ord. (Bsp. of Down and Connor); K.B., S.C., 10 Dec. 1705; sett. St. Paul's Par. (Colleton) S.C., 1706-1707; left S.C., 1707; Ep.

PETER du PLESSIS, son of the Rev. Franc du Plessis of Shoreditch, London; matric. Oxford, 1730; K.B., S.C., 3 June 1736; arriv. S.C., Sept. 1736; sett. St. James's Parish, Santee, S.C., Sept. 1736-1742; left S.C., 1742; Hug.-Ep.

LEVI DURAND, A.M., b. London, 1706, son of James Durand, merchant; pens. Trinity Coll., Dublin, 9 July 1724, a. 18; A.B., 1737, A.M.; ord. (Archbishop of Dublin), 19 Nov. 1739; arriv. S.C., 1740 as S.P.G. missionary; sett. Christ Chh. Par. (Berkeley) S.C., 15 Nov. 1740-Nov. 1750; sett. St. John's Par. (Berkeley) S.C., Nov. 1760-1765; Ep.; d. St. John's Par. (Berkeley) S.C., 1765.

DANIEL DWIGHT, A.M., b. Northampton, Mass., 28 Apr. 1699, son of Nathaniel and Mehitable (Partridge) Dwight; A.B., Yale Coll., 1721, A.M.; A.M., Oxford U., 19 July 1729; ord. (Bsp. of London), 1 June 1729; K.B., N.E., 2 June 1729; S.P.G. missionary; came to S.C., 1729; sett. St. John's Par. (Berkeley) S.C., 1729-1748; chaplain at Fort Dummer, Brattleboro, Vt., 1724; Ep.; d. St. John's Parish (Berkeley) S.C., 28 Mar. 1748, a. 49 (bur. in the Strawberry Chapel).

EDWARD DYSON, came to S.C., 1729; sett. Christ Chh. Par. (Berkeley) S.C., 1 Feb. 1729/30-19 July 1730; left S.C., 1730; Ep.

JAMES EDMUNDS (See *C.C.Ga.*), b. London, England, ca. 1720; sett. Wando River, S.C., 9 Dec. 1753-1754; ord. Charleston, S.C. (Independent Chh.), Feb. 1755; sett. Charleston, 1754-1767; sett. Dorchester, S.C., 9 Aug. 1767-1770; itinerant missionary and supply for Presb. chhs. of S.C.; Cong.-Presb.; d. Charleston, S.C., Apr. 1793, a. 73.

JOSHUA EDWARDS, b. Pembrokeshire, Sou. Wales, 11 Feb. 1704; came to Welsh Tract, Pa., 1709; sett. S.C., 1749; ord. Welsh Neck Chh., Society Hill (Chesterfield-Darlington) S.C., May 1752-1758; sett. Cashaway Neck, Mt. Pleasant (Charleston) S.C., 1758-1761; sett. Little Pedee Chh., S.C., 1761-1768; sett. Catfish, near Latta (Dillion) S.C., 1761-1768; Bapt.; d. S.C., 22 Aug. 1784.

WILLIAM ELBERT, lic. Euhaw Chh., near Beaufort, S.C., 18 May 1746-1750; Bapt.

EDWARD ELLINGTON, A.M. (See *C.C.Ga.*), K.B. Ga., 12 May 1767; sett. St. Bartholomew's Par. (Colleton) S.C., 15 Dec. 1770-Apr. 1772; sett. St. Helen's Par., Beaufort, S.C., 20 Apr. 1772-22 Oct. 1772; sett. St. James's Par., Goose Creek (Berkeley) S.C., 16 Apr. 1775-1793; removed to Savannah, Ga., 1793; Ep.; d. Savannah, Ga.

CALEB EVANS, A.M., b. Llanafon-faur, Brecknockshire, Wales, 30 Mar. 1743; A.B. and A.M., Aberdeen U.; ord. Farnham,

England, 1768; sett. Stono, S.C., 4 Nov. 1768-1772; Bapt.; d. Charleston, S.C., 22 Apr. 1772.

JOHN EVANS, A.M., K.B., S.C., 24 Mar. 1760; came to S.C., 1762; sett. St. Bartholomew's Par. (Colleton) S.C., 23 July 1764-1770; preacher at the 19th annual meeting of the clergy of S.C., 1767; Ep.; d. St. Bartholomew's Parish, S.C., 5 Mar. 1770.

RICHARD FARMER, A.M., arriv. S.C., 26 Feb. 1769; sett. St. John's Parish (Berkeley) S.C., 1769-1769; Ep.; d. St. John's Parish, S.C., 1769.

SAMUEL FAYERWEATHER, A.M. (See *C.C.N.E.*), A.B., H.C., 1743; sett. Charleston, S.C. (Independent-Cong.-Presb. Chh.), 1748-1749; ord. (Bsp. of Carlisle), 25 Mar. 1756; K.B., N.E., 14 Apr. 1756; A.M., Oxford U., 21 Apr. 1756; arriv. S.C., June 1757; sett. Prince George Parish at Winyaw, S.C., June 1757-25 July 1760; sett. Prince Frederick Parish at Prince Frederick Town, S.C., 5 Apr. 1758-1760; Cong.-Presb.-Ep.; d. Kingston, R.I., 1781.

JOHN FEVRIER (also called Feveryear), K.B., Bermuda, 23 Oct. 1755; sett. Bermuda Islands, 1755-1766; came to S.C., 1766; sett. St. Helena's Par. (Beaufort) S.C., 1766-1766; Ep.; d. St. Helena's Parish, S.C., 1766.

ALEXANDER FINLAY, K.B., Ga., 27 Sept. 1770; came to S.C., 1771; sett. St. Stephen's Parish, Santee, S.C., 1773-1783; Ep.; d. St. Stephen's Parish, S.C., 1783.

HUGH FISHER, sett. Dorchester (Dorchester) S.C., ca. 1720-1734; Presb.; d. Dorchester, S.C., 6 Oct. 1734.

JOHN FORDYCE, A.M., ord. (Bsp. of St. David's), 22 Mar. 1729/30; K.B., Jamaica, 2 June 1730; S.P.G. missionary; arriv. S.C., 1736; sett. Prince Frederick's Parish at Prince Frederick Town, S.C., 1736-1751; sett. Prince George's Parish at Winyaw, S.C., 1736-1746; preacher, 9th visitation, S.C., 1739; preacher, 2nd annual meeting of clergy, 1750; Ep.; d. Prince Frederick Town, S.C., 1751.

JAMES FOULIS (See *C.C.Va.*), came to S.C., 1770; sett. St. David's Parish at Cheraw Hill, S.C., 1770-1770; Ep.; left S.C., 1779.

JOHN GEORGE FRIEDRICKS, sett. Charleston, S.C., Luth. Chh., 1755-1761; sett. St. Matthew's Chh., at Amelia (Orangeburg) S.C., 1761-1774; Luth.; d. after 1774.

WILLIAM FRY, ord. Edisto Island (Beaufort) S.C., 1726-1731; Bapt.

JOHN FULLERTON, A.M. ord. (Bsp. of London), 1734; came to S.C., 1735; S.P.G. missionary; sett. Christ Church Parish (Berkeley) S.C., 5 Feb. 1734/5-1735; Ep.; d. Christ Church Parish, S.C., 4 Sept. 1735.

JOHN FULTON, A.M. (*prob.* b. near Raphoe, Ireland, 1699, son of William Fulton, farmer; sizar, Trinity Coll., Dublin, 14 June 1720, a. 21; A.B., 1724, A.M., 1729), ord. (Bsp. of London) 22 Feb. 1729/30; K.B., S.C., 4 Apr. 1730; came to S.C., 1730; sett. Christ Church Parish (Berkeley) S.C., 26 July 1730-1734; Ep.

RICHARD FURMAN, D.D., b. Esopus, N.Y., 9 Oct. 1755, son

of Wood and Rachel (Brodhead) Furman; A.M., Brown U., 1792; D.D., Brown U., 1800; D.D., Sou. Carolina Coll.; began preaching, 1773; ord. High Hills of Santee, at Statesburg, S.C., 16 May 1774; sett. High Hills, 1773-1787; sett. Charleston, S.C., 1787-1825; member, S.C. constitutional convention; Bapt.; d. Charleston, S.C., 25 Aug. 1825.

COMMISSARY ALEXANDER GARDEN, A.M., b. Scotland, ca. 1685; Bishop's Commissary for S.C., 1726-1748; sett. St. Philip's Church, Charleston, S.C., 1719-29 Oct. 1753; Ep.; d. Charleston, S.C., 27 Sept. 1756, a. 71.

ALEXANDER GARDEN, JR., A.M., nephew of Commissary Alexander Garden; ord. (Bsp. of Gloucester), 17 Apr. 1743; K.B., S.C., 28 Apr. 1743; sett. St. Thomas and St. Dennis Parish (Berkeley) S.C., 1743-1783; preacher, 16th visitation, 1746; Ep.; d. St. Thomas and St. Dennis Parish, S.C., 1783.

JOHN GASSER, chaplain of a Swiss regiment before 26 May 1755; came to S.C., 1754; sett. Upper and Lower Forks, Santee, S.C., 20 Dec. 1754-1759; Germ.-Ref.

JEAN LOUIS GIBERT, b. near Alais, Languedoc, France, 22 July 1722; ed. Lausanne, Switzerland, 1745; sett. Saintogne, France, 1745-1763; arriv. S.C., 14 Apr. 1764; sett. New Bordeaux, S.C., at Hillsborough, 1764-1773; Hug.; d. Badwell, New Bordeaux, S.C., Aug. 1773, a. 52.

JACOB GIBSON, b. Va.; ord. Little River, S.C., 7 Nov. 1771; sett. Little River of Broad River Chh., S.C., 1771-1790; Bapt.; d. Fairforest Dist., S.C., 1793.

JOHN ULRICH GIESSENDANNER, SR., b. Lichtensteig, St. Gall, Switzerland, 30 Jan. 1660, son of Andreas and Barbara (Steger) Giessendanner; teacher at Halle, Germany; sett. St. Matthew's Chh., Orangeburg (Orangeburg) S.C., 1737-1738; sett. Saxe-Gotha (Lexington) S.C., 1737-1738; Luth.-Germ.-Ref.; d. Orangeburg, S.C., 1738.

JOHN ULRICH GIESSENDANNER, JR., nephew of the above; ord. Charleston, S.C. (Presb.), 1739; sett. St. Matthew's Luth. Chh. at Orangeburg (Orangeburg) S.C., 1739-1761; Luth. Chh. at Saxe-Gotha (Lexington) S.C., 1739-1761; sett. Amelia, S.C., 1739-1747; ord. (Bsp. of London), 24 Sept. 1749; sett. St. Matthew's Chh. (Ep.), 1749-1761; Luth.-Germ.Ref.-Presb.-Ep.; d. Saxe-Gotha (Lexington) S.C., 1761.

JAMES GIGUILLET (or Gigwillatt); K.B., for America, 15 Nov. 1709; sett. St. James's Parish, Santee, S.C., at Jamestown, 1710-1710; Fr.Ref.-Ep.

CHARLES GORDON, came from Scotland; inst. Walterborough (Colleton) S.C., Pon Pon Chh., 31 Oct. 1759-1760 et post; Presb.

JAMES GORLAY, b. 1732; sett. Tullicoultry (Clackmannan) Scotland; sett. Walterborough (Colleton) S.C., Pon Pon Chh., 1774-

1780; sett. Stoney Creek (Prince William Parish) S.C., 1774-1802; Presb.

ROBERT GOWIE, A.M., ord. (Bsp. of London), 21 Oct. 1733; K.B., S.C., 23 Oct. 1733; S.P.G. missionary; sett. St. Bartholomew's Par. (Colleton) S.C., 1733-1733; Ep.; d. St. Bartholomew's Parish, S.C., 7 Nov. 1733.

JOHN GRANT, sett. Charleston, Scot's Presb. Chh., 1740-1747; Presb.

JOHN GREEN, A.M., St. Peter's Coll., Cambridge; (N.B.: Joseph Green was K.B., S.C., 24 Mar. 1762, obviously a mistake for John); came to S.C., 1762; sett. St. Helena's Par. (Beaufort) S.C., 28 Sept. 1762-1765; Ep.; d. St. Helena's Parish, S.C., 1765.

RICHARD GREGORY, son of John Gregory of Broad River, S.C.; sett. Tuckaseeking, Ga., 1759-1764; sett. Edisto, S.C., 1764 *et post;* 7th Day Bapt.

FRANCIS GUICHARD, sett. Charleston, S.C., Hug. Chh., 1734-1752; sett. St. James's Par. (Berkeley) S.C., at Goose Creek, 1734-1752; Hug.

WILLIAM GUY, A.M. (See *C.C.N.E.*), sett. St. Philip's Chh., Charleston, 1711, 1713, 1716-1717; St. Helena's Par. (Beaufort) S.C., 1713-1717; St. Andrew's Chh., on Ashley River near Charleston, S.C., 1719-1751; Ep.; d. St. Andrew's Parish, S.C., 1751.

JOHN SEVERIN HAHNBAUM, arriv. Charleston, S.C., 12 June 1767; sett. St. John's Chh., Charleston, S.C., 1767-1770; Luth.; d. Charleston, S.C., 10 Feb. 1770.

JOHN HARRIS, A.B. (See *C.C.Del.*), A.B., Princeton, 1753; Boonsborough, S.C., 1772-Nov. 1779, at Long Cane Creek; Greenville, S.C., Saluda Chh., 1772-1773; Bulltown, S.C., 1772-1779; Long Canes (Abbeville) S.C., 1772-Nov. 1779; Ninety-Six (Abbeville) S.C., 1776-1779; member, S.C. Provincial Congress; physician; Old Side Presb.; d. 1790.

JAMES HARRISON, A.B., b. 1726, son of Leonard Harrison of Bongate, Westmoreland; matric. Queen's Coll., Oxford, 18 Nov. 1743, a. 17; A.B., 1748; ord. (Bsp. of Bangor), 23 Sept. 1750; Curate at Battersea, Surrey, Eng.; K.B., S.C., 1 July 1752; came to S.C., Dec. 1752 as S.P.G. missionary; sett. St. James's Parish (Berkeley) S.C., at Goose Creek, 18 Dec. 1752-7 Nov. 1774; sett. St. Bartholomew's Par. (Colleton) S.C., 8 Apr. 1776-1784; preacher, 8th annual meeting of the clergy of S.C., 1756; Ep.; d. St. Bartholomew's Parish, S.C., 1788.

OLIVER HART, A.M., b. Warminster (Bucks) Pa., 5 July 1723; lic. 20 Dec. 1746; ord. 18 Oct. 1749; A.M. (Hon.), Brown U., 1769; sett. Charleston, S.C., inst. 16 Feb. 1749/50-1780; inst. Hopewell, N.J., 16 Dec. 1780-1795; Bapt.; d. Hopewell, N.J., 31 Dec. 1795, a. 72.

SAMUEL HART, K.B., West Florida, 10 May 1764; came to S.C., 1765; sett. St. Michael's Chh., Charleston, S.C., asst., 10 June

1765-2 June 1770; Rector, St. John's Parish (Berkeley) S.C., 2 June 1770-1779; Ep.; d. St. John's Parish (Berkeley) S.C., 1779.

THOMAS HASELL, A.M. (or Hassill), b. England; K.B., N.C., as schoolmaster, 13 Feb. 1705; came to Charleston, 1705; sett. Charleston, S.C., 1705-1708; ord. London, Eng., 31 July 1709, S.P.G. missionary; sett. West Parish or Chuckatuck (Nansemond) Va., 1709; sett. Rector, St. Thomas and St. Dennis Parish (Berkeley) S.C., 1709-1744; Ep.; d. St. Thomas and St. Dennis Parish, S.C., 9 Nov. 1744.

THOMAS HENDERSON, b. Scotland, ca. 1740; chaplain of the Royal Scots at St. Augustine, Fla.; ord. Salt Ketcher (Colleton) S.C., 1775; sett. Edisto Island (Charleston) S.C., 1770-1775; sett. Salt Ketcher, S.C., 1773-1776; sett. Wilton (Colleton) S.C., 1776-1780; Presb.

ROBERT HERON, came from Scotland; sett. Williamsburg, S.C., Aug. 1736-1740; ret. to Ireland; Presb.

ALEXANDER HEWATT, D.D., b. Scotland, 1739; came from Edinburgh to S.C.; sett. Charleston, S.C., Scot's Presb. Chh., before 20 Mar. 1763-1776; ret. to England ca. 1776, and settled in or near London; he was the *first historian of S.C.;* Presb.; d. London, England, ca. 1828.

HENRY HEYWOOD, came from Farnham, near London, England, to S.C., 1739; sett. Stono (Charleston) S.C., 3 May 1740-1755; General Bapt.; d. Charleston, S.C., 29 Oct. 1755.

BARTHOLEMI HENRI HIMELI, sett. Charleston, S.C., Hug. Chh., 1759-1772; Hug.; ret. to France between 1773-Nov. 1785.

GEORGE LEWIS HOCKHEIMER, arriv. in America, 1 Nov. 1755; sett. York, Pa., 1756-1758; sett. Sandy Run, at Saxe-Gotha (Lexington) S.C., 1765-1774; Luth.; d. after 1774.

JOHN HOCKLEY, A.M., b. 1736, son of John Hockley of Southampton, England; matric., Magdalen Coll., Oxford, 17 Dec. 1754, a. 18; A.B., 1758, A.M., 1761; K.B., S.C., 13 Sept. 1765; arriv. S.C., 1765; sett. St. John's Par. (Berkeley) S.C., 10 Nov. 1765-10 May 1767; ret. to England, 1767; sometime of Parson's Green, Fulham; Ep.; d. London, England, 24 Oct. 1824.

BRIAN HUNT, A.B., b. Kent; adm. Corpus Christi Coll., Camb., 1704; A.B., 1722; ord. priest, 10 Mar. 1709/10; Vicar of Quadring, Lincs, 1717; marine chaplain; came to S.C., 1722; K.B., Va., 8 May 1722; sett. St. John's Par. (Berkeley) S.C., 1723-1726; ret. to Eng., ca. 1728; Ep.; was prob. K.B., Barbadoes, 16 Mar. 1709/10.

SAMUEL HUNTER, came to S.C., 1734 or 1735; sett. Black Mingo, S.C., 1744-1754; Presb.; d. Black Mingo, S.C., June 1754.

WILLIAM HUTSON, b. England, 14 Aug. 1720, son of a clergyman; studied law; sett. Orphan House, Ga., 1743; ord. Stoney Creek, Prince William's Parish, S.C., 20 May 1743-1757; sett. Charleston, S.C., Independent Chh., 1757-1761; Presb.; d. Charleston, S.C., 11 Apr. 1761, a. 41 y.

ABRAHAM IMER, b. Switzerland; deacon and master of the Latin School at Neuville, Switzeralnd, 1759; ord. London, England (Ep.), 1759; K.B., S.C., 31 Jan. 1760; sett. St. Peter's Parish, Purysburg (Jasper) S.C., 1760-1766; Swiss and Germ. Ref. with Ep. ord.; d. St. Peter's Parish, S.C., 1766.

ROBERT INGRAHAM, b. Lincolnshire, Eng.; came to S.C., 1735, from Farnham near London; sett. Stono (Charleston) S.C., 1735-1738; Bapt.; d. Stono, S.C., 1738.

PHILIP JAMES, b. Pennepack, Pa., 1701, son of James James, Esq.; came to S.C., 1737; ord. Welsh Neck Chh., Society Hill (Chesterfield-Darlington) S.C., 4 Apr. 1743-1754; Bapt.; d. Catfish, Welsh Neck, S.C., 31 Jan. 1754.

EDWARD JENKINS, D.D., b. 1744, son of Edward Jenkins of Cowbridge, Glamorganshire; matric. Jesus Coll., Oxford, 29 Oct. 1762, a. 18; A.B., 1767; D.D. (Hon.), Brown U., 1803; D.D. (Hon.), Columbia U., 1804; K.B., S.C., 11 Sept. 1772; Rector, St. Bartholomew's Par. (Colleton) S.C., 1 Nov. 1772-1776; St. Michael's Par., Charleston, S.C., 1797-17 Dec. 1804; St. Philip's Chh., Charleston, S.C., 24 Dec. 1804-1809; elected Bishop of S.C., 20 Feb. 1804, but declined; Ep.; d. England, after 1819.

COMMISSARY GIDEON JOHNSTON, A.M., b. Loony, co. Mayo, Ireland, 1668, son of James Johnston, gent.; pens. Trinity Coll., Dublin, 19 June 1684, a. 16; A.B., 1692, A.M., 1692; ord. Vicar, Castlemore, Ireland; K.B., Carolina, 18 July 1707; also 28 Jan. 1707/8 and 11 Feb. 1707/8; Bishop's Commissary, S.C., 1708-1716; sett. St. Philip's Chh., Charleston, S.C., 1708-1716; Ep.; d. Charleston, S.C., 26 Apr. 1716 (drowned).

GILBERT JONES, A.M., (prob. b. Welchpool, Montgomeryshire, 1688, son of John Jones; matric. Jesus Coll., 21 Mar. 1703/4, a. 16; A.B., 1707); K.B., Carolina, 11 May 1711; arriv. S.C., Mar. 1711/2; sett. Christ Chh. Par. (Berkeley) S.C., 24 Mar. 1711/2-1721; S.P.G. missionary; ret. to England, 1721; Ep.; (Vicar of St. Michael Mancton, Pembroke, 1722).

LEWIS JONES, A.M. (prob. b. Llanfynnydd, Carmarthenshire, 1694, son of John Jones; matric. Jesus Coll., Oxford, 5 June 1712, a. 18; A.B., Univ. Coll., Oxford, 19 Feb. 1718/9; A.M., 19 June 1719; vicar, Merthrys Cynog, Brecon, 1723); K.B., S.C., 30 Sept. 1725; S.P.G. missionary; came to S.C., 1725; sett. St. Helena's Par. (Beaufort) S.C., 1725-1744; bequeathed £100 to S.P.G.; Ep.; d. St. Helena's Parish, S.C., 24 Dec. 1744.

MORGAN JONES (poss. b. Penmoyne, Glamorgan, 1621, son of Thomas Jones; matric. St. Edmund's Hall, Oxford, 24 May 1639, a. 18); sett. St. Helena's Par., Port Royal (Beaufort) S.C., 19 Apr. 1660-1660; Ep.

ALEXANDER KEITH, ord. (Bsp. of London), 21 Oct. 1733; lic. for S.C., 26 June 1745; K.B., S.C., 3 July 1745; came from Eng., 1746; sett. Prince George's Parish, at Winyaw, S.C., 29 Sept. 1746-1 Dec. 1749; sett. St. Philip's Chh., Charleston, S.C., as asst., 5 Dec.

1749-2 May 1753; sett. St. Stephen's Parish, Santee. S.C., 1754-1773; preacher at 18th visitation, 1748; Ep.; left S.C., 1773.

RICHARD KELLY, ord. ca. 1772; sett. Goucher Creek, Goshen, S.C., 1772-1775; Bapt.

THOMAS KENNEDY, sett. Charleston, S.C., Scot's Presb. Chh., 1747; Presb.; d. Charleston, S.C., ca. 31 Aug. 1747.

THOMAS KENNEDY, came from Ireland to S.C., May 1772; sett. Williamsburg, S.C., 1772-1775; Presb.; ret. to Ireland.

PATRICK KIER, sett. James Island, S.C., 1760-1765; Presb.; d. James Island, S.C., before 14 Oct. 1765, an old man.

MR. KIRKPATRICK, sett. Stoney Creek, S.C., 1773-1774; Presb.

WILLIAM KNOX (poss. b. Dublin, pens. Trinity Coll., Dublin, 18 Sept. 1756, son of William Knox, gent.); came from Ireland; sett. Indian Town, S.C., 1767-1768; Black Mingo, S.C., 1768-1800; Salem Chh., Black River, S.C., ca. 1768; Presb.

JOHN LAMBERT, A.M., K.B., S.C., 21 Oct. 1727; S.P.G. missionary; sett. as schoolmaster and minister at St. Philip's Chh., Charleston, S.C., 1727-1729; Ep.; d. Charleston, S.C., 14 Aug. 1729.

WILLIAM LANGHORNE, ord. (Archbishop of York), 24 Sept. 1749; curate at Pickering, England; K.B., S.C., 3 Aug. 1750; came to S.C., 1751; S.P.G. missionary; sett. St. Bartholomew's Par. (Colleton) S.C., 1751-Sept. 1752; sett. St. George's Par. (Dorchester) S.C., Nov. 1752-1759; preacher at 4th annual meeting of the clergy of S.C., 1752; Ep.; left S.C., 1759.

JOHN de LA PIERRE, A.B. (See C.C.N.C.), sett. St. Dennis's Parish, Orange Quarter (Berkeley) S.C., 1711-1728; sett. Charleston, S.C., Fr. Prot. Chh. 1712-1713; 1728-1728; in N.C., q.v., 1729-1735; Hug.-Ep.; d. S.C., 1735.

JAMES LATTA, D.D., b. Ireland, 1732, son of James and Mary (Alison) Latta; A.B., U. of Pa., 1757, A.M.; D.D., 1799; tutor, U. of Pa., 1756-1759; ord. 19 Feb. 1762; sett. Deep Run Chh., Bedminster (Bucks) Pa., 1761-12 Apr. 1770; sett. John's Island (Charleston) S.C., 1768-1770; sett. Drumore Chh., Chesnut Level (Lancaster) Pa., Nov. 1771-1801; pvt. and chaplain, Pa. militia, Rev. war; Presb.; d. Chestnut Level, Pa., 29 Jan. 1801, a. 68.

HENRY LEDBETTER (See C.C.N.C.), sett. Lynches Creek, S.C., 1755-1761; Bapt.

FRANCIS LE JAU, D.D., b. Angiers, France, 1665; Trinity Coll., Dublin, A.M., 1693, B.D., 1696, D.D., 24 Jan. 1700; Canon, St. Paul's Cathedral, London; missionary, St. Christopher's, W.I., 1700-1701; K.B., S.C., 27 Nov. 1705; arriv. S.C., Oct. 1706; sett. Hug. Chh. and St. James's Par. Goose Creek (Berkeley), Cooper River, S.C., 13 Oct. 1706-1717; Hug.-Ep.; d. Goose Creek, Cooper River, S.C., 15 Sept. 1717.

PAUL L'ESCOT, ord. (Anglican), 1719; sett. Charleston, S.C., Hug. Chh., Dec. 1700-Mar. 1719; sett. Dover, England. Fr. Chh. 1720-1728; sett. Charleston, S.C., Hug. Chh., 1731-1734; Hug.-Ep.;

will made, Charleston, S. C., 24 Aug. 1752; proved, 13 Oct. 1752.

ANDREW LESLIE, A.M., ord. (Bsp. of Derry), 14 July 1728; lic. 3 July 1729; K.B., S.C., 5 Aug. 1729; arriv. S.C., 13 Sept. 1732; sett. St. Paul's Par. (Colleton) S.C., 15 Sept. 1729-1740; S.P.G. missionary; Ep.; d. St. Paul's Parish, S.C., 1740.

PIERRE LEVRIER, sett. Pensacola, Fla., 1766-1772; sett. New Bordeaux, Hillsborough, S.C., 1772-1774; sett. Charleston, S.C., Hug. Chh., 1774-1780; Hug.

JOHN LEWIS, A.M. (perhaps, b. 1741, son of Rev. John Lewis of Rhoscoln, Isle of Anglesey; matric. Oriel Coll., Oxford, 2 Apr. 1759, a. 18; A.B., 1762); K.B., S.C., 1 Sept. 1768; came to S.C., 1768; sett. as Rector, St. John's Par. (Colleton) S.C., 1 Jan. 1769-1773; sett. Rector, St. Paul's Par. (Colleton) S.C., 1773-1784; preacher at the 22nd annual meeting of the clergy of S.C., 1770; prisoner as an American patriot, 27 Aug. 1780-May 1781; Ep.; d. St. Paul's Parish, S.C., 1784.

WILLIAM LIVINGSTON, b. Scotland or Ireland; sett. Charleston, S.C., Independent Chh., 1704-1720; Presb.; d. Charleston, S.C., after 1720.     ,

JOSEPH LORD, A.M. (See *C.C.N.E.*), Harvard Coll., 1691; ord. Dorchester, Mass., for S.C, 22 Oct. 1695; sett. Dorchester (Dorchester) S.C., Cong. Chh., 1695-1716; inst. Chatham, Mass., 15 June 1720; sett. Chatham, 1718-1748; Cong.; d. Chatham, Mass., 6 June 1748.

CHARLES LORIMER, sett. Wilton (Colleton) S.C., 1750-1752; sett. Charleston, S.C., Scotch Presb. Chh., 1750-Oct. 1754; sett. John's Island, S.C., (inst. 18 Apr. 1755), 1754-1764; Presb.; embarked for England, 8 July 1764.

SAMUEL FREDERIC LUCIUS, K.B., S.C., 9 Nov. 1769; came to S.C., 1770; sett. Cuffee Town (Edgefield) S.C., Chh. at Londonderry, 1770-1783; Ep.; refugee in Charleston, S.C., during the Rev.

RICHARD LUDLAM, A.M., K.B., S.C., 6 June 1723; came to S.C., 1723 as S.P.G. missionary; sett. St. James's Par. (Berkeley) at Goose Creek, S.C., 31 Aug. 1723-1728; left a bequest of £2,000. to the S.P.G.; Ep., d. Goose Creek, S.C., Oct. 1728.

JOHN McCALLISTER, sett. Walterborough (Colleton) S.C., Pon Pon Chh., 1737-1739; Presb.; d. Walterborough, S.C., 1738/9.

MR. McCLELAND, came from Northern Ireland; sett. Salem Chh., Sumter, S.C., 1759-1770; Presb.; d. Salem Church, S.C., 1770.

ROBERT McCLINTOCK, b. co. Antrim, Ireland, son of Timothy and Eleanor (Hamilton) McClintock; ed. in Scotland; came to America, 1772; supply, Pedee, Hopewell Chh., (Pedee) S.C., 1772-1775; ret. to Ireland, 1775; sett. Indian Creek, Concord and Rocky Spring, 1785-1796; Presb.; d. in S.C., soon after 5 June 1803.

WILLIAM McGILCHRIST, A.M. (See *C.C.N.E.*), b. 1711; matric. Balliol Coll., Oxford, 17 Dec. 1728, a. 17; ord. (Bsp. of Gloucester), 17 Aug. 1735; K.B., S.C., 2 Oct. 1741; sett. St. Philip's

Chh., as asst., Charleston, S.C., 1741-1745; ret. to England, 1745; Ep.; preacher, 14th visitation, 1744; d. Salem, Mass., 19 Apr. 1780, a. 73.

DAVID McKEY, ord. by the Presb. of Bangor, Ireland; sett. Williamsburg, S.C., 1769-1772; sett. Salem (Sumter Dist.), S.C., 1770-1770; Presb.; d. Salem, S.C., ca. 1772.

JOHN McLEOD (See *C.C.Ga.*), came from Isle of Skye, Scotland; ord. Edinburgh, Scotland, 13 Oct. 1735; sett. Edisto Island, S.C., 1741-1767; Presb.

JOHN MAITLAND, K.B., S.C., 15 Mar. 1707/8; came to S.C., 1708; sett. St. Paul's Par. (Colleton) S.C., 1708-1709; Ep.; d. St. Paul's Parish, S.C., 1709.

JOHN MALTBY, A.M., b. New Haven, Conn., 3 Apr. 1727, son of Capt. Wm. and Sarah (Davenport) Maltby; A.B., Yale Coll., 1747, A.M.; Tutor at Princeton, 1749-1752; A.M., Princeton; ord. Elizabethtown, N.J., 9 Apr. 1751; sett. Bermuda, 1752-1768; sett. Wilton (Colleton) S.C., inst. Dec. 1768-1771; Presb.; d. Hanover, N.H., 30 Sept. 1771, a. 44.

RICHARD MARSDEN (See *C.C.Md.*), Rector, St. Philip's Chh., Charleston, S.C., 1707-1708; sett. Christ Chh. Par. (Berkeley) S.C., 9 Aug. 1708-1709; Ep.

DANIEL MARSHALL (See *C.C.Ga.*), sett. Beaver Creek, S.C., 1760-1771; sett. Horse Creek, S.C. (about 15 miles north of Augusta, Ga.), 1760-1771; sett. Stephen's Creek, S.C., 1766-1772; Bapt.; d. Kioka Creek, Ga., 2 Nov. 1784, a. 78.

SAMUEL MARSHALL, A.M., sett. St. Philip's Chh., Charleston, S.C., 1696-1699; Registrar of the Colony of S.C., 1698-1699; Ep.; d. Charleston, S.C., 1699, of yellow fever.

EDWARD MARSTON, A.M., b. 1659, son of William Marston of Lawsen, co. Leicester; matric. Christ Chh. Coll., Oxford, 23 Apr. 1675, a. 16; A.B., Queen's Coll., Cambridge, 1678/9; K.B., S.C., 18 Sept. 1700; Rector, St. Philip's Chh., Charleston, S.C., 1700-1705; deprived, 1705; sett. Christ Chh. Par. (Berkeley) S.C., 1706-1708; Ep.; left S.C., 1712.

DAVID MARTIN, b. Conestoga, Pa., 8 Oct. 1737; came to S.C., 1754; ord. Beaver Creek, S.C., 28 Sept. 1770; sett. Beaver Creek, 1759-1775; Tunker Bapt. or Dunkard.

JOHN MARTIN, A.M. (See *C.C.Va.*), missionary to the Cherokee Indians, 1757-1759; sett. Wappetaw, S.C., Cong. Chh. at Wando Neck, 9 June 1757-1772; sett. Cainhoy, S.C., 1760-1770; sett. Wilton (Colleton) S.C., 1772-1774; Presb.; d. Wilton, S.C., June 1774.

JOHN NICHOLAS MARTIN (See *C.C.Ga.*), sett. Amelia (Orangeburg) S.C., 1750-1760; sett. Zion's and St. Michael's Chhs., Saluda River, S.C., 1750-1760; sett. Forks of the Saluda and Broad Rivers, S.C., 1750-1760; 1767-1774; sett. Charleston, S.C., St. John's Luth. Chh., 24 Nov. 1763-1767; 1774-1778; 1786-1787; Luth.; d. Charleston, S.C., 27 July 1795.

CHARLES MARTYN, A.B., b. 1725, son of Rev. Roger Martyn of Aylescomb, Devon; matric. Balliol Coll., Oxford, 10 Apr. 1742, a. 17; A.B., 1745; ord. (Bsp. of Exeter), 25 Sept. 1748; curate, Devonshire; K.B., S.C., 25 Sept. 1751; came to S.C., as S.P.G. missionary, 1752; sett. St. Andrew's Par., Ashley River, near Charleston, S.C., Mar. 1752-10 Apr. 1770; preacher at 7th and 11th annual meeting of the clergy of S.C., 1755, 1759; left S.C., 1770; sett. Octagon Chapel, Bath, Eng.; Ep.

ROBERT MAULE, A.B., b. Killebagh, co. Down, Ireland, 1681, son of the Rev. Robert Maule; sizar, Trinity Coll., Dublin, 4 July 1700, a. 19, A.B., 1703; K.B., North America, 20 Feb. 1706/7; came to S.C., 1707, as S.P.G. missionary; schoolmaster at Charleston, S.C.; sett. St. John's Par. (Berkeley) S.C., 1707-1717; bequeathed £750 to the S.P.G.; Ep.; d. St. John's Parish, S.C., 1716/7.

TIMOTHY MELLICHAMP, A.B., b. 1696, son of Richard Mellichamp, of Abdon, Salop; matric. Univ. Coll., Oxford, 9 Apr. 1715, a. 19; A.B., 1718; ord. (Bsp. of Salisbury), 21 Sept. 1729; lic. for S.C., 2 June 1732; K.B., S.C., 6 June 1732; S.P.G. missionary; sett. St. James's Par. (Berkeley) S.C., at Goose Creek, 25 Oct. 1732-1746; on sick leave, 1748-1748; sett. Colisbourne, Gloucestershire, Eng., 25 Mar. 1748; Ep.

FRANCIS MERRY, A.B., b. 1692, son of Thomas Merry of Coventry; matric. Balliol Coll., Oxford, 2 Mar. 1710/11, a. 19, A.B., 1714; K.B., S.C., 9 July 1721; came to S.C., 1720; sett. St. Helena's Par. (Beaufort) S.C., 1720-1720; sett. St. James's Par. (Berkeley) S.C., at Goose Creek, 1721-1722; left S.C., 1723; Ep.

ROBERT MILLER, lic. to preach, 7 Feb. 1755; schoolmaster; well advanced in years; sett. Waxhaw Chh. (Lancaster) S.C., and Fishing Creek Chh., at Richardson, S.C., 1755-1758; deposed at Charleston, S.C., 22 June 1758; Presb.

WILLIAM MILLER, A.M., came to S.C., 1772; sett. St. Bartholomew's Par. (Colleton) S.C., 16 Aug. 1772-1772; Ep.; d. St. Bartholomew's Parish, S.C., Oct. 1772.

MR. MOORE, sett. Edisto Island (Charleston) S.C., ca. 1723-1733; Presb.; d. Edisto Island, S.C., 1733.

CHARLES FREDERICK MOREAU, K.B., S.C., 16 Feb. 1773; sett. St. Helena's Par. (Beaufort) S.C., 14 June 1773-1776; sett. St. Philip's Chh., Charleston, 1780-1784; Hug.-Ep.; d. Charleston, S.C., 1784.

PHILIP MORRISON, sett. Charleston, S.C., Scotch Presb. Chh., inst. 19 Mar. 1757-1763; Presb.

THOMAS MORRITT, ord. (Bsp. of Winchester), 22 Feb. 1717/8; K.B., S.C., 18 Jan. 1722/3; S.P.G. missionary; schoolmaster at Charleston, S.C., 1723-1727; sett. Prince George's Parish, at Winyaw, S.C., 1728-1734; sett. Prince Frederick Parish, at Prince Frederick Town, S.C., 1734-1735; sett. Christ Chh. Par. (Berkeley). S.C., 1735-1736; Ep.; d. S.C., 1740.

PHILIP MULKY (See *C.C.N.C.*), sett. Broad River, S.C., Aug. 1760-1762; Fairforest, S.C., 13 Dec. 1762-1776; Lawson's Fork, S.C., 1772-1776; Cheraw Hill, S.C., 1782-1790; Bapt.; d. 1801.

THOMAS MURRAY, sett. John's Island (Charleston) S.C., 1740-1753; Presb.; d. John's Island, S.C., 15 Aug. 1753.

SAMUEL NEWMAN, came from Va.; ord. Bush River, S.C., Aug. 1771-1771; Bapt.; d. Bush River, S.C., Nov. 1771.

JOHN NEWTON (See *C.C.N.C.*), sett. Congaree, S.C., Feb. 1768-1768; Bapt.; d. Ga., 1791.

THOMAS NORRIS, b. N.C., 1743; ord. Bush River, S.C., 1771-1780; Bapt.; d. Bush River, S.C., 1780.

LAWRENCE O'NEILL, A.M., ord. (Archbsp. of Dublin), 16 Nov.1719; came to S.C., 1734; sett. Christ Chh. Par. (Berkeley) S.C., 2 June 1734-5 Feb. 1734/5; left S.C., 1735; Ep.

WILLIAM ORR, A.M. (See *C.C.Md.*), ord. (Bsp. of London), 29 Sept. 1736; K.B., S.C., 7 Oct. 1736; sett. St. Philip's Chh., Charleston, S.C., 20 Jan. 1736/7-1741; sett. St. Paul's Par. (Colleton) S.C., 1741-1744; sett. St. Helena's Par. (Beaufort) S.C., 1746-1747; sett. St. John's Par. (Colleton) S.C., May 1750-1755; preacher, 10th visitation, 1740; Ep.; d. St. Paul's Parish, S.C., 1755.

NATHANIEL OSBORNE, K.B., S.C., 24 Sept. 1712; came to S.C., 1713; sett. St. Bartholomew's Par. (Colleton) S.C., 1713-1715; escaped from Indians, 1715, to Charleston; Ep.; d. Port Royal, S.C., 13 July 1715.

JOHN OSGOOD, A.M., b. Dorchester, S.C.; A.B., Harvard Coll., 1733, A.M.; ord. Dorchester, S.C., 24 Mar. 1734/5-1752; sett. Midway (Liberty) Ga., 1752-1773; Cong.; d. Midway, Ga., 2 Aug. 1773.

WILLIAM PALMER, sett. Terrell's Bay, in Pedee Section, S.C., 1775-1775; Bapt.

THOMAS PANTING, A.M., b. Oxford, 1773, son of Dr. Matthew Panting; matric. Lincoln Coll., Oxford, 27 Jan. 1749/50, a. 17; A.B., Merton Coll., Oxford, 1753, A.M., 1765; came to S.C., 1769; headmaster of the Free School in Charleston, S.C., 1769-1770; sett. St. Andrew's Parish, Ashley River, S.C., 1770-1771; Ep.; d. St. Andrew's Parish, S.C., 23 Sept. 1771.

JAMES PARKER, b. Leicester, England; ord. London, ca. 1773; sett. Gravesend, Eng., 1733-1740; arriv. Charleston, S.C., 9 Nov. 1740; sett. Charleston, S.C., Independent Congregational, Brick or Circular Presb. Chh., 1 Jan. 1740/1-1742; Cong.-Presb.; d. Charleston, S.C., 6 July 1742, a. 37 (GS).

JOB PARKER, A.M., prob. came from Martha's Vineyard; A.B., Harvard Coll., 1729, A.M., 1732; sett. Wappetaw Chh., at Wando Neck (Christ Church Par.) S.C., 1733-1735; Arminian; Cong.; d. Wappetaw, S.C., 28 Oct. 1735.

CHARLES PATE, b. Bertie co., N.C., 1 May 1729; ord. Bear Creek (Dobbs) N.C., 7 Aug. 1769; sett. Beauty Spot Chh., S.C., 1768-1772; Bapt.; d. after 1790.

OFFSPRING PEARCE, A.M., Cambridge Univ.; curate, St. Paul's Chh., Shadwell, Eng.; K.B., S.C., 8 Oct. 1761; arriv. in S.C., Jan. 1762; sett. Prince George's Parish, at Winyaw, S.C., 1762-(inst. 22 June 1763)-24 June 1767; sett. St. George's Parish, Dorchester, S.C., 1767-1782; preacher at the 16th and 18th annual meetings of the clergy of S.C., 1764 and 1766; Ep.; d. St. George's Parish, Dorchester, S.C., 1782.

WILLIAM PEART, ord. before 1717; sett. Charleston, S.C., Bapt. Chh., 1717-1723; Bapt.; d. Charleston, S.C., 1723, *s.p.*

FRANCIS PELOT, A.M., b. Neuville, Switzerland, 11 Mar. 1720, son of Jean Pelot; A.M., Brown Univ., 1771; came to S.C., 28 Oct. 1734; ord. Ewhaw (Beaufort) S.C., 12 Jan. 1752; sett. Ewhaw Chh., 1746-1774; Bapt.; d. Ewhaw, S.C., 12 Nov. 1774.

WILLIAM PERCY, D.D., b. Bedworth, Warwickshire, England, 15 Sept. 1744, son of William Percy; matric. Edmund Hall, Oxford, 10 July 1767, a. 22; A.B.; D.D., Coll. of S.C., 1807; Pres. of Bethesda Coll., 1772; ord. 1767; curate at West Bromwich, Staffordshire, ca. 1773; sett. Charleston, S.C., 1773-1781, ret. to Eng., 1781; minister of Westminster Chapel, 1783-1798; minister of Queen's Square Chapel, 1798-1804; sett. St. Michael's Chh., Charleston, S.C., 1805-1809; sett. St. Philip's Chh., Charleston, S.C., 1805-1810; sett. St. Paul's Chh., Radcliffeborough, Charleston, S.C., 1810-1819; Ep.; d. London, Eng., 13 July 1819.

JAMES PIERCE, A.B., b. 1745, son of Caleb Pierce of Tiverton, Devon; matric. Balliol Coll., Oxford, 19 May 1763, a. 18; A.B., 1767; K.B., S.C., 12 Oct. 1769; came to S.C., 1769; sett. St. Helena's Par. (Beaufort) S.C., 1769-1771; Ep.; d. St. Helena's Parish, S.C., 1771.

BENJAMIN PIERPONT, A.M., b. Roxbury, Mass., 26 July 1668, son of John and Thankful (Stow) Pierpont; A.B., Harvard Coll., 1689, A.M.; sett. Independent-Cong.-Presb. Chh., Charleston, S.C., 1691-1698; Cong.; d. Charleston, S.C., 3 Jan. 1697/8, a. 29 y.

AARON PINSON, ord. ca. 1772; sett. Raeburn's Creek, S.C., 1772-1794; Bapt.; will dated 21 Feb. 1794.

WILLIAM PORTER, sett. Wappetaw Chh. at Wando Neck (Charleston) S.C., 1710-1733; Cong.; d. Wappetaw, S.C., 1733.

ALBERT POUDEROUS, b. France; a learned divine and convert form the Roman Catholic Chh.; became Fr. Hug. and Ep.; K.B., S.C., 9 Nov. 1720; came to S.C., 1720; sett. St. James's Parish, Santee, S.C., 1721-1731; d. St. James's Parish, Santee, S.C., 7 Feb. 1730/1.

BENJAMIN POWNALL, A.M., b. ca. 1690, son of William Pownall of Warford, Cheshire, Eng.; matric. Queen's Coll., Oxford, 25 Feb. 1705/6, a. 16; A.B., 1709, A.M., 1715; in Va., 1719; K.B., S.C., 4 July 1715; came to S.C., Nov. 1722, as S.P.G. missionary; sett. Christ Chh. Par. (Berkeley) S.C., 5 Dec. 1722-1722; resigned; Ep.; ret. to Eng., 1724.

ELIAS PRIOLEAU, b. Saintonge, France, son of Rev. Samuel

Prioleau; ed. at Univ. of Geneva; minister at Saintonge, Pons, France, 4 May 1683-1686; escaped, Apr. 1686; naturalized in England, 15 Apr. 1687; came to Charleston, S.C., 1687, and founded the Fr. Hug. Chh. there; sett. Charleston, S.C., 1687-1699; Hug.; will made at Charleston, 8 Feb. 1689/90; d. Black River, S.C., 1699.

EVAN PUGH, A.M., b. Matachin, Pa., 2 Apr. 1729; A.B., Brown U., 1802; lic. to preach at Euhaw, S.C., 5 June 1763; ord. Yadkin, 22 Nov. 1764; sett. Head of Yadkin, N.C., 1762-1765; sett. Welsh Neck Chh., Society Hill (Darlington) S.C., 4 Jan. 1766-26 Dec. 1766; Cashaway Neck Chh., at Mount Pleasant (Charleston) S.C., 1766-1802; sett. Muddy Creek Chh., Pedee region, S.C., 1769-1802; Bapt.; d. Black Creek, S.C., 2 Dec. 1802.

HENRY PURCELL, D.D., b. Herefordshire, Eng., 1742, son of George Purcell; matric. Wadham Coll., Oxford, 13 Dec. 1759, a. 17; A.B., Christ Chh. Coll., Oxford, 1763; D.D., Princeton; ord. (Bsp. of London), 25 Sept. 1768; sett. Great and Little Warley and Childerditch; Chaplain, Br. Army; K.B., S.C., 3 Apr. 1770; came to S.C., 1770; sett. (supply) St. George's Par. (Dorchester) S.C., 1770; sett. Rector, Christ Chh. Par. (Berkeley) S.C., 1775-1776; Rector, St. Michael's Chh., Charleston, S.C., 1783-1802; Chaplain, 2nd S.C. Regt., 1776; Dep. Judge Advocate Gen., S.C., 1778; Ep.; d. Charleston, S.C., 24 Mar. 1802.

ROBERT PURCELL, D.D., b. 1732, son of Rev. Robert Purcell of Bristol, England; matric. Wadham Coll., Oxford, 24 Oct. 1751, a. 19; Rector, Shipton-Mallet, Eng., 1761-1769; K.B., S.C., 1 Apr. 1769; came to S.C., 1769; sett. St. Philip's Chh., Charleston, S.C., 12 July 1769-1775; ret. to Shipton-Mallet, Eng., 1775, where he later died; Ep.

SAMUEL QUINCY, A.M. (See C.C.Ga.), sett. St. John's Par. (Colleton) S.C., 5 July 1742-1745; St. George's Par. (Dorchester) S.C., 1746-1747; asst., St. Philip's Chh., Charleston, S.C., 6 July 1747-1749; Ep.

JOHN RAE, b. 1716; ord. (Presb. of Dundee), 1742; arriv. S.C., Apr. 1743; sett. Williamsburg, S.C., Mar. 1743/4-1761; Presb.; d. Williamsburg, S.C. 1761, a. 45.

JOSEPH REESE, b. Duck Creek, Kent co., Del., 1736; came to S.C., 1745; ord. Congaree, S.C., Feb. 1768; sett. Congaree, 1760-1795; Bapt.; d. Congaree, S.C., 5 Mar. 1795, a. 63.

OLIVER REESE, A.B., Princeton, 1772; ord. Wilton (Colleton) S.C., 27 Mar. 1775-1775; Presb.; d. Wilton, S.C., 1776.

THOMAS REESE, D.D., b. Pa., 1742; A.B., Princeton, 1768; D.D., Princeton, 1794; sett. Mecklenburg, N.C., 1775; sett. Salem Chh., Sumter Dist., S.C., 1773-1792; sett. Old Stone Chh., Pendleton Dist. (Anderson) S.C., 1793-1796; Presb.; d. Pendelton Dist., S.C., 1796, a. 54.

JEREMIAH RHAME (See C.C.N.C.), sett. Little Pedee Chh., Catfish, near Latta (Dillon) S.C., 1752-1758 and 1772-1805; sett. Cashaway Neck, S.C., 1772-1805; Bapt.; d. S.C., 1805.

WILLIAM RICHARDSON, b. Egremont near Whitehaven, Eng., 1729; ed. Univ. of Glasgow; came to Philadelphia, Pa., 1750; missionary to the Cherokee Indians, 1750-1758; ord. Cumberland, Va., 18/25 July 1758; sett. Waxhaw Chh. (Lancaster) S.C., 1759-1771; Fishing Creek Chh., at Richardson, S.C., 1759-1771; Catholic Congregation, at Rocky Creek, S.C., 1759-1771; Presb.; d. Waxhaw (Lancaster) S.C., 20 July 1771, a. 42.

PIERRE ROBERT, son of Daniel and Marie Robert; ord. Basel, Switzerland, Huguenot Chh., 19 Dec. 1682; sett. Hug. Chh. at St. James's Santee, Jamestown, S.C., 1686-1710; Hug.-Ep.; d. St. James's Santee, S.C., ca. 1710.

STEPHEN ROE, A.M. (or Rowe) (See *C.C.N.E.*), ord. (Archbishop of Dublin), 5 June 1732; lic. for S.C., 19 Mar. 1736/7; K.B., S.C., 5 Apr. 1737; sett. St. George's Parish, Dorchester (Dorchester) S.C., 1737-1742; left S.C., 1742; preacher, 11th visitation, S.C., 1741; sett. Boston, Mass., King's Chapel, 1743-1744; Ep.

MR. ROSS, sett. Wilton (Colleton) S.C., 1741-1747; Presb.; d. Wilton, S.C., 1747.

JOHN ROWAN, K.B., N.C., 24 Sept. 1747; came to S.C., 1751; sett. St. Paul's Par. (Colleton) S.C., 1751-1753; in Va., 1754; sett. St. James's Parish, Santee, S.C., 1755-1757; left S.C., 1757; Ep.

JAMES RYMER, b. St. Andrew's, Scotland; arriv. S.C., 24 Jan. 1753; inst. Walterborough (Colleton) S.C., Chh. at Pon Pon, 14 Feb. 1754-1755; Presb. d. Walterborough, S.C., 8 July 1755.

RICHARD SAINT JOHN, A.B., pens., Trinity Coll., Dublin, 2 July 1736; A.B., 1740; K.B., Bahamas, 1 Oct. 1745; sett. New Providence, Bahamas, 1746-1747; came to S.C., 1747; sett. St. Helena's Par. (Beaufort) S.C., 7 Dec. 1747-1750; left S.C., 1750; Ep. and S.P.G. missionary.

MR. SANFORD, sett. Charleston, S.C., 1st Bapt. Chh., 1706-1717; Bapt.; d. Charleston, S.C.

PETER SCHMIDT, converted Jacob Weber to his views, May 1756; sett. Saluda Forks, at Youngineer's Ferry, S.C., 1760-1761; Weberite; Peter Schimdt personified Christ in this cult. (See Jacob Weber).

GEORGE SCHULIUS, arriv. Savannah, Ga., 15 Oct. 1738; sett. Purysburg (Beaufort) S.C., 1738-1739; Moravian; d. Purysburg, S.C., 4 Aug. 1739.

JOHN CHRISTOPHER ERNEST SCHWAB, b. Franconia, Germany; K.B., S.C., 11 June 1771; came to S.C., 1771; sett. St. Andrew's Parish, Ashley River, S.C., 25 Nov. 1771-1773; Ep.; d. St. Andrew's Parish, S.C., 5 July 1773.

WILLIAM SCREVEN (See *C.C.N.E.*), sett. Charleston, S.C., Bapt. Chh., 1696-1713; Bapt.; d. Georgetown, S.C., 10 Oct. 1713, a. 84.

WINWOOD SERJEANT (See *C.C.N.E.*), K.B., S.C., 1 Feb. 1757; came to S.C., 1757; sett. St. Philip's Chh., Charleston, S.C., 1759-25 Nov. 1759; sett. Christ Chh. Par. (Berkeley) S.C., 1759-

1759; sett. St. George's Par. (Dorchester) S.C., 1760-1767; preacher 14th annual meeting of the clergy of S.C., 1762; Ep.; d. Bath. Eng., 20 Sept. 1780.

CAPTAIN ISRAEL SEYMORE, sett. Broad River, S.C., ca. 1757-1759; captain of a vessel; joined the army; 7th Day Bapt.

THOMAS SIMMONS, b. England; ord. Philadelphia, Pa.; sett. Charleston, S.C., Bapt. Chh., 20 Mar. 1725-1749; Bapt.; d. Charleston, S.C., 31 Jan. 1749.

ARCHIBALD SIMPSON, b. Glasgow, Scotland, 1 Mar. 1734/5, son of William and Susanna (Gardner) Simpson; adm. Univ. of Glasgow, 1748; came to S.C., 6 Mar. 1753; ord. Wilton (Colleton) S.C., 2 Apr. 1755; sett. Wilton, S.C., 1754-1756; sett. Stoney Creek, S.C., 16 June 1756-1772; sett. Beaufort, S.C., 1756-1772; sett. Salt Ketcher (Colleton) S.C., 1766-1772; ret. to Scotland, June 1772; sett. Port Glasgow, Scotland, 1774; Presb.

JOHN SIMPSON, A.M., b. N.J., 1740; A.B., Princeton, 1763, A.M.; lic. 1770; ord. Poplar Tent, N.C., 6 Apr. 1774; sett. Fishing Creek, S.C., at Richardson, 1772-1774; sett. Bethesda, S.C., 1774-1775; Presb.; d. 1808.

GEORGE SKEENE, A.M., ord. (Bsp. of Peterborough), 22 Nov. 1761; K.B., S.C., 17 Dec. 1762; came to S.C., 1762; sett. Prince Frederick Parish, at Prince Frederick Town, S.C., 1762-1766; Ep.; d. Prince Frederick Parish, S.C., 1766.

ROBERT SMALL, A.M., ord. (Bsp. of London), 16 Apr. 1738; lic. for S.C., 15 May 1738; K.B., S.C., 21 June 1738; arriv. S.C., Oct. 1738; S.P.G. missionary; sett. Christ Chh. Par. (Berkeley) S.C., 1738-1739; Ep.; d. Christ Church Parish, S.C., 28 Sept. 1739.

JAMES SMART (See C.C.N.C.), sett. Lynches Creek, S.C., 1755-1759; sett. Coosawhatchie (Jasper) S.C., 1759-1788; Bapt.; d. Coosawhatchie, S.C., 1788.

HEZEKIAH SMITH, D.D. (See C.C.N.E.), ord. Cashaway Neck, at Mount Pleasant, S.C., Pedee Chh., 1763-1765; sett. N.E., 1766-1805; Bapt.

JOSIAH SMITH, A.M., b. Charleston, S.C., 25 Dec. 1704, son of Dr. George and Dorothy (Archar) Smith, and grandson of Landgave Thomas Smith; A.B., Harvard Coll., 1725, A.M.; ord. Boston, Mass., 11 July 1726, for Bermuda; sett. Cainhoy, S.C., 1728-14 May 1734; sett. Charleston, S.C., Independent Chh., 14 May 1734-1749, became sole minister, 21 Nov. 1742; was stricken with paralysis, 1749; published 25 works; Cong.; d. Philadelphia, Pa., 19 Oct. 1781.

MICHAEL SMITH, A.M., b. co. Meath, Ireland, 1698, son of Rev. Robert Smith; pens. Trinity Coll., Dublin, 22 Dec. 1713, a. 15, A.B., A.M.; ord. (Bsp. of London), 1747; curate in Hertfordshire, 5 yrs.; came to S.C., 1753; sett. Prince Frederick Parish, Prince Frederick Town, S.C., 1753-1756; sett. Prince George's Parish, at Winyaw, S.C., 1753-1756; left S.C., 1756; sett. St. James's Parish, Wilmington (New Hanover) N.C., 1759-1760; Ep.

BISHOP ROBERT SMITH, D.D., b. Norfolk, England, 25

Aug. 1732; A.B., Gonville & Caius Coll., Cambridge, 1753, A.M.; D.D., Univ. of Pa., 1789; ord. (Bsp. of Ely), 21 Dec. 1756; came to S.C., 1757; sett. St. Philip's Chh., Charleston, S.C., 3 Nov. 1757-1780; 1783-1801; was in England, 1768-1770; K.B., S.C., 12 Oct. 1769; sett. St. Paul's Parish (Queen Anne's) Md., 1780-1783; preacher at 13th annual meeting of the clergy of S.C., 1761; president of Charleston Coll., 1783-1798; Bishop of S.C., 1795-1801.; d. Charleston, S.C., 28 Oct. 1801, a. 70.

GEORGE SOELLE, received a college education; arriv. N.Y.C., 9 Sept. 1753; sett. York, Pa., 1756-1757; sett. Staten Island, N.Y., 1761-1762; sett. Amelia (Orangeburg) S.C., 1773-1773; Moravian; ord. a Lutheran minister in Denmark, 1741; sett. Lows' Luth. Chh (Guilford) N.C., ca. 1762-1769; became a Moravian, ca. 1769-1771.

DAVID STANDISH, A.M., K.B., S.C., 5 Aug. 1724; came to S.C., 1724, as S.P.G. missionary; sett. St. Paul's Par. (Colleton) S.C., 1724-1728; Ep.; d. St. Paul's Parish, S.C., Spring of 1728.

JOHN STEPHENS, b. Staten Island, N.Y.; ord. Oyster Bay, L.I., N.Y., 1747; sett. Horse Neck, Conn., 1747-1750; sett. N.Y.C., 1747-1750; sett. Ashley River, S.C., 22 June 1750-1769; left for drunkenness; Bapt.; d. Black River, S.C., 1785.

HUGH STEWART, sett. Charleston, S.C., Scotch Presb. Chh., 1731-1739; sett. Walterborough (Colleton) Pon Pon Chh., Aug. 1739-1748; Presb.; d. Walterborough, S.C., ca. 1748.

SAMUEL STILLMAN, D.D. (See C.C.N.E.), ord. Charleston, S.C., 26 Feb. 1759; sett. James Island, S.C., 1759-1761; sett. Bordentown, N.J., 1762-1763; Bapt.; d. Boston, 1807.

ARCHIBALD STOBO, A.B., b. Scotland; A.B., Edinburgh U., 25 June 1697; ord. 1699; came to Charleston, S.C., 3 Sept. 1700; sett. Charleston, S.C., Independent Chh., Sept. 1700-1704; Wilton (Colleton) S.C., 1704-9 Sept. 1739; Walterborough, Pon Pon Chh., 1728-1737. On 1 June 1710 there were "five churches of British Presbyterians" in S.C.: viz. Wilton, James Island, Cainhoy, John's Island and Edisto.; Presb.; d. Wilton, S.C., shortly before 15 Oct. 1741 (will proved 28 Nov. 1741).

ROBERT STONE, A.B., b. 1720, son of Robert Stone of Taunton Dean, Esq.; matric. Hart Hall, Oxford, 8 May 1739, a. 19; A.B., Hertford Coll., 11 Feb. 1742/3; sett. St. James's Par. (Berkeley) S.C., at Goose Creek, June 1748-1751; S.P.G. missionary; preacher, 3rd annual meeting of the clergy of S.C., 1751; Ep.; d. Goose Creek, S.C., 21 Oct. 1751, bur. Charleston.

PIERRE STOUPPE, A.M., b. France, 1690; A.B., U. of Geneva, Switzerland, A.M.; sett. Hug. Chh., Charleston, S.C., 1722-1723; ord. London, England, 25 Dec. 1723; K.B., N.Y., 15 Feb. 1723/4; sett. New Rochelle, N.Y., Trinity Chh., 20 July 1724-1760; Fr. Ref.-Ep.; d. New Rochelle, N.Y., July 1760.

JAMES STUART, lic. for Va., 21 Sept. 1766; K.B., Va., 2 Oct. 1766; S.P.G. missionary in N.C., 1767-1768; came to S.C., 1772;

sett. Prince George's Parish at Winyaw, S.C., 1772-10 Nov. 1777; left S.C., 1777; Ep.

EBENEZER TAYLOR (See *C.C.N.C.*), came to S.C., 1711; K.B., S.C., 13 Nov. 1711; S.P.G. missionary; sett. St. Andrew's Parish, Ashley River, S.C., 1711-1717; left S.C., 1717; Ep.

WILLIAM TENNENT III, A.M. (See *C.C.N.E.*), sett. Independent Chh., Charleston, S.C., 1772-1777; member, S.C. Provincial Congress; Presb.-Cong.; d. High Hills of Santee, S.C., 11 Aug. 1777, a. 36.

JEAN PIERRE TETRARD (See *C.C.N.Y.*), b. Switzerland, 1722; sett. Hug. Chh., Charleston, S.C., 1753-1764; sett. N.Y. state, 1764-1787; d. 1787.

CHRISTIAN THEUS, b. Switzerland; ord. (Presb.), 1739; sett. Saxe-Gotha (Lexington) S.C., both Germ.-Ref. and Luth. Chhs., 1739-1789; Germ. Ref.; d. (bur. near Columbia, S.C.), ca. 1789.

JOHN THOMAS, b. Wales, 1746; ord. Charleston, S.C., Independent Chh., 7 June 1767-1771; Presb.; d. N.Y.C., N.Y., 29 Sept. 1771, a. 25.

SAMUEL THOMAS, of Ballydon, Sudbury; K.B., N.C., 11 Aug. 1702; 1st S.P.G. missionary in S.C., 1702; sett. Cooper River, S.C., June 1702-1706; sett. St. James's Par. (Berkeley) S.C., at Goose Creek, 1702-1706; Ep.; d. Goose Creek, S.C., Oct. 1706.

THOMAS THOMSON, A.M. (See *C.C.Va.*), Fellow, Christ Coll., Cambridge, A.M.; ord. (Bsp. of Litchfield), 15 Nov. 1730; sett. St. Bartholomew's Par. (Colleton) S.C., 1734-1744; sett. St. George's Parish, Dorchester (Dorchester) S.C., 1744-1746; ret. to Eng., 1746-1748; sett. St. John's Parish (Colleton) S.C., Sept. 1748-1750; sett. Chester, Pa., 1750-1758; sett. Concord, Pa., 1750-1756; sett. Antrim Parish (Halifax) Va., 1762-1763, as an aged man; Ep.

WILLIAM TILLEY, b. Salisbury, Eng., 1699; ord. Charleston, S.C., Bapt. Chh., 1731-1744; sett. Edisto Island, S.C., 1731-1744; Bapt.; d. Edisto Island, S.C., 14 Apr. 1744, a. 45.

· JOHN JAMES TISSOT, ord. (Bsp. of St. David's), 20 Aug. 1729; K.B., S.C., 5 Aug. 1729; came to S.C., 1730; sett. St. Dennis's Parish, Orange Quarter (Berkeley) S.C., 1730-1763; Hug.-Ep.; d. Orange Quarter, S.C., 3 July 1763.

JOHN TONGE, A.M., b. St. Peter's, Oxford, Eng., 1729, son of William Tonge; matric. Hertford Coll., Oxford, 17 Dec. 1746, a. 17; A.B., 1750; A.M., 1753; came to S.C., 1759; sett. St. Paul's Par. (Colleton) S.C., 1759-1773; Ep.; d. St. Paul's Parish (Colleton) S.C., 1773.

LAURENT PHILIPPE TROUILLARD, b. La Ferté-au-Vidame, France, son of the Rev. Pierre and Marie Trouillard (his father was Professor of Theology and minister of the French Prot. Chh. in Canterbury) came to S.C., 1686; sett. French Reformed Chh. at Goose Creek (Berkeley) S.C., 1686-1712; sett. Hug. Chh., Charleston, S.C., 1686-1699; sett. St. Dennis's Par., Orange Quarter (Berkeley) S.C., 1700-1712; sett. St. John's Par. (Berkeley) S.C., 1699-1712; sett. Western Branch of Cooper River (which later became St. John's Par. (Colleton) S.C., Ep.), 1699-1712; Hug.; d. Orange Quarter, S.C., 1712.

MR. TURNBULL, sett. John's Island (Charleston) S.C., 1710-1737; Presb.; d. John's Island, S.C., 1737 (bur. 27 Oct.).

PAUL TURQUAND, b. London, Eng., 1735, of French ancestry; ord. 1761; sett. St. Matthew's Par. (Berkeley) S.C., 28 Apr. 1768-1786; sett. Orangeburg, S.C., St. Matthew's Chh., Lutheran, 1768-1786; Luth.-Ep.; d. St. Matthew's Parish, S.C., 18 Sept. 1786.

PETER TUSTIAN, A.M., b. Warwickshire, Eng., 1696, son of Peter Tustian of Hardwick; matric. Christ Coll., Oxford, 5 May 1710, a. 14; A.B., 18 Feb. 1713/4, A.M.; K.B., S.C., 4 Nov. 1719; came to S.C., 1719, as S.P.G. missionary; sett. St. George's Parish, Dorchester (Dorchester) S.C., 1719-1721; sett. St. James's Par. (Anne Arundel) Md., 1721-1736; Ep.

JOHANNES FREDERICUS VAN HANNOVER, minister at Santee, S.C., 1755; Germ. Ref.; only mention.

FRANCIS VARAMBANT, b. 1699; sett. Charleston, S.C., Hug. Chh., 1742-1753 (and perhaps later); Hug.; d. Charleston, S.C., Sept. 1767, a. 68.

FRANCIS VERNOD, ord. (Bsp. of London), 25 July 1723; K.B., S.C., 7 Aug. 1723; came to S.C., 1723 as S.P.G. missionary; sett. St. George's Parish, Dorchester (Dorchester) S.C., 1723-1736; "a foreigner," naturalized 23 Feb. 1733; Ep.; d. St. George's Parish (Berkeley) S.C., 1736.

JOHN VILETTE, K.B., Ga., 25 Sept. 1771; arriv. S.C., 1772; sett. Prince Frederick Parish, at Prince Frederick Town, S.C., 1772 ff.; Ep.

JEPTHA VINING, b. Sutton, Mass., 15 Feb. 1738; sett. Lynches Creek, S.C., 1772-1775; Upper Falls of Lynches Creek, S.C., 1772-1775; sett. Rocky Comfort Creek, Ga., 1780-1792; sett. Long Creek Chh., Ga., 1780-1792; Bapt.

NATHANIEL WALKER, came from Eng. or Ireland; sett. Lynches Creek, S.C., 1772-1775; sett. Edisto, S.C., 1786-1798; Bapt.; d. Edisto, S.C., Nov. 1798.

THOMAS WALKER, K.B., S.C., 28 Feb. 1772; came to S.C., 1772; sett. St. Mark's Parish, S.C., 1772-1773; Ep.; left S.C., 1773.

JOHN WARDEN, A.M., came to S.C., 1725; sett. Christ Chh. Par. (Berkeley) S.C., 15 Aug. 1725-1726; Ep.; d. Christ Church Parish, S.C., 1726.

SAMUEL FENNER WARREN, A.M., b. 14 Dec. 1728, son of Rev. Richard Warren, Rector of Cavendish, Suffolk, Eng.; Trinity Hall Cambridge; ord. (Bsp. of Peterborough), 17 June 1753; curate, South Colingham, Notts.; and Eastey, Kent, Eng.; lic. for S.C., 12 Jan. 1758; K.B., S.C., 18 Jan. 1758; sett. St. James's Parish, Santee, S.C., 4 June 1758-Jan. 1789; Ep.; d. St. James's Parish, Santee, S.C., 3 Mar. 1789.

HENRY BURCHER GABRIEL WARTMANN, arriv. America, 1753; sett. Reading, Pa., 1753-1753; sett. Muhlenberg (Berks) Pa., 1753-1753; sett. Trinity Chh., Lancaster (Lancaster) Pa., 1753-1753; sett. Savannah, Ga., 1760-1761; sett. Charleston, S.C., Lutheran Chh., 1761-1763; Luth.

JACOB WEBER, b. Stifferschweil, Zurich, Switzerland; converted by Peter Schmidt, May 1756; sett. Saluda Fork, S.C., Weberite Chh. at Youngeneer's Ferry. Jacob Weber personified God; Peter Schmidt was Christ; the wife of Weber was the Virgin Mary; two others personified the Holy Spirit and Satan. The congregation turned on Satan and killed him. Weber was hung for murder soon after 16 Apr. 1761.

DANIEL WHEELER, b. Calne, Wilts., Eng., 1706; ord. Lindherst, Hampshire, Eng.; came to Charleston, S.C., 1757; sett. Stono, S.C., 25 Nov. 1757-1767; Bapt.; d. Charleston, S.C., Nov. 1767, a. 61.

MR. WHITE, sett. Charleston, S.C., Bapt. Chh., 1706-1717; Bapt.

JOHN WHITEHEAD (possibly b. 1682, son of William Whitehead of Little Dawley, Salop; matric. Pembroke Coll., Oxford, 26 Feb. 1700/1, a. 19; A.B., 28 Feb. 1704/5); K.B., S.C., 30 Apr. 1714; sett. Charleston, S.C., S.P.G. catechist and asst., St. Philip's Chh., 1714-1716; Ep.; d. Charleston, S.C., 8 Nov. 1716.

ATKIN WILKINSON, sett. St. Philip's Chh., Charleston, S.C., 14 Jan. 1680/1-1 Mar. 1710/11; Ep.; d. after 1711.

ROBERT WILLIAMS, b. Northampton, N.C., 20 Dec. 1717; ord. Welsh Neck, Society Hill (Chesterfield-Darlington) S.C., 30 Sept. 1752-1759; Bapt.; d. Welsh Neck, S.C., 8 Apr. 1768.

JOSEPH DACRE APPLEBY WILTON, A.M., b. 1730, son of the Rev. Anthony Wilton of Kirk Levington, Cumberland; matric. St. Alban's Hall, Oxford, 6 May 1761, a. 27; K.B., S.C., 28 Oct. 1761; curate, Greenwich Chapel, Eng.; sett. St. Philip's Chh., Charleston, S.C., (ass't.), 9 Jan. 1762-1767; Ep.; d. Charleston, S.C., 6 Oct. 1767, a. 37.

ELHANAN WINCHESTER (See C.C.N.E.), sett. Welsh Neck, Society Hill, S.C., 1775-1779; Bapt.—later Universalist.

JOHN WINTELEY, A.M. (poss. b. 1688, son of Rev. John Winteley of Tunbridge, Kent; matric. All Soul's Coll., Oxford, 18 Apr. 1706, a. 18; A.B., 1710); K.B., S.C., 3 Aug. 1726; arriv. S.C., 1 Mar. 1726/7; sett. Christ Chh. Par. (Berkeley) S.C., 5 Mar. 1726/7-1 Jan. 1728/9; Ep.; left S.C., 1729.

JOHN WITHERSPOON, b. Glasgow, Scotland; sett. co. Down, Ireland; sett. James Island, S.C., 1710-1734; Presb.; d. James Island, S.C., 14 Aug. 1734.

ALEXANDER WOODS, A.M., came to S.C., 1707, as S.P.G. missionary; K.B., S.C., 6 June 1707; sett. St. Andrew's Parish, Ashley River, S.C., 1707-1708; Ep.; d. St. Andrew's Parish, S.C., 1708.

WILLIAM WOOD, sett. Enoree, S.C., 1772 and ff.; Bapt.

CHARLES WOODMASON, ord. England, 1766; K.B., S.C.,

as S.P.G. missionary, 1 May 1766; sett. St. Mark's Parish, S.C., 1766-1770; Ep.; went to Md., 1770.

BARTHOLOMEW ZAUBERBUEHLER, Sr., b. Herisau, Appenzell, Switzerland, 7 Apr. 1678, son of Rev. Bartholomew Zauberbuehler; matric. Marburg Univ., 2 June 1714; ord. 1700; chaplain and minister at Trogen, Switz.; sett. at Grub, 1704; and at Appenzell, 27 Mar. 1726; came to S.C., 1736; arriv. 2nd time at Charleston, Feb. 1737; sett. Purysburg (Jasper) S.C., 22 May 1738-1738; Germ.Ref.; attempted to get Ep. ord. without success; d. Purysburg (Jasper) S.C., 1738.

BARTHOLOMEW ZAUBERBUEHLER, Jr. (See *C.C.Ga.*), sett. Londonderry (Abbeville) S.C., St. George's Chh. at Hard Labor Creek, 1752-1766; Germ.Ref.-Luth.-Ep.; preached in German, French and English.

JOHN JOACHIM ZUBLY, D.D. (See *C.C.Ga.*), b. St. Gall, Switzerland, 27 Aug. 1724; D.D., Princeton, 1774; ord. Germ.Ref. Chh., London, Eng., 19 Aug. 1744; sett. St. John's Chh., Germ.Ref. at Amelia (Orangeburg) S.C., 1747-1749; St. Matthew's Chh., Luth. at Amelia, 1747-1749; Purysburg (Jasper) S.C., Germ.Ref. Chh., 1744-1748; Cainhoy, S.C., Presb. Chh., 1748-1757; Charleston, S.C., St. John's Chh., Germ.Ref., 1749-27 Jan. 1759; Wappetaw, S.C., Cong. Chh. at Wando Neck, 1753-1759; Savannah, Ga., 1760-1778; patriot; Germ.Ref. but also preached in Luth., Cong., Presb. and Ep. churches as noted above; d. Savannah, Ga., 26 Aug. 1781.

\* \* \* \* \*

Summary: Baptists, 51; Congregationalists, 12; Episcopalians, 127; German Reformed, 5; Huguenots (French Reformed), 11; Lutherans, 6; Moravians, 3; Presbyterians, 59; Weberites, 2. Total: 276.

1678 Accomack (Accomac).
Accomac Shore, see Pongey (1678).
1755 Amelia (Amelia).
1678 Annamesia (Accomac).
Banister, see Halifax (1755).
1698 Barbican (Nansemond).
1766 Bear Garden (Hampshire) W.Va.
1762 Bennett's Creek (Nansemond).
1699 Black Creek (New Kent).
1760 Black Creek (Southampton).
1705 Blackwater (Surry).
1770 Botts (Nottoway).
1718 Burleigh (Prince George).
1755 Bush Creek (Fairfax).
Buskins, see South Branch (1678).
1774 Camp Creek (Louisa).
1738 Caroline (Caroline).
1721 Cedar Creek (Hanover).
1660 Chuckatuck (Isle of Wight).
1759 Crooked Run (Warren).
1672 Curles (Henrico).
1757 Dan (Halifax).
1700 Denbigh (James City).
Douglas, see Orange (1748).
1723 Dover (Goochland).
1698 Edward Thomas's (York).
1735 Fairfax (Loudoun).
Fawcett's, see Crooked Run (1759).
Fawcett's, see Mt. Pleasant (1771).
1730 Fork Creek (Louisa).
1760 Gap (Louisa).
1755 Genito (Goochland).
1756 Goose Creek (Loudoun).

1751 Gravelly Run (Dinwiddie).
1741 Green Spring (Louisa).
17— Green Spring (James City).
1755 Halifax (Halifax).
1698 Hicquotan (Elizabeth City).
1734 Hopewell (Clarke).
1701 Howard's (Charles City).
1706 John Crews (Charles City).
1762 Johnson's (Isle of Wight).
Johnson's, see Amelia (1755).
Kirby's, see Dan (1757).
1708 Ladd's (Charles City).
1755 Langley's (Dinwiddie).
1698 Lawne's Creek (Surry).
1657 Massawadox (Northampton).
1699 Merchant's Hope (Prince George).
1761 Mill Creek (Jefferson) W.Va.
1771 Mount Pleasant (Clarke).
1680 Muddy Creek (Accomac).
1710 Murdaugh's (Norfolk).
Nusswattocks, see Massawadox (1657).
1668 Occahannock (Accomac).
1754 Old Goose Creek (Roanoke).
1748 Orange (Orange).
1663 Pagan Creek (Isle of Wight).
1766 Pattison's (Amelia).
1738 Perquimans (New Kent).
1768 Picquinocque (Henrico).
1678 Pocomoke Bay (Accomac).
1678 Pongey (Accomac).

1698 Poscin (Elizabeth City).
Potts, see Gap (1760).
Providence, see Tuscarora (1735).
Queen's Creek, see Ed. Thomas's (1698).
Salem Turnpike, see Old Goose Creek (1754).
1758 Seacock (Sussex).
Sedley, see Black Creek (1760).
1698 Skimino (York).
1738 Smith's Creek (Shenandoah).
1672 Somerton (Nansemond).
1678 South Branch (Nansemond).
1769 South Fork (Loudoun).
1754 South River (Campbell).
1738 Stanton's (Sussex).
1744 Sugar Loaf (Orange).

1700 Surry (Surry).
Sussex, see Seacock (1758).
Swamp, see The Swamp (1719).
1698 Terrascoe Neck (Isle of Wight).
1719 The Swamp (New Kent).
1735 Tuscarora (Berkeley) W. Va.
1762 Vicks (Southampton).
1703 Warwick (James City).
Waterford, see Fairfax (1735).
1679 Western Branch (Nansemond).
1714 Weyanoke (Charles City).
1759 Whipanock (Dinwiddie).
1722 White Oak Swamp (Henrico).

## FRIENDS MEETINGS IN NORTH CAROLINA
### 1680-1776

1751 Cane Creek (Alamance).
1773 Center (Guilford).
1772 Contentnea (Wayne).
1733 Core Creek (Carteret).
1748 Falling Creek (Johnston).
1754 New Garden (Guilford).
1698 Pasquotank (Pasquotank).
1680 Perquimans (Perquimans).

Piney Creek, see Perquimans (1680).
1760 Rich Square (Northampton).
1773 Spring (Alamance).
1736 Sutton's Creek.
Symons Creek, see Pasquotank (1698).
1760 Tar River (Granville).
1764 Wells.

## MEETINGS FOUNDED IN 1770 OR EARLIER
### Dates unknown

Clubs Foot (Craven), Little River (Pasquotank), Newbegun Creek (Pasquotank), Old Neck (Pasquotank), The Narrows (Pasquotank), Trueblood's (Pasquotank), Upper and Lower Trent (Jones) and Vosses Creek.

# FRIENDS MEETINGS IN SOUTH CAROLINA
## 1718-1776

1770   Bush River (Newberry).    1774   Padget's (Union).
1775   Cane Creek (Union).             Wateree, see Freder-
1718   Charleston (Charleston).       icksburg (1770).
1750   Fredericksburg (Ker-
        shaw).


# FRIENDS MEETING IN GEORGIA

1773   Wrightsboro (McDuffie).

\*     \*     \*     \*

Summary: Virginia, 74; North Carolina, 21; South Carolina, 5; Georgia, 1. Total: 101.

# ADDENDA TO THE COLONIAL CLERGY OF MARYLAND, 1629-1776.

COMMISSIONER THOMAS BRAY, D.D., b. Marton, Shropshire, England, 1656, son of Richard Bray; matric. All Soul's Coll., Oxford, 12 Mar. 1674/5, a. 17; A.B., 1678; A.M., Hart Hall, Oxford, 1693; B.D., Magdalen Hall, Oxford, 1696; D.D., 1696; sett. as Curate, Bridgenorth, Salop; Vicar, Over Whitacre; Rector, Sheldon, Warwickshire, 1690-1696; Commissioner for the Bishop of London in Maryland, 1692, 1700-1701; originator of the Society for Promoting Christian Knowledge, 1699; Vicar, St. Botolph's Without Aldgate, London, 1706-1730; Ep.; d. London, England, 15 Feb. 1729/30, a. 73.

JASPER DANKAERTS (or Dankers); came to America, 1679, to find a place for settlement; chose Bohemia Manor, Md., and returned to Holland, 1680; arriv. N.Y.C., 27 July 1683; sett. Bohemia Manor, Md., 1684; Labadist; d. Bohemia Manor, Md.

EDWARD LARRAMORE, sett. South Sassafras Par. (Cecil) Md., 1712-1713; Ep.; d. South Sassafras Parish, Md., 1713.

ROBERT MADDOX, sett. Wicomico and Manokin (Somerset) Md., Nov. 1671-Mar. 1674/5; Presb.

SAMUEL McMASTER, grad. Newark Academy; lic. 26 Mar. 1776; ord. 20 Apr. 1779; sett. Snow Hill, Del., 1774-1811; sett. Pitt's Creek, Del., 1774-1811; sett. Rehoboth, Md., 1774-1811; Presb.; d. 1811.

JOHN MYERS, sett. St. Anne's, Annapolis, Md., 18 Apr. 1754-1755; Ep.

DAVID RICHARDSON, sett. Somerset co., Md., 9 Nov. 1679-1689; "clerk, minister of the Gospel, etc." in deeds; d. Somerset co., Md., 1696.

NATHANIEL WHITAKER, A.M., b. Cambridge, Mass., 4 Dec. 1707, son of Nathaniel and Hannah Whitaker; A.B., Harvard Coll., 1730, A.M.; ord. (by Bishop of St. David's), 1740; inducted, St. Margaret's Parish, Westminster (Anne Arundel) Md., 7 May 1743-11 July 1748; Rector, Coventry Parish (Somerset and Worcester) Md., 1748-1766; Ep.; d. Coventry Parish, Md., 3 Nov. 1766.

# ADDENDA TO THE COLONIAL CLERGY OF
## GEORGIA, 1733-1776

JONATHAN BARBER, A.M. (See *C.C.N.E.*), Yale College, 1730; superintendent and chaplain at the Orphan House, Bethesda, Ga., 1740-1747; Cong.; Presb.; d. Groton, Conn., 8 Oct. 1783, a. 71.

JOHN BOEHNER, came from Krumberg, Bohemia; arriv. Savannah, Ga., 20 Feb. 1736; sett. Savannah, Ga., 1736-1740; sett. Nazareth, Pa., 1740-1742; sett. as a missionary in the West Indies, 1742-1785; visited Bethlehem, Pa., 1754; Moravian; d. St. Thomas, W.I., 1785.

GABRIEL FALK (See *C.C.Pa.*); Swedish Luth.

BENJAMIN INGRAHAM, A.B. (or Ingram), b. 1712, son of William Ingram of Dewsbury, Yorks.; matric. Queen's Coll., Oxford, 13 Nov. 1730, a. 18; A.B., 1734; arriv. Savannah, Ga., 6 Feb. 1735/6; assigned to Frederica, Ga., Aug. 1736-1737; returned to England and became a Methodist under John Wesley; m. 1741, Lady Margaret Hastings, dau. of Theophilus, 7th Earl of Huntingdon; Ep.-Meth.

JOHN FRANCIS REGNIER, came from Pa. to Ga., sett. Savannah, Ga., 1735-1738; sett. as a missionary at Surinam, W.I.; Moravian; broke with the church after his return to Pa.

GEORGE WHITEFIELD, A.M. (See *C.C.N.E.*), ord. Gloucester, England, 20 June 1736; ord. priest, Oxford, Jan. 1739; sailed for Ga., Dec. 1737, and Charleston, S.C., ret. to England, Aug. 1738; arriv. again at Philadelphia, Pa., Nov. 1739; dedicated the Orphan House at Bethesda, near Savannah, Ga., 25 Mar. 1740; preached in all the colonies; ret. to London, Mar. 1741; ret. to America, Aug. 1744; landed at York, Me.; arrived again at Savannah, Ga., Oct. 1751; ret. to London, Apr. 1752; arriv. at Beaufort, S.C., 27 May 1754; ret. to England, 1755; came again, 1763-1765; returned finally to America, and d. at Newburyport, Mass., 30 Sept. 1770 (GS); Ep.-Meth.

www.ingramcontent.com/pod-product-compliance
Lightning Source LLC
Chambersburg PA
CBHW030257030426
42336CB00009B/423